THE DEEPER STATE

INSIDE THE WAR ON TRUMP BY CORRUPT ELITES, SECRET SOCIETIES, AND THE BUILDERS OF AN IMMINENT FINAL EMPIRE

LT. COL. ROBERT MAGINNIS

Defender

Crane, MO

The Deeper State: Inside the War on Trump by Corrupt Elites, Secret Societies, and the Builders of an Imminent Final Empire
By Lieutenant Colonel Robert Maginnis, USA, RET.

Defender Crane, MO 65633 ©2017

ISBN: 9780999189412

A CIP catalog record of this book is available from the Library of Congress.

Cover illustration and design by Jeffrey Mardis.

All Scripture quotations from the King James Version; in cases of academic comparison, those instances are noted.

Dedicated to all the patriots who bought
our freedom with their
blood, sweat, and tears.

Acknowledgments

I gratefully acknowledge…

I'm eternally grateful for my wife, Jan, who tolerated my absence while I labored over this important volume. These efforts, though important and a commitment to truth, are understandably a sacrifice for both of us.

I continue to be indebted to my Christian brother Don Mercer, who once again stepped up to assist with editing as this volume grew. His wisdom and encouragement are much appreciated.

Many others participated in interviews, and for their time and permission to use their insights I'm indebted.

The Lord put on my heart the idea and the insights to assemble this important work, which I pray will serve His purposes.

Robert Lee Maginnis
Woodbridge, Virginia

CONTENTS

Section One
THE WORLD'S NEW COLD WAR

Section Two
GLOBALISTS ELITE

Section Three
PUSHING BACK GLOBALISTS

Foreword

Globalization is more than a process of corporate expansion, free trade, and instant communications; it is also about a radical ideology, a humanist religion, an effort to replace national sovereignty with global governance and deliver great wealth to the few elite. It is empowered by progressivism and other nefarious societal engines like Marxism, communism that promises utopia but results in massive vulnerabilities for most people and robs those citizens of their basic freedoms.

Do you want to understand this sort of chaos that is now threatening every corner of our world? Then you better investigate globalization and all its prickly tentacles.

Why did the election of Donald Trump and the rise of European populists seem to turn our political world upside down? Unfortunately, that sort of turmoil has only started, and it's fueled by a visceral reaction to an insidious agenda exposed in *The Deeper State*.

Are globalists and their unseen co-conspirators really seeking to control the world's power centers like "puppeteers" and do they really intend to take over every aspect of our lives? Yes, and it's getting worse. In fact, those same "puppeteers" really believe they are superior to the rest of us—genetically predisposed, "entitled" to rule the world.

What does the Bible say about these globalists elite who possess world-changing power? Are they seeding the prophetic end times? Yes, events are building to a crescendo and fulfilling the Scriptures.

Detailed answers to these and other tough questions are addressed in *The Deeper State,* which is a well-documented primer for those uninitiated to the contemporary battle for control of this world, a fight being waged both in the visible and invisible realms.

The Deeper State is especially critical for those who desperately want to put all the geopolitical so-called "conspiracies" erupting almost daily into context. This mixed-up world does frighten us, and it makes us feel hopeless—vulnerable, because events really do seem to be spinning out of control.

The Deeper State begins by introducing stories about the world's contemporary "cold war" between the globalists elite and the nationalists/populists who now fill the front pages of most newspapers and scroll across the bottom of our cable channel screens. The long-term consequences are pervasive, undeniable.

This volume explains many strange terms and introduces the key global players—both historic and contemporary—as well as their means and intentions.

What do you know about the globalists elite's secret societies? Are they really dark enclaves of secret global conspiracies, and if so, what is the relevance for me and mine? It's significant!

Do you believe someone is actually manipulating world events to fit a nefarious agenda? Who controls the world's power centers—much less, what are those "power centers"—and to what end?

The Deeper State concludes with a call to action similar to one used two-plus millennia ago by an ancient biblical builder who blazed a trail in his time to secure from evil the "city of God." Today we must retrace those ancient steps in order to reverse the globalists' gains—that is, if it isn't already too late.

The Deeper State is a blend of history, sociology, scriptural interpretation, geopolitics, and dark motivations. It addresses contemporary issues and challenges to help the reader step out to make a difference, first by making him/her aware of the unvarnished truth and then by providing a strategy for him/her to fight against a global enemy that is influential, wealthy, clever, insidious, and—dare I say—spiritual, but in a demonic way.

Explore these pages only if you can't resist understanding these times. If you do accept this challenge, then it will open your eyes as nothing else before to help you become informed and therefore be prepared for what is certainly the future new world order.

Robert L. Maginnis
Woodbridge, Virginia

THE WORLD'S NEW COLD WAR

INTRODUCTION

The Cold War between the U.S. and Russia lasted for decades and pitted those superpowers against one another with dangerous levels of nuclear weapons at the ready to utterly destroy the earth and all its inhabitants. A new cold war pits two equally dangerous and global adversaries armed with very different weapons against one another, and perhaps this war has a truly end-times outcome. These modern adversaries, backed by entities in the unseen realm, are fighting over and with the very things that bind societies together: government, faith, culture, jobs, national identity, and much more—all fueled by ideologies that are diametrically opposed.

This first section of three includes five chapters that provide the foundation for understanding the globalists' instigated cold war and where it will logically lead—the end times.

The first chapter, "Globalism's Lexicon," addresses the terms critical to helping the reader understand the players on the world stage and the "weapons" they employ in the global, multidimensional fight.

The second chapter, "Impact of Globalism," explores the impact globalism is having on planet earth and her inhabitants, both the negative and positive outcomes.

The third chapter, "Scoping the Cold War," introduces the adversaries in the new war and provides evidence of their rapidly escalating fight.

The fourth chapter, "What the World Public Understands about the Ideological New Cold War—Not Much and Why," addresses the globalists' victims (we the people) and how the world's public is a mere pawn in this global conflagration. Most of us are utterly clueless as to what's happening about us, in part because we don't pay attention as well as the fact that much of the war is fought in the unseen realm, the occupants of that world are good and evil and the dwelling place of God and Satan. The beings are the actors who play the roles.

The fifth chapter, "Globalism over the Horizon," demonstrates why globalism is a bankrupt idea when taken to its logical conclusion. Further, God settled the globalist aim at the Tower of Babel, and it is His plan to bring about a spiritual globalism called heaven.

CHAPTER ONE

Globalism's Lexicon

We will no longer surrender this country, or its people, to the false song of globalism.[1]

—Presidential candidate Donald Trump, April 27, 2016

Arguably, Donald Trump won the presidency because he never stopped attacking the dangers of globalization, the deceit of jet-setting elites and their multicultural agenda robbing Americans of jobs, our culture, and security. Trump said the "nation-state," not the international order, was "the true foundation for happiness and harmony."[2]

Trump repeatedly denounced the "false song of globalism" to champion "America First," his campaign slogan, and labeled his presidential opponent, former secretary of state Hillary Clinton, a "globalist" who was enthralled with interests beyond America's borders and eager to open the floodgates to aliens, no matter the consequences for America.

"I think we haven't organized ourselves for the 21st Century globalization," Clinton admitted in an interview. But her rare and honest admission fell flat for many voters who responded in droves to what Trump campaign CEO Steve Bannon said a week before the election: "People want more control of their country. They're very proud of their countries. They want borders. They want sovereignty. It's not just a thing that's happening in any one geographic space."[3]

Trump tapped into America's growing antiglobalist sentiment. He understood, as do many Americans, that globalists have captured much of American society's elite institutions—the media, academia, big corporations, and big finance. The elites running these institutions thought their political victories were complete, that is, until Donald Trump came and upended their world. Trump successfully rode the globalist boogeyman to victory in 2016.

What is globalism, and did the election of Mr. Trump really end the threat posed by globalists like Hillary Clinton?

Globalism is a synonym for globalization, the system of global economic interconnection that is embraced by liberal groups like labor unions, climate change alarmists, and the wealthy, self-righteous elite. Many of those same advocates mistakenly claim globalization is a dispassionate concept that describes the associated increasing connectivity throughout the world that makes our lives better. That's at best a half-truth.

Most people would support globalization if it was indeed limited to making life easier, but it is a nefarious concept spun by its proponents. Yes, globalization gave us easier, faster travel, and instant communication across the world; less-expensive clothing; improved automobiles; better returns on our investments; and a food menu that is no longer confined to just meat and potatoes. These benefits, explain globalists, are made possible when supply chains cross borders, cultures meld, and capital flows freely across the world.

The problem with globalization is that its advocates believe the world "ought" to be interconnected, no matter the consequences. That's the catch. Modern globalism will have very significant and potentially devastating consequences for all our lives.

Yes, globalism is much more than the offering of a diverse menu for dinner or access to social media for the developing world. It is a concept that promotes the supremacy of the global community over the individual. Globalists are ostensibly believers in the rights of the masses over the individual who endorses such a belief system, and they are found in all occupations and professions and represent every political stripe: liberal, conservative, and libertarian—but their globalist philosophy is in fact the antithesis of the U.S. Constitution, especially our Bill of Rights.

The core of the world's globalist community is a worldwide network of self-consumed elitists and their mass of naïve supporters (sycophants)—international financiers, the royal land owners and wealthy political figures who seek to control everything and everyone on earth. They use their wealth to exercise control over the globe's power centers—corporations, the media, education, governments, religion, medicine, and even the military.

Yes, there is a conspiracy of these globalists elite who are at war—a cold war—being waged against the unsuspecting, naïve masses. The globalists-versus-masses war is an age-old problem, but things are now different in the twenty-first century, because the likelihood of the globalists' success is vastly better than ever.

Today, the globalists have access to modern tools to manipulate the world's centers of power. Modern travel and communications afford them the means to better organize than in the past, and they now control the global means (tools) to be truly effective—in particular, within the media and education system, which are psychological manipulation tools of the masses.

Globalists and their media megaphones claim that such criticism is unwarranted, and in fact, they spew hatred at those who make such claims by calling them racists, xenophobic, and anti-Semitic because much of their opposition is over the sovereign concern of unfettered immigration, a key globalist agenda item.

The fact is those who embrace core globalism are true radicals. They are at their core fascists, socialists, communists, and crony capitalists—always endorsing the group over the individual—while espousing a utopian world aim run by people like them who pretend to care for the masses, like Plato's philosopher king.

No right-minded, sovereignty-loving person should want such people to rise to positions of power, because many of these elite are in fact psychopaths. Unfortunately, the world has a long history of such people rising to positions of great power.

Former Republican president candidate and then-Senator Barry Goldwater exposed the influential Trilateral Commission's globalist agenda in his 1964 book, *With No Apologies*.

David Rockefeller's newest international cabal [The Trilateral Commission]…is intended to be the vehicle for multinational consolidation of the commercial and banking interests by seizing control of the political government of the United States.… The Trilateral Commission represents a skillful, coordinated effort to seize control and consolidate the four centers of power: political, monetary, intellectual, and ecclesiastical. What the Trilateral Commission intends is to create a worldwide economic power superior to the political governments of the nation states involved. As managers and creators of the system, they will rule the future.

In 1991, David Rockefeller, billionaire and founder of the Trilateral Commission, confirmed Goldwater's globalist allegation:

We are grateful to *The Washington Post, The New York Times, Time Magazine* and other great publications whose directors have attended our meetings and respected their promises of discretion for almost forty years. It would have been impossible for us to develop our plan for the world if we had been subject to the bright lights of publicity during those years.

But, he added:

The work is now much more sophisticated and prepared to march towards a world government. The supranational sover-

eignty of an intellectual elite and world bankers is surely preferable to the national auto determination practiced in past
centuries.[4]

There is much more on the Trilateral Commission and other "secret
societies" later in this volume.

Even former Vice President Joseph Biden showed his globalist colors
while serving as a U.S. senator in a 1992 article in the *Wall Street Journal*.
In Biden's article, entitled "How I Learned to Love the New World Order,"
he extolled "collective security" through the United Nations, and called for
a "permanent commitment of forces for use by the Security Council."
Biden then asked, "Why not breathe life into the U.N. Charter?"[5]

Biden continued to promote a new world order outcome at least
through 2013 when he spoke to the thirty-eighth annual conference
of the Export-Import Bank of the United States. Biden asserted at that
conference that "the affirmative task we have now is to actually create a
new world order." This means global governance and world government
and all that implies.[6]

There are hundreds of such indicting quotes and reports regarding
the globalists' agenda—world control, one-world economy, one-world
religion, and much more. The problem is that most of the public hasn't
a clue about the danger posed by elite globalists, which reminds me of
something Adolf Hitler, the genocidal Nazi dictator, once said about the
German masses: "How fortunate for Leaders that men do not think."[7]
It's time the masses awaken to the globalist threat and think about the
likely consequences of their agenda.

Globalists literally want to destroy anyone who stands in their way as
they have in the past. They want total control of every aspect of our lives
and will do whatever is necessary to reach that goal.

The *New York Times*, a mouthpiece for the globalist agenda, fondly
attacked Donald Trump throughout the 2016 campaign for president,
and it has ever since because of the president's antiglobalist rhetoric—
and especially for his America-focused actions once in office.

Mr. Trump has repeatedly pushed back on the globalist agenda. Predictably, leftist groups and their surrogates complain that Trump's views are fear-mongering. "Globalism is a principle driver for the fears that animate the radical right in the United States," said Ryan Lenz, a blogger for the radical left Southern Poverty Law Center. "It is the enemy, ultimately."

The fact is that Mr. Trump has a healthy view of globalism. Shortly after his election in November 2016, his spokeswoman provided Mr. Trump's definition for globalism:

> An economic and political ideology which puts allegiance to international institutions ahead of the nation-state; seeks the unrestricted movement of goods, labor and people across borders; and rejects the principle that the citizens of a country are entitled to preference for jobs and other economic considerations as a virtue of their citizenship.[8]

Lauren Southern, the hostess for the Canadian media site Rebel Media, agrees with Mr. Trump. For Southern, globalization means rule by autocrats such as former President Barack Obama and the United Nations, whom she explains value "the false flag of diversity" and "unchecked immigration from the third world."[9]

"Globalists almost always sneer down their nose at tradition, disdain national culture, laugh at religion and generally despise the west while holding a creepy affection for the third world," Southern said. "They want open borders, cheap labor and antinationalism to benefit their business and political visions, and is all too willing to shaft the little people to achieve it."[10]

Globalism is more than a concept. It's a dominant ideology, even a cult-like religion, which for some is a world ordered like that described in Plato's *Republic*. Some globalists have a sense of being destined to rule like Plato's philosopher kings as the wisest of humans, and a few openly admit their goals, perhaps never expecting the uneducated commoner to read their tomes.

Carroll Quigley was a mentor to former President Bill Clinton and a member of the globalist Council on Foreign Relations. He wrote in *Tragedy and Hope*:

> The powers of financial capitalism had (a) far-reaching aim, nothing less than to create a world system of financial control in private hands able to dominate the political system of each country and the economy of the world as a whole. This system was to be controlled in a feudalist fashion by the central banks of the world acting in concert, by secret agreements arrived at in frequent meetings and conferences. The apex of the systems was to be the Bank for International Settlements in Basel, Switzerland; a private bank owned and controlled by the world's central banks which were themselves private corporations. Each central bank...sought to dominate its government by its ability to control Treasury loans, to manipulate foreign exchanges, to influence the level of economic activity in the country, and to influence cooperative politicians by subsequent economic rewards in the business world.[11]

Globalists like Quigley are waging an outright war against the ideal of sovereign people, an ideological guerrilla war fought by elites against the rest of us.

Globalists are not uniformly behind one neat set of beliefs, however. Manfred Steger, a professor at the University of Hawaii, classifies the globalists' ideologies into three groups: market, justice, and religious.

Professor Steger defines globalist ideologies as powerful systems of widely shared ideas and patterned beliefs that are accepted as truth by significant groups in society, such as globalists elite. Ones ideology, says Steger, creates one's worldview endowing us with values and meaning, shaping the ways in which we speak and think about ourselves and our world, the way it is and the way it ought to be.

Steger says ideologies are political. "What makes an ideology 'political' is that its concepts and claims select, privilege, or constrict social meanings related to the exercise of power in society." He continues, "If you subscribe to the ideology's world-view, it will prescribe particular kinds of actions and proscribe others."[12]

The three types of globalist ideologies compete for adherents around the world. The dominant ideology, writes Steger, is market globalism, which "seeks to endow 'globalization' with free-market norms and neoliberal meanings." It is supported by global power elites who include corporate managers, influential journalists, celebrities, and many politicians. They "saturate the public discourse with idealized images of a consumerist, free-market world" and "they portray globalization in a positive light as an indispensable tool for the realization of such a global order."

Microsoft CEO Bill Gates is a powerful advocate of market globalism, and he is joined by most of the financial world's media—*Business Week*, the *Wall Street Journal*, and the *Financial Times*—that daily feed their readers a diet of market-globalist propaganda. Steger explains that market globalism has become a "strong discourse" that is difficult to resist because of the powerful social forces "that have already pre-selected what counts as 'real' and, therefore, shape the world accordingly."

Justice globalism contests market globalism as an alternative vision based on egalitarian ideals of global solidarity and distributive justice. These globalists believe extreme corporate profit strategies lead to widening global disparities in wealth and well-being. This ideology gave rise to the "social justice movement" that sees itself as a "global civil society" dedicated to protecting the global environment, fair trade, human rights, and women's issues.

Justice globalists rally around the slogan "another world is possible," evidence of their vision of a new world order based on a global redistribution of wealth and power. They accuse market-globalists for pushing policies that result in greater global inequality, high levels of unemployment, environmental degradation, and the demise of social welfare.

The third globalist ideology is the religious. The religious globalist seeks "to mobilize a religious community imagined in global terms in defense of religious values and beliefs that are thought to be under severe attack by the forces of secularism and consumerism."

The September 11, 2001, attack on America is the by-product of religious globalism, according to Steger. Al Qaeda is an extreme example of an organization that subscribes to religious globalism. Such groups desire for their version of a global religious community to be all-encompassing, to be given primacy and superiority over state-based and secular political structures. Like al Qaeda, they are occasionally prepared to use violent means to achieve their end goal.

Jihadist Islamism is the most spectacular manifestation of religious globalism. It feeds on a common perception in the Muslim world that Western modes of modernization have not only failed to put an end to widespread poverty in the Middle East and North Africa, but that they have also enhanced political instability and strengthened secular tendencies.

Steger ignores the underlying influence of Islam's radical teachings, however. Those teachings—the Koran, Hadith, and Sira—explain the extreme behavior by conservative adherents, Islamists, more so than do the social consequences of the West's alleged oppression.

The globalist, religion-based ideology is an important aspect of the globalist movement, the role played out in the unseen world.

A sidebar is appropriate here because of the nexus between globalists driven by Marxist/communist ideology and Islamists. There is growing evidence, especially in the U.S., of an unholy alliance between some groups, like the well-entrenched Muslim Brotherhood and the radical globalists. This is a very dangerous association, which will become more evident in the coming years.

Finally, what role does the unseen world—the spiritual realm— play in the globalist agenda of one-world government and domination?

Likely, it plays a decisive role, but one the spiritually blind will never discern, much less address.

The globalists' radicalism and ideology is "demonic" and even "anti-Christ" in nature. For many Christian theologians, globalist ideology has a dark agenda. "Globalism is far more than 'geographical' or 'eliminating national borders and boundaries,'" explained Dr. Jim Garlow, pastor at Skyline Church in San Diego. "It is spiritual and demonic at its core."[13]

Senior Associate Pastor Wallace Henley, with the Second Baptist Church in Houston, Texas, warned that "a major objection to globalism from a spiritual and biblical point of view is that many of the globalists are pushing for a global value system." Henley said the globalists oppose the kingdom of Christ, which he defines as "righteousness, peace, and joy in the holy ghost."[14]

There are biblical prophecies that warn of the rise of global government, a totalitarian system that opposes God and His people. Those prophecies will be explored later in this volume.

CONCLUSION

This chapter identifies many of the significant aspects of the globalist agenda and the lexicon and explores the threats. Next, we will explore globalism's true influence across the world, and further in this volume, I will define the contemporary globalist ideology as a dangerous enemy.

CHAPTER TWO

Impact of Globalism

Globalization began impacting the world during China's Han Dynasty (200 BC), when the Silk Road, a network of trade routes that originated in Chang'an (an ancient Chinese dynastic capital) and ended at the Mediterranean, linking China with the Roman Empire. That connection opened both good and bad trade outcomes.

No one could have anticipated the impact of those trade outcomes introduced by the Silk Road, however. The riches of the East exposed Western nations to different cultures, philosophies, and products. It also brought east-central Asian ethnic groups such as Mongol entrepreneurs to the West, and those same merchants unwittingly transported fleas infected with virulent bacteria in their stomach, which attached themselves to Western rats. Soon, Europeans were infected with a plague that eventually killed 60 percent of the known world.

The fourteenth century's devastating Bubonic Plague exposed the downside of East-West globalism: massive death, quarantines, and the temporary end to trade. Although the spread of disease continues to be a concern associated with globalization today, such as the 2015 outbreak of the deadly Ebola virus in Liberia, most contemporary global trade proponents look beyond such risks to boast globalism's considerable positive promises, such as easy access to goods, sharing of medical and technical innovations, higher living standards, and the promotion of democratic values.

Globalization critics such as the disease-devastated, Middle-Age Europeans claimed then, as some skeptics do today, that significant negative consequences are associated with globalization beyond the obvious spread of deadly diseases and viruses. They claim that globalization introduces not only unfair and immoral distribution of income, but the loss of national integrity (sovereignty), homogenized culture, the loss of jobs, and much, much more.

Yes, modern globalization is a mixed bag of good and bad outcomes, and one size certainly doesn't fit all. Consider the following vignette of the good and bad consequences associated with globalization as applied generally to the African continent.

Africans are apprehensive about globalization. A Pew Research Center survey found 58 percent of Nigerians and less than half of Kenyans, Ugandans and South Africans view globalization very positively. However, the same survey found four in five Africans view globalization as a serious threat to African traditions.[15]

Globalists cite positive outcomes from globalization for Africans: economic growth and diversification, which fosters political stability, gender equality, and cultural development. Those outcomes are indeed desirable, but there are counterbalancing negative impacts for Africans in the age of globalization, and they aren't just related to the threats to African cultures.

The United Nations Development Program found that after globalization started on the continent 22 sub-Saharan African countries saw a decline in their per capita incomes. That disappointing outcome happened in part because African industries suffered significant losses due to cheap imports and in particular in countries such as Nigeria and Tanzania textile industries were devastated by cheap imports triggered by premature and indiscriminate free trade.

Harvard Professor Calestous Juma throws a wet blanket on Africa becoming a viable member of the globalized world anytime soon. He outlines four attributes needed to satisfy his "systems" approach to successful globalization. Africa fails miserably on all four counts.[16]

Africa needs the capability nodes and corridors to operate in a global system, which means the nation-state can take part in international transactions. Unfortunately, most African countries lack this capability.

The second attribute is connectivity to the World Wide Web, because information is the currency of all human interactions. Once again, most of Africa has limited or no widespread access to the Internet, which denies all but a few countries new opportunities.

Global mobility is the third attribute, according to Juma, which is sadly lacking on the continent. Road transportation accounts for the largest share of freight movement globally and Africa's poor road networks makes road-bound freight movement prohibitive across much of the continent.

The final attribute of successful globalization is the growing interdependence among countries. "This depends on having competent capability nodes in government, industry and academia, at both the national and regional level," according to Juma. But there is very little interdependence across Africa.

The African continent may be the least prepared region to join the modern globalization revolution. Other continents and countries suffer from the same globalization shortcomings as well.

What follows is a synopsis of a number of public sectors impacted positively and negatively by globalization. This background information is important to consider before exploring the broader issue of globalization, because as it stands today, this phenomenon is not the panacea its proponents claim.

TRADE

Trade is the sector that comes to mind for most people when considering the impact of globalization. Clearly, the benefits and drawbacks of open and free global trade depends on where you sit. For the American consumer, inexpensive clothing and affordable electronics are readily available at local stores or on many websites, thanks to globalized trade, but our economic blessings come with a moral stigma, because the production of those items abroad comes more often than not thanks to workers who are poorly paid and who work under sub-optimal conditions.

Globalization encourages open and free global trade, which results in more efficient markets. This happens when there is equilibrium between the provider (the manufacturer) and the customer—i.e., the price is right for both parties. Then, of course, those producers who improve the way they manufacture and/or deliver a product naturally benefit. That improvement might come by outsourcing certain aspects of the manufacturing process or buying discounted ingredients from new suppliers, and then the manufacturer can afford to lower the price for the consumer, share some of the profits with his/her investors, and/ or raise worker wages.

Global competition for the same product across multiple producers is good for consumers in terms of price and quality of goods as well. When businesses compete internationally, new standards enter the marketplace, giving consumers more options and forcing the competitors to fight over market share, which results in improved goods or services. That's a win-win combination.

International competition also leads to partnerships across countries and corporations, an important benefit as well. This can result in both stability and security for developing countries while prospering all involved, as well as allowing economies to grow. And, when one sector grows in a country, it potentially spurs others that are connected.

Globalization of trade can be especially helpful for developing countries, because it creates new opportunities that help local entrepreneurs tap into global markets. In turn, this can lead to more capital flows, better access to new technology, cheaper imports, and larger export markets. Further, some businesses can become part of international production networks and supply chains that further bolster trade.

There are some potentially serious negative consequences of globalized trade as well. Globalization can exacerbate income inequalities, both among industrialized and less-developed nations. This can happen because global commerce is dominated by transnational corporations, which focus on profits while failing to meet the needs of less-privileged countries.

American manufacturing has been badly impacted by global competition. Specifically, U.S. companies can't compete with international manufacturers that pay ultra-low wages like in China, and in fact that explains why most former, highly compensated American factory jobs disappeared. But industrialized countries like America aren't totally without the means to level the playing field.

Industrialized country governments often create protectionist policies that prevent developing country producers from accessing export markets. That outcome can then create competition among those shut-out countries to attract foreign investment, which leads to a "race to the bottom," meaning the inevitable lowering of environmental standards to reduce the cost of their products and the wages to their desperate work forces. We see that outcome, the acceptance of low environmental standards and low wages, is tragically too common a tool used by developing nations to cut production costs in order to gain foreign investment.

Invariably, some companies don't survive because of globalized trade. Some fail because of protectionist policies while others find it impossible to compete in markets operated by borderline monopolies like some of the largest companies in America, such as Google and Apple. Small-time innovators have an incredibly difficult time competing against these giants, no matter their home country.

Finally, globalization encourages unwise dependence on other countries for essential goods. A country may come to believe there is no point in producing a product, choosing to depend on imports and special-ize in something different. That happened to the United States regard-ing so-called rare-earth metals, an industry currently cornered by the Chinese. Rare-earth metals are chemical elements vital to many modern technologies, including computers, communications, national defense, and other important products. Only in the past few years has the Pen-tagon sounded alarms that many of our most important weapons now depend on Chinese rare-earth products, a very unwise development for America's national security.

LABOR AND IMMIGRATION

Globalization transfers jobs from developed countries like the United States to less-developed countries. That issue spurred considerable politi-cal debate during the 2016 U.S. presidential campaign as Mr. Trump pointed out that America has bled many of its manufacturing jobs to other countries. One report states the U.S. has shed five million manu-facturing jobs since 2000 alone.[17]

What America has experienced is what some business observers call the Great Shift. Workers transitioned from fields to factories and then to service counters. Consider that in 1960, about one in four American workers had a job in manufacturing, but today, fewer than one in ten are employed in that sector. That's not bad news, according to some.[18]

Global trade and immigration have been a net positive for the United States, argues Professor Kislaya Prasad, director of the Center for International Business Education and Research (CIBER) at the Uni-versity of Maryland's Robert H. Smith School of Business. Even though "globalism has been good for much of our history and even now," it is "not necessarily for everybody." Prasad continued, "When people are aggrieved, foreigners [migrants] make an easy target, and people are receptive to a populist message [e.g., President Trump's campaign message on losing American jobs to overseas manufacturers] accompanied by no realistic solutions."[19]

The Great Shift started in the last century. Much of the West lowered its trade and immigration barriers after World War II, which spurred economic growth. After all, countries with lower cost structure (lower wages, cheaper energy), which is much of the non-Western world, are able to out-compete developed countries. Manufacturers quickly realized they could find cheaper labor overseas or import cheap labor using liberal immigration policies, which led to new factories in China and Mexico and laid off factory workers in America.

This development was an opportunity. "Once the economy opens, there's a pressure on you to be more efficient," Prasad says. "You have to compete with imports, and it makes you better." However, as Prasad explained, "If countries wall themselves out of the global trading system, they put this prosperity at risk."

There are plenty of negative consequences associated with globalization's job displacement phenomenon. Some globalists naively argue that those who lose their jobs thanks to globalization can be retrained but, as Prasad explains, "The problem is, there's not a whole lot of evidence to show that these [retraining] programs actually work.... Do you retrain a coal miner to be a nurse? It's not that easy." Do you relocate those people to better job markets? "People are not so easily mobile to leave a community and networks and ties and historical associations to a [new] place," Prasad says.

Another response to the loss of jobs to migrants is to tighten borders and immigration policies to keep out low-wage (legal and illegal) job seekers, but that, according to Prasad, leads to higher costs. "If you add up the amount by which you're paying less for all these goods, that amount is much greater than the cost of all the displaced jobs," Prasad argues.

Protectionism protects unsustainable jobs with false hope and makes domestic products more expensive. "As a society we haven't tackled the issue of stagnant wages in blue collar jobs with creative solutions," Prasad says. "As a consequence, we're paying for it in our politics."[20]

Juxtapose the protectionist tendency with the impact of unfettered immigration. America has by some estimates twelve million illegal aliens spread across the country, arguably performing jobs many U.S. citizens won't accept, but at the same time, as critics explain, they soak up social services (schooling, health care, and welfare), but don't contribute their fair share to the government's coffers.

On February 28, 2017, President Trump addressed the nation in a joint session of Congress and specifically spoke to the immigration job issue. He cited a report by the National Academy of Sciences and then said, "Protecting our workers also means reforming our system of legal immigration. The current, outdated system depresses wages for our poorest workers, and puts great pressure on taxpayers."[21]

The president's statement is not consistent with the National Academy of Sciences report, especially regarding legal immigration. The report finds that state and local governments do "bear the burden of providing education benefits to children;" however, the federal government benefits from "the resulting educated taxpayers" who work and pay taxes. It also found that among those who immigrate, the initial costs are relatively high, but by the third-plus generations, there are significant annual benefits for the nation.

There's a serious problem with that analysis. We may never see those alleged "significant annual benefits" unless immigration controls are put in place to slow the flow into this country. Pew Research indicates that America's immigration flow will continue, thus failing to mitigate the alleged third-generation benefit.

The Pew Research Center reports that future immigrants and their descendants in the U.S. will "be an even bigger source of population growth" than in the past. Nearly fifty-nine million immigrants have arrived in the U.S. over the past fifty years, pushing our foreign-born share to a near record 14 percent, which accounted for just over half of the nation's population growth. Pew anticipates by 2065, the foreign-born share of the U.S. population will account for 88 percent of the growth, or 103 million, as the nation expands to 441 million.[22]

The National Academy of Sciences report concludes that "immigration is integral to the nation's economic growth" and "has an overall positive impact on long-run economic growth in the U.S." That's a rosy, pro-globalist conclusion and certainly not supported by the stark sustained immigration flow outlined by Pew Research Center.

CULTURE

Globalization pushes Western capitalism into every corner of the world, which inevitably impacts those cultures. Along with Western products come aspects of Western culture to non-Western countries. Anthropologists indicate that Western capitalism promotes profit, modernization, and individualism, which often push aside indigenous ideas of tradition and social responsibility. Thus, for much of the non-Western world, globalization becomes synonymous with Westernization, moving all countries together into a single, global economy and, by association, one culture.[23]

The evidence of "Westernization" abounds across the world. Travel abroad to virtually any country and you notice that most places visited have some things in common with your American hometown, such as fast-food restaurants like McDonald's and Starbucks, which has nearly twenty thousand shops in sixty countries. That's an example of cultural globalization, which is the process by which one culture—especially the American—disseminates its values and ideas, which happens via the Internet (e.g., Facebook and Twitter), popular cultural media (*The Simpsons* and the latest Hollywood movie), and especially thanks to Western celebrities such as Madonna or Bono, who reach large audiences with their opinions as well as international travel for business and tourism.

Culture is dynamic, thanks to the above process, according to the World Commission on Culture and Development. That organization notes that a society's culture is not static but in a constant state of flux. That dynamism is accelerated by globalization, which is accelerating and intensifying the global flow of capital, labor, and information, and results in what's known as a homogenizing influence on local culture.

Cultural homogenization occurs when cultural globalization reaches maturity, or when there is a marked reduction in cultural diversity through the mechanism of popularization. The homogenization process works both ways as well for Western countries like the United States. Americans, for example, have adopted aspects of other cultures to include foreign cuisine like Chinese, Thai, and Mexican food. Europeans routinely listen to music in many languages, and business people from across the world frequently exchange ideas about their markets and the latest technology.

Cultural globalization manifests itself in other ways as well. We see it evidenced in words and gestures such as "okay" or the use of the thumbs-up sign for "all is well."

There are downsides to cultural homogenization, such as the loss of uniqueness of local culture, which can result in loss of identity and even conflict. This process can be especially dysfunctional for traditional societies, which experience difficulties adapting to Western cultural mores.

The rapid pace of cultural homogenization and therefore the loss of diversity raises an important question: Why have humans had so many different cultures over the ages? Is cultural diversity rooted in our DNA, and if so, what impact might the homogenization of culture have for our future world?

Group psychology demonstrates that our formation of small groups (tribes) eventually made it possible for us to form larger social networks and then nations of many millions of people. This metamorphosis demonstrates with each step that cooperation can produce better outcomes, so we continue to seek to get along in ever-larger groups.

How might this tribal psychology of forming ever-larger groups be impacted by rapidly growing globalization? Are we destined for a "one-world" culture? That's unlikely anytime soon, because, as Mark Pagel, a professor at the University of Reading, United Kingdom, writes for the BBC, two factors will likely slow the rate of cultural homogenization: resources and demography.

Cooperation has grown globally "because large collections of people have been able to use resources more effectively and provide greater prosperity and protection than smaller groups," Pagel explains. However, cooperation will inevitably decline as resources become scarce. "After all," Pagel rhetorically asks, "why cooperate when there are no spoils to divide?"[24]

Over the next century, we anticipate experiencing the movement of large groups of people from poorer to richer regions of the world. This diversity of people brought together will be because of declining resources, and most will have little common cultural identity with the people in their new country—which will exacerbate the problem of cultural integration and assimilation.

This phenomenon is quite evident in Western Europe today, which over the past decade has welcomed more than a million migrants from Northern Africa and the Middle East. Large migrant communities in Europe form into ghettos, refusing to embrace local language and culture and grant allegiance to those governments. The failure by these growing groups to assimilate has given rise to nationalist groups and political parties such as Marine le Pen's Front National in France, as well as those who the supported the 2016 Brexit vote in Great Britain and similar movements rising to prominence elsewhere in Western Europe.

Perhaps in spite of the lack of assimilation, cultural homogenization does seem somewhat inevitable, thanks to travel, the global job market, the Internet, and social networking. "In fact, breaking down of cultural barriers—unfashionable as this can sound—is probably one of the few things that societies can do to increase harmony among ever more heterogeneous peoples," says Pagel.

EDUCATION

The globalization of the Christian religion in the nineteenth and twentieth centuries had a significant collateral effect on the education of the masses. Although the Christian missionaries' motivation was spiritual, virtually all Christian missions operated schools that educated the people to help improve their lives. This is the first evidence of a positive globalized outcome for education.

Globalized trade has also positively impacted education, but not until the past century and only after the United States demonstrated the correlation between an educated labor force and prosperity. Americans should thank the American Legion in part for that success.

The United States led the world in education after World War II, thanks to the Servicemen's Readjustment Act of 1944, also known as the G.I. Bill and pushed by the American Legion. The bill granted millions of wartime veterans benefits to attend high school, college, or vocational/technical school and grant them loans to start a business. The G.I. Bill ultimately supplied America with a highly qualified labor force, which propelled the United States to become the dominant economy in the world.

Today, globalists seek to harness education to do for the rest of the world that which the G.I. Bill did for America, and, to a certain extent, their efforts are paying off.[25] Today, high school graduation has become the norm in most industrialized countries, and it is growing in the developing world.

Yes, globalization has played an important role in the education of the world. This is especially true because of the recent growth of global networking—e.g., the Internet. But the revolution in education-related technology has both positive and negative impacts.

The positive impacts of globalization for education are undeniable. It created opportunities for sharing knowledge, technology, social values, and behavioral norms, and promoted developments at different levels, including individuals, organizations, communities, in addition to promoting international understanding, collaboration, harmony, and acceptance of cultural diversity across countries and cultures.

Globalization has also contributed to an increasing interest in English-language education worldwide, a boon for America and the rest of the English-speaking world. Certainly, a common language fosters better access to education globally, much like using English for global air traffic control makes air travel safer.

Globalization's negative impact for education comes in various forms, according to Sadegh Bakhtiari with Isfahan University (Iran), such as creating the cultural colonization of education by advanced countries in developing and underdeveloped countries, as well as the promotion of dominant cultures and values. Education is also negatively impacted where there are technological gaps and digital divides between advanced and less-developed countries. Another negative and major concern for globalizing developing countries is the plethora of local languages, which adds a layer of complexity to the education task.[26]

MEDIA AND COMMUNICATIONS

The world experienced a technological revolution over the past century as the means of communication globalized. Modern communication is a conduit for spreading knowledge quickly and efficiently to large sectors of the world. Of course, the ready access to information has a downside as well, because those with nefarious goals can easily acquire the knowledge to build a bomb, spread a dangerous virus, or use the medium to radicalize some, such as the propaganda spawned by the Islamic State.

Globalization has spread information access across the globe, even into some of the most remote areas. Interactive communications platforms like the iPhone and iPad tethered to the World Wide Web allow the user to communicate around the world in an instant, as well enabling users to entertain and educate themselves or help those in distress. These tools are used to influence as well as separate and isolate people from one another.

Commercial use of communications platforms such as television, radio, and Internet websites allow self-representation and information-sharing across the entire globe. It can depict images and portrayals of self-identity—social media—and can provide the means by which truth is established or false truths are spread.

It has become an invaluable instrument for Christians to spread the Word of God through websites and streaming of Christian programs. Untold millions of people across the world learn of the claims of Christ today because of modern media outlets.

Global media outlets also grant cultures a distinctive voice to promote awareness, knowledge, and understanding. They possess the persuasive power to revitalize and restore cultures, language, and customs.

Unfortunately, modern communication platforms and especially the so-called commercial media outlets have become increasingly concentrated, until today we have only a few corporations and governments owning most of the major outlets. This is dangerous, because those outlets have created a socially engineered construct to fabricate a version of reality for their constituents. Of course, this is one of the aims of the globalists elite.

Media maintain a fabricated reality through censorship of news and, in some cases, the media spews pure propaganda using lies of obfuscation, distortion, and omission. This topic became part of the national debate during the 2016 presidential campaign because Mr. Trump frequently attacked media outlets for fabricating news: "fake news."

The globalists elite who control many of these media outlets have the potential to use this incredibly powerful weapon of mass psychology to manipulate the minds of the masses. They use these platforms to manipulate for a variety of purposes by employing well-known psychological tools.

Consider contemporary media examples that illustrate the medium's value as a weapon of mass psychology pushing a radical, anti-Christian agenda, using manipulative tools like predictive programming...and then ask yourself about their potential globalization impact.

Destruction of the Traditional Family: Long gone are television series such as *The Donna Reed Show* or *Father Knows Best*, which typified an ideal home life. Today's television families are typically dysfunctional and push an anti-Christian radical agenda such as single motherhood, as portrayed in *Keeping Up with the Kardashians* or the parenting of a homosexual couple in *Modern Family*.

Christian leader Franklin Graham said Disney is using the medium of a popular children's story made into a television and movie to normalize homosexuality and "push the LGBT [lesbian, gay, bisexual, transgender] agenda into the hearts and minds of your children." In a March 2, 2017, post on Facebook, Reverend Graham, son of the evangelist Billy Graham, said, "Disney has aired a cartoon with same-sex couples kissing. It has also been announced that their new movie 'Beauty and the Beast' will feature a gay character in an attempt to normalize this lifestyle."[27]

"Disney has the right to make their cartoons, it's a free country," said Graham. "But as Christians we also have the right not to support their company. I hope Christians everywhere will say no to Disney."

Gender and Role Reversal: Gender is described by behaviors, attitudes, and beliefs a culture associates with the roles of men and women. There are classic gender roles of the past, such as men are thought to be the financial providers, strong, dominant, and logical, while women are believed to be weak, passive, and emotional, and focused on being loving wives and mothers raising children and doing housework.[28]

In the past, much of the commercial media promoted those classic gender roles, but more recently it has redefined male and female roles in society. Today, media more often than not portrays a different family model, more a partnership than based on patriarchy. Certainly, entertainment media reinforces new stereotypes such as the television series, *Two and a Half Men* and the *Big Bang Theory*. More recently, big media is pushing a gender role reversal to further confuse distinctions between the sexes as well.

Media's manipulation of gender roles is offensive for more traditional cultures, but clearly demonstrates the direction the globalists are pushing the masses.

Even former President Obama tried in many venues to push his radical view of gender and acceptability. In 2015, the president visited Africa and made the LGBT agenda one of the centerpieces of his foreign policy. He compared the discrimination of homosexuals in Africa to the treatment of black Americans prior to the Civil Rights movement. "As an African American in the United States I am painfully aware of what happens when people are treated differently under the law," Obama told an African audience.[29]

A Nigerian university student said Obama's pro-gay push in Africa made things worse. "There's more resistance now. It's triggered people's defense mechanism," said the student to a *New York Times* reporter.

The U.S. government has spent more $700 million of taxpayer money to advance the homosexual agenda globally, and half of the money has targeted sub-Sharanan Africa, according to the *New York Times*.

Following Obama's Africa visit, some African bishops and other leaders attacked the president for his Western "cultural imperialism," and asked Obama to respect Africa's values.

Cardinal John Onaiyekan, the Catholic Archbishop of Abuja Diocese in Nigeria, said, "Unfortunately, we are living in a world where these things have now become quite acceptable but for the fact that they are acceptable doesn't mean that they are right." [30]

Moral Relativism: Moral relativism is the belief that there are no absolutes that are used to determine right and wrong. Much of the entertainment media appears to be moral relativists who believe that there is no permanent or standard basis for moral values—and in fact, moral values are only opinions, a view shared by most modern Western adults.

A survey by Barna Research found that three in four American adults believe truth is always relative to the person and situation. That view is more prevalent among teenagers, with more than four in five (83 percent) believing that moral truth depends on the circumstances, while only 6 percent said moral truth is absolute.[31]

That outcome should not surprise anyone who watches entertainment media. Moral relativism is pervasive across the wide screen and most popular entertainment media outlets today. One of the "moral relativism" issues media pushes is the so-called pro-choice (abortion-on-demand) agenda.

Most media luminaries push mindless abortion-rights slogans such as "Pro-choice, but personally opposed," so they say. This is an attempt to find a "middle ground" and to avoid being labeled "an extremist." Of course, the pro-abortionist's assumption of moral relativism to solve the abortion debate reveals a tremendous ignorance of the pro-life position, which is if one believes that the unborn are fully human, then the unborn carried in the wombs of pro-choice women are just as human as those carried in the wombs of pro-life women.[32]

Moral relativism in this situation is truly a blood offering to Satan, the real power behind the abortion movement. This is similar to the blood sacrifices the Mayans and Aztecs made to Satan, albeit under another name.

Joseph Farah writes in worldnetdaily.com examples of modern moral relativism in America. They seem to boost the globalists' view of the future world.[33]

- You can get arrested for expired tags on your car or truck, but not for being in the country illegally.
- You will need your parents' signature to get an aspirin or go on a school field trip, but not to get an abortion.
- An 80-year-old nun traveling by air will be strip-searched by a TSA employee who is a Muslim woman in a burqa.
- How do you deal with a $16 trillion debt problem? By borrowing more money.
- Six-year-old boys can be suspended from school for playing cowboys and Indians with make-believe guns and bows.

- Kids in school are suspended for sexually harassing classmates while they learn about how to perform "safe" sex without emotional or physical consequences.
- The Supreme Court of the United States can rule that lower courts cannot display the Ten Commandments, while justices sit under a display of the Ten Commandments.
- Hard-working Americans are penalized with higher taxes and government intrusion, while unproductive and lazy Americans are rewarded with free cell phones, food stamps, subsidized housing, and government checks.
- Being self-sufficient is considered a threat to the government.

Farah concludes, "In America today, right is left, black is white, up is down and right is wrong."[34]

This conclusion should remind the Christian of a statement made 2,500 years ago by the prophet Isaiah: "Woe unto them that call evil good, and good evil; that put darkness for light, and light for darkness; that put bitter for sweet, and sweet for bitter! (Isaiah 5:20, KJV)."

Predictive Programming: It is a tool of media elites who sprinkle our popular culture with mostly subtle references to future events in order to make us accept them without question. Predictive programming is evident in hundreds of movies and television shows, such as in the movie *Dark Knight Rises*, wherein the words "Sandy Hook" (the 2012 scene of the Connecticut school massacre) were written on a map, and *The Simpsons* predicting the ebola outbreak and the death of prince. (It is noteworthy that Suzanne Collins, the author of the *Hunger Games* trilogy, lives in Sandy Hook and her writings deal with child sacrifices.)[35]

Predictive programming may be used for signaling others, hypnosis, and what's called manifestation. Signaling others is predictive programming that messages certain operators to carry out a particular event such as Project Monarch, a covert Central Intelligence Agency operation known as MKUltra, which subjected the victims to intense trauma to the point their minds dissociate from the experience. This allegedly causes a form of multiple-personality disorder, which makes them controllable. That allows the "programmer" or "handler" to put in place within popular media a "trigger" that causes these mind-controlled "slaves" to perform whatever actions they have been programmed to do.[36]

The "slaves" don't even know they are under control but, once triggered, their programmed personality surfaces and they respond as planned. Consider that various well-known movies, *The Wizard of Oz* and *Alice in Wonderland* allegedly employ Monarch programming to plant triggers.[37]

Predictive programming is also used to destroy existing norms. Marketing experts understand the use of creative disruption to break an existing pattern of behavior of the target audience in response to a highly creative message (advertisement).

Creative disruption messaging also helps to disrupt the normal flow in the way the media consumer processes marketing messages, so they stop to consider the message. Techniques include contrasting messaging, exaggerated presentation, and out-of-place presentations. The aim is to develop marketing messages that are remembered and acted upon.[38]

You should feel violated because much of mass media manipulates your thinking about issues and your preferences for products.

ENVIRONMENT AND RESOURCES

Globalization impacts both our environment and the rate of consumption of our limited natural resources. For example, globalized trade has increased the need for energy and industry, and at the same time, as industry grew to satisfy production demands, it contributed to global pollution as well as the abuse of the land, such as unnecessary bulldozing of the world's tropical forests.

China illustrates the problem of abuse of the environment to advance trade. Beijing joined the World Trade Organization in December 2001 and by the end of 2002 its coal use for power generation skyrocketed making the air around Chinese factory cities dangerous to breath.

The air quality in Beijing becomes incredibly dangerous as a result of air pollution. The World Health Organization measures air quality by counting particles known as PM2.5. Breathing these particles can damage the lungs. WHO states a safe level of air quality is 10–25 micrograms per cubic meter of PM2.5. Beijing reached levels as high as 400 micrograms per cubic meter in late December 2016.[39]

Globalization has also led to significant fluctuations in oil prices as demand failed to keep up with supply. Although the prices have waxed and waned over the decades, the supply still won't catch the demand, especially in developing countries. This view is supported by a recent market analysis.

An energy market projection through 2025 prepared by LUKOIL anticipates global population will grow by more than 1.1 billion people, especially in India and African countries. At the same time, developing countries will experience movement to cities, known as urbanization, which in turn will promote increased demand for energy resources.[40]

Globalization, which connects markets, impacts resource volatility as outlined above and will in the future across most resources, especially as globalization grows. "The globalized world increases the pressure on resources, making even basic food volatile, and especially increasing the pressure on energy and metals," says Kai Goerlich, SAP's iIdea director.[41]

Clearly, environmental and resource challenges are ahead, and globalization does not seem to help, at least as yet, to resolve these challenges.

FINANCE

Globalization does make international investing available to developing countries. Investment money flows to those countries that offer a competitive advantage, which often results in the sacrifice of the country's environment and exploitation of cheap labor.

Certainly, for the wealthy Western stockholders, globalization can become a financial security blanket. For example, one of the benefits of investment diversification can be as U.S. stocks may go down, stocks overseas may go up in value to balance out the loss. However, in a thoroughly globalized stock market where international stocks become more correlated with those in the U.S., they will provide less benefit for a diversified investment portfolio.

Globalization also has led to huge U.S. balances of trade deficits. The deficit is so high because the U.S. dollar is the world's reserve currency and is likely to remain high because the rest of the world takes its surpluses and buys U.S. debt with the balance. This situation means the globalized world funds American overspending. That situation can't last forever, and that end will be ugly.

The 2016 U.S. trade deficit was $502 billion, down from a record high of $762 billion in 2006. That decrease means U.S. exports are growing faster than imports, as well as that the dollar is changing in value. That's a good trend. However, continuing to carry a trade deficit hurts our economy in several ways, according to Kimberley Amedao, who writes for *The Balance.*

First, that trade debt must be financed, and at some point, the debt must be repaid.[42] "One day, the lending countries could decide to ask America to repay the debt. On that day, the party is over," Amedao cautions.

Second, the dollar's long-term value is pressed down by the growing debt, which makes American exports cheaper, a benefit. However, global oil prices rise as the dollar buys less, which means our reliance on oil translates into difficulty escaping a growing trade deficit.

Finally, a growing trade deficit indicates weakened American competitiveness. Buying more from others means we lose our expertise with our factories to make competitive products.

HEALTH

Globalization of health care offers many possibilities for good, such as responses to catastrophes and epidemics like the 2015 Ebola outbreak in Liberia.

Consider some of the medical pro and con impacts of globalization for health.

One of the great health benefits of globalization is the flow of information, goods, capital, and people across all kinds of boundaries, such as the movement of medical advances. This is thanks to the global growth in communication and transportation technologies, which enable rapid response to epidemics and catastrophes, saving thousands of lives every year.

There is a medical downside to globalization mentioned earlier in this chapter: the rapid spread of infectious diseases, especially among the world's poor. The fact is that no microbe in the world is more than twenty-four hours away from every industrialized country.[43]

Globalization also contributes to the promotion of radical health issues, such as family planning, which is code for abortion. America shares in that tragic agenda, but thanks to President Trump, one of the first executive orders he signed after taking office blocked foreign aid or federal funding for international nongovernmental organizations that provide abortions.[44]

President Ronald Reagan in 1984 established the so-called Mexico City policy blocking federal funding for international family planning organizations, but the policy has been subjected to a game of political football over the years, with Democratic presidents rescinding the policy and Republicans reinstating it.

President Obama reinstated the policy in 2009, and his final budget included $607 million for "reproductive health internationally," according to the Guttmacher Institute, a research group that supports abortion rights.

Likely, globalized health services are here to stay. Pam Matthews, the CIO of American Healthcare Services, anticipates globalization of healthcare is helped when developing countries push their services into developed countries. The most common offshore medical services now include transcription, physician credentialing, tele-radiology, claims processing, programming, report writing, interface development, and call center and help desk support services.[45]

Information technology makes healthcare offshore services more attractive. This is especially true in terms of research outsourcing.

GOVERNMENT

Globalization contributes to the growth of government, primarily because their bureaucracies tend to grow as they wrestle with the intricacies of being more interconnected to the world economy. Further, public transfers and subsidies increasingly pervade nations as they globalize, and personal income taxes become more burdensome because globalization tends to move taxation away from corporations and onto individual citizens. Corporations tend to have an advantage because they can flee the government's taxman while citizens tend to stay in place.

Also, bureaucracies grow because worker citizens competing in a globalized economy tend to demand more protection from their governments. That creates more government policies such as tariffs and a variety of expensive safety nets.

Globalization also makes it virtually impossible for government regulators in one country to foresee the worldwide implications of their actions, which requires more government oversight and policy bureaucracies.

Further, globalization compels countries to try to sell their goods and services at the lowest prices as possible. That means they accept more pollution, because they use cheaper polluting fuels, and governments like China lower the value of their currency to make their goods and services cheaper to foreign buyers.

There is another serious problem that globalization introduces for every involved country. It links countries in a vulnerable way so that, should one country collapse financially, others fall as well. Certainly, we see how the European Union is now suffering due to terrible fiscal policy in member countries like Greece, Italy, and Spain. History demonstrates that such interdependence can be self-defeating, because when a large number of countries are involved, they become increasingly interdependent and, like the English nursery rhyme, "Humpty Dumpty," they could all fall: "All the king's horses and all the king's men, Couldn't put Humpty together again."

Globalists will counter this argument that such vulnerability is due to the wide disparity in conditions in each member country, and ,therefore, a one-world government will be more attractive as it demands and enforces changes in standards and operations in each member country. Of course, that argument depends on stripping countries of their sovereignty and ignores the nature of man and the diversity of the earth's nation-states.

RELIGION

There are a number of approaches to understanding the nexus between religion and globalization. Author Peter Beyer of Religion and Globalization identifies roles religion plays vis-à-vis globalization in the *Encyclopedia of Religion: A Transnational Institution and a Cultural & Political Resource*. Some of those perspectives are outlined below.[46] Each renders positive and negative outcomes.

Religion's response to globalization: The world's religious communities generally consider that globalization results in violence and unjust oppression. It threatens culture and poses a particular burden on women, the most vulnerable sex. It is also a significant contributor to environmental degradation and tends to marginalize humanity. Such views are shared by significant parts of the major religious groups: Christians, Muslims, Buddhists, Jews, and others.

These negative views of globalization communicate that religion in general and specifically religious sensibilities are fundamentally incommensurate with globalization. Not surprisingly, some within the world's religious communities argue that religion should help shape globalization by espousing a positive global ethic.

Hans Kung, a former Swiss Catholic priest and president of the Foundation of Global Ethic, believes that the globalized world needs a guiding global ethic and that religion ought to influence that effort. Peter Beyer explains, "The globalized whole depends for its viability on the contribution of religion, yet this contribution presupposes a plurality of particular religions that come to understand themselves in positive relation to one another. Unity and diversity are both constitutive of the global."[47]

It is highly unlikely that orthodox believers among the world's religious community will ever "come to understand themselves in positive relation to one another," however. Certainly, the fact that religion is often the basis (cause) for wars, then Kung's "positive relation to one another" idea is really a utopian dream.

Religion as a transnational institution. Religion's diverse manifestations operate relatively independently of other globalization structures to bind regions together much as do media and global trade.

European powers expanded their influence around the globe between the sixteenth and twentieth centuries through colonization and Christian evangelization. This was evidence of worldwide globalization, because as missionaries accompanied the colonizers to Africa, the Americas, and elsewhere, Christian missionaries evangelized people in all corners of the globe. Little wonder today that the vast majority of globally extended religious institutions are Christian.

This extensive network of mostly Christian institutions and global migrants undoubtedly influence the globalization process. After all, these institutions and their believers work with migrants, advocate integration policies, and help shape attitudes in host countries. Further, the migrants help shape the global character of local communities across the world.

There is a problem with Beyer's theory that all faith groups advocate integration. He evidently doesn't understand the Islamic phenomenon of Hijra, an Islamic organizational strategy that has the goal of jihad by nonviolent means—also known as civilizational jihad. For the Muslim, to emigrate in the cause of Allah—to move to a new land in order to bring Islam—is considered a meritorious act. "And whoever emigrates for the cause of Allah will find on the earth many locations and abundance," states the Qur'an.

Hijra, as experienced in places like Western Europe, is especially threatening, according to Sam Solomon and E. Al Maqdisi in their book, *Modern Day Trojan Horse: The Islamic Doctrine of Immigration:*[48]

> One can see that the threat from Islam doesn't just come in the form of Islamic terrorism by suicide bombers trying to wreak havoc in our cities. More often, it comes in the form of gradual and incremental transformation of our societies and legal systems, or what is termed "Islamisation" of our democratic societies by the vast growing numbers of Muslim immigrants who are importing Islam into our Western way of life.[49]

Orthodox Islam is counter to assimilation for the good of all peoples and dangerous when embraced by globalists.

Powerful as cultural and political resource. Religion helps the less powerful and marginalized populations to assert their identity and inclusion in a globalized system.

People who migrate to another country often depend on their religion and local religious institutions to help them adjust to the new environment. In fact, churches, temples, mosques, and other religious centers serve as a home away from home where the migrant hears someone speak his language, eat familiar food, and gather with like-minded others to share. This is evident across America, where millions of Mexican migrants find fellow Mexicans at local churches that help the newcomers through the period of adjustment.

The migrant-friendly religious institutions also provide a platform for effective religion-political movements across the world. Politicized religion has been a constant feature dating back to the nineteenth century and a significant contributor to globalization. That happens when religions, even those with great differences, rally resources on similar political issues that eventually impact government policies, such as the Islamic revolution in Iran and the Christian right in the United States.

CONCLUSION

This chapter is a primer regarding the impact of globalization for nine community sectors. Understanding the degree to which globalization has and might impact all aspects of human life is important, especially as we dissect the coming worldwide "cold war" in the next chapter.

CHAPTER THREE

Scoping the Cold War

There is a new global Cold War raging between two diametrically opposed old adversaries with irreconcilable differences, and the fight is expected to intensify, leading to a true global war. Unlike past world wars, this one is truly global pitting citizens in every country against one another as well as against their neighbors. The "fighting" is between those divided by ideology, and the fight will be on many fronts crossing all socioeconomic strata, and joined by the forces of the unseen realm with grave eschatological implications.

The indicators of this current and growing war abound, and the modern battlefields are already littered with the faceless masses victimized by global elitist adversaries who better today than ever before have harnessed mass manipulation in order to exercise draconian power over every sector of society. Their global ambitions know no bounds, and one-world control is their chief aim.

Much of the evidence of this globalist fight is still only found in the shadows, with the powerful elite pulling the strings of power as puppeteers all so subtly manipulate the power structures like strings on a marionette. There are less subtle examples of this fight, which on first glance may appear to be replays of the past, but in fact demonstrate what is truly at stake in this emerging global war.

The spiking tensions between Russia and the West are evidence of this new ideological cold war, at least in part. Why? Because the Russian Federation acted predictably against Western globalist aggression to recover that which was lost with the fall of the former Soviet Union, their national pride and control over Russia's periphery, a legitimate security concern.

The most visible evidence of this fight surfaced as tensions mounted over Russian aggression in the Ukraine, which the globalists claim was an affront to freedom and democracy. But in reality, the Russia-West fight over Ukraine is evidence of a difference in ideology, especially for Russian leaders who are mostly nationalists opposed to the small cabal of globalists dead-set on seeding the fight now consuming much of Eastern Europe. How are they seeding the fight? The West (the European Union [EU] and its partner the U.S.) want to recruit the former Soviet satellites into the globalist West by pushing membership in the North Atlantic Treaty Organization (NATO) and the EU. That push is a serious threat to Russian sovereignty, according to the powers in Moscow.

The Russian leadership responded to globalist pressures against the West's push for former satellites to join NATO and the EU from a nationalist perspective, rejecting the globalists elite's agenda, which hid behind their calls to "give democracy a chance" in places like Eastern Ukraine whileRussian actions in places like Syria and confrontations across the globe in the air and on the sea demonstrate a real ideological fight emerging.

A retired Russian general characterized the Russia-West standoff by reminding the world of a historic and grave parallel: "If we talk about the last Cold War, we are currently somewhere between the erection of the Berlin Wall and the Cuban Missile Crisis." That's very dangerous ground. The general continued, "In other words, teetering on the brink of war, but without the mechanisms to manage the confrontation."[50]

Russian President Vladimir Putin, a staunch nationalist with very high popularity ratings at home, understands the new cold war and the stakes. Putin said a new cold war has indeed started, and he responded to the globalist aggression by a host of actions such as cancelling the decades-old reprocessing deal over the U.S.' "unfriendly" policies,[51] placement of missiles in Kaliningrad, and launching cyber-attacks and releasing indicting materials against globalist Hillary Clinton during the 2016 American presidential campaign.

The Russia-West conflict is just an indicator of the new cold war, and many others are outlined at the end of this chapter, but first, consider a brief history of the competing sides (ideologies) in the new cold war.

THE GLOBALIST CABAL

Globalists are a cabal of ruling elites known for their goal of taking over the whole planet to control every aspect of humanity best known as the new world order (NWO). That aspiration also includes an effort to control every natural resource and all sovereign nation-state governments.

We will identify some of these globalists elite by name (past and present in the next section of the book) and their extremist agenda, their secret societies (Bilderberger Group, Trilateral Commission, and others to include dark brotherhoods like the Freemasons) in this volume. For now, understand that these elites are behind the emerging cold war.

These NWO globalists are a relatively small group of individuals. Some label them as transnationalists who have very deep pockets, and they sit atop and leverage multinational power centers. Those power centers and how the elite leverage them will also be explored in detail in this volume, but for now, understand that their influence is comprehensive, especially today.

It is also important to appreciate that this cabal of transnationalist powerhouse elites have a long, albeit secretive, history of trying to dominate global power—and some engage in bizarre rituals, which are rightly labeled occultism. They are also enjoying success today unlike their ideological predecessors for reasons to be explained later.

For now, as a primer of sorts, let's consider a brief history of the globalist ideology to set the stage for further examination.

Although as explained in the last chapter we saw evidence of globalism as early as the second century before Christ, thanks to the adventurous Chinese seeking to sell their wares to the Romans. Certainly in the underbelly of Europe, globalism lost its hold with the fall of the Ottoman Empire due to the growing view that large, multinational empires were inherently weak due to the mixture of many nationalities and languages. This grassroots view led to major European powers like the British, French, and Russians helping those under the heel of the Ottomans.

Those grassroot movements soon caught fire throughout the Ottoman Empire, such as the Greek Revolution of 1821–1832, which was fueled by European powers that opposed Ottoman rule. Eventually, the Ottomans were unable to defeat the Greeks backed by European powers. Other nations under Ottoman control revolted, and eventually that rebellious, anti-globalist streak crept into the heart of the Ottoman Empire, Turkey. By the start of World War I, the Ottoman Empire was a shell of its former self with former occupied lands—Greece, Bulgaria, Serbia, and Bosnia—back under European control.[52]

Around the same time, globalized trade really rocketed to the forefront—especially in the West, as international exports expanded, raising gross domestic product eightfold between 1820 and 1913. Fueling this boom period was the significant advance in modes of transportation, with the invention and wide use of both the railway and steamships that carried significant freight to new and distant destinations. Further, capital investments followed the new modes of transport, as did global trade. Predictably, migration followed, with at least at first mostly Europeans flocking to the new jobs, many of which were in America.[53]

Globalization's nineteenth-century gains suffered a major reverse with the outbreak of World War I, in part because of the widespread eruption of nationalism, driven by the global economic downturn.

Great Britain, like other European countries at that time, suffered strikes on their railways and in their mines, both which had fueled global economic expansion, but brought about what became known as "the strange death of liberal England." Globalism for the time being in England stopped dead in its tracks. The British hunkered down to wait out the economic storm. Meanwhile, workers in Germany and Russia pushed back at globalized trade, and others did as well—some in a violent way, as Europe experienced a rise in anti-globalism-related terrorism by jobless citizens, such as at the Barcelona opera house in 1893 and the Parisian café bombing in 1894.[54]

The nineteenth-century losses were set aside as Europe recaptured prosperity in the wars of the first half of the twentieth century. Soon, a near-religious faith in the vision for a "European Union" fueled the globalist ideology once again and put nationalism into political exile. This resurgence came about only after two terrible twentieth-century wars tore apart the continent, whereby the center of gravity in Europe shifted away from nation-states and to the new centralized EU headquarters in Brussels, with its continent-wide market, a single economy, and government. EU-favoring globalists soon came to ask expectantly: Why can't the rest of the world embrace an EU-like project and inevitably realize a one-world government?

Americans understood that the EU isn't a template for global government and certainly not for the United States. America was isolationist from the time of independence through the early part of the twentieth century, at least until World War I and the ascension of President Woodrow Wilson. America didn't take the globalist bait to join other nations in the post-World War I hysteria to embrace Wilson's League of Nations, principally because of their reluctance over sovereign interests. At that time between the world wars, America continued to have a strong majority anti-interventionist movement led by Charles Lindbergh, the famed Atlantic-crossing pilot who vigorously fought to keep us out of foreign entanglements even as the Japanese and Germans aggressively gobbled up their adversaries during the 1930s.

It took the December 7, 1941, unprovoked Japanese attack on Pearl Harbor to persuade the American people to enter the war against the Axis powers. Until that time, President Franklin Roosevelt, an avowed globalist, had insufficient popular support to persuade the majority of Americans to support war. In fact, just prior to the Japanese attack, most members of Congress and citizens across the country held to an isolationist foreign policy view in spite of the country's brief foray decades earlier in World War I.

American attitudes post-World War II were primarily focused on national interests, not internationalism—much less globalism. After all, as Lord Ismay famously said about Europe's push to create the North Atlantic Treaty Organization (NATO), his motives were clear and geopolitically savvy: "To keep the Russians out, the Americans in, and the Germans down." America, with few exceptions, after the war wanted to return to isolationism, not foreign adventure—much less one world government.[55]

President Roosevelt knew most Americans didn't share anything like his objective of "governing the world." They were ready to shut down the borders and return to an insular lifestyle. Meanwhile, Secretary of State Edward Stettinius Jr., trying to deflect criticism from FDR's policy to create a successor to the failed League of Nations, said in 1945 that "the thought of fashioning any kind of super state is repugnant to us."[56]

Roosevelt's push to realize the full potential of the globalists' United Nations had limited popular support at the time and even less today because of its many failings. Further, America, in spite of the globalist push by President Obama, still stands apart because of national consensus on limiting government and thus rejecting the globalists' broader governance schemes. But there are cracks in that defense thanks to Obama, who abused our constitutionally-based limited government ethos and seeded a globalist view at every turn.

The same arrogant disregard for the framers' limited government approach for America is the very same ideological push globalists seek today by forcing us to "share" national sovereignty with international institutions, because as climate change advocates often argue, so many problems today are really "global."

THE NATIONALISTS

Author Dani Rodrick explains in *The Globalization Paradox: Democracy and the Future of the World Economy* that the natural political reaction to the ravages of globalism are job loss and failing trade. "We cannot simultaneously pursue democracy, national determination and economic globalization. If we want to push globalization further, we have to give up either the nation state or democratic politics," writes Rodrick.[57] That's in part why the nationalists are rising up believing that globalism intends to take a wrecking ball to every nation-state to destroy their national sovereignty, deny their territorial integrity (no borders), and homogenize every culture. The nationalists are diametrically opposed to everything embraced by the globalists.

Nationalists tend to take a decentralized view to government, believing people are best served at the local level but are not opposed to cooperating with others when global issues are at stake, such as wars when national interests are at risk. But they have no intention to surrender sovereignty, jobs, language, borders, and culture.

American nationalists trace their background to the eighteenth-century Boston Tea Party. On a cold December night in 1773, a large group of men disguised as Mohawk Indians boarded British merchant ships moored in Boston Harbor and set about destroying 342 chests of tea in protest to taxes imposed by the British Parliament.[58]

The British considered this a lawless act of unheard-of political activism. The British writer Samuel Johnson published a pamphlet at the time denouncing the colonials' tea parties and their arguments against imperial taxation, writing, "These antipatriotic prejudices are the abortions of folly impregnated by faction."

American nationalism has a rich history, which some historians like Jill Lepore, who writes in *The Whites of Their Eyes* that nationalism did indeed begin with the original Tea Party in Boston Harbor. That nationalism as an ideology grew with America to represent resentment of the well-bred, well-connected, and well-paid elite. In the early nineteenth century, this form of populist rebellion against the establishment came to be known as "Jacksonianism" after the former President Andrew Jackson, the leader who remade the American party system and introduced electoral politics.[59]

Jacksonian populists were known for being anti-establishment, which was a mixed record, especially when they rallied to universal white male suffrage and forced the country to accept a wrong-headed financial system. On the positive side, they fought against monopolistic corporations, for worker protection, and for support of threatened minorities. They also demanded land, which led to the Homestead Act and the Western movement of millions.

Intellectually, Jacksonian ideas are rooted in the common-sense tradition of the Scottish Enlightenment. This philosophy—that moral, scientific, political, and religious truths can be ascertained by the average person—is more than an intellectual conviction in the United States; it is a cultural force. Jacksonians regard supposed experts with suspicion, believing that the credentialed and the connected are trying to advance their own class agenda. These political, economic, scientific, or cultural elites often want to assert truths that run counter to the common-sense reasoning of Jacksonian America. That federal deficits produce economic growth and that free trade with low-wage countries raises Americans' living standards are the kind of propositions that clash with the common sense of many Americans. In the not-too-distant past, so did the assertion that people of different races deserve equal treatment before the law.

Similarly, a nationalist backlash grew in Europe as a result of the simultaneous rise of the threatening Ottoman Empire centered in Istanbul, Turkey, and the rapid industrialization across the continent that resulted in the concentration of factory workers in major West European cities.[60]

A nationalist backlash at the time spawned domestic terrorism traceable to international trade and its byproducts. After all, the expansionists, globalists, pushed for rapid change in industries that many people found difficult to accept, much less to adopt. So, they resisted the change or looked to others to blame, which explains the rise in terrorism. For example, opening the vast American markets led to Britain's "great agricultural depression" of 1873–96 that created resentment against international trade.[61]

Predictably, international trade soured some economies, giving rise to emergency government measures to protect domestic jobs. That's when we saw a rise in protectionist policies and the devaluation of currencies to make home products more competitive abroad.

Nationalist support for trade policies was difficult, but not nearly as challenging was gaining populist support for foreign adventures. President Roosevelt, as outlined earlier in this chapter, struggled to build support for intervention against the Axis powers. Certainly, the Japanese attack helped Roosevelt overcome the Jacksonian opinion, albeit temporarily, but he knew there were limits among the nationalists for adventures too far, such as taking a post-World War II harder line with the Soviets.

President Harry Truman faced much the same resistance after the war, particularly in his attempt to limit Moscow's ambitions. Truman's Secretary of State Dean Acheson pushed for a sustained global reach for the United States because no longer was the United Kingdom capable of exercising world power. Acheson pushed that agenda, believing only the U.S. could stop the Soviets' disruption of the balance of power in Europe and the Middle East. That launched America into what became the first Cold War juxtaposing the U.S. against the Soviet Union.

America's global engagements continued in spite of its strong isolationist desires, and for decades our country fought wars—Korea, Vietnam, and more recently Afghanistan and Iraq—contrary to our natural tendency and partly because Acheson was right: We were the only power capable of keeping a lid on the aggressive Soviet Union.

Now, in the second decade of the twenty-first century, we are seeing a renewed push-back to contemporary advances to globalization. The Brexit vote in the United Kingdom was a reaction against international cooperation, with the loss of sovereignty, unacceptable immigration, and slumping standard of living.

Thus far, the nationalist backlash across the rest of Europe hasn't sparked armed conflict, but that's still possible. But nationalism is growing, in part fueled by the European Union's allowance for mass immigration from North Africa and the Middle East and unacceptable anti-sovereignty globalism.

The 2016 presidential election in the United States may be a bell-wether for the nationalists who responded to the globalist overreach. Specifically, Russell Jones of Llewellyn Consulting writes of President Trump's trade policies: "Trump's trade stance would risk deepening already burgeoning global protectionist pressures, while at the same time resulting in higher prices, lower quality, and less choice for domestic consumers. It could also conceivably usher in a full-blown trade war akin to that of the 1930s."[62]

Jones says of the whole Trump policy package that:

Reviewing this inventory of policy proposals, what is striking is its naiveté and incoherence. It is a litany of simplistic ideas, with no guiding principle, little clear direction, and no over-arching notion of how these various initiatives might fit together to deliver short-term macroeconomic stability, or improved long-term growth potential and flexibility. Trumponomics is hyper-active, myopic, inward-looking, and never escapes the traps of equating a country with a business, or more generally of partial equilibrium analysis. It also runs against the grain of much that the US has stood for since 1945, and which has been the key-stone of the post-WWII global institutional architecture.[63]

At this point, angry voters are backing nationalist politicians across the world.

The election of Trump was, in part, according to Rush Limbaugh, the country's leading radio talk show host, a serious nationalist apprehension to electing Hillary Clinton, an avowed globalist. "People that voted for Donald Trump," said Limbaugh, were people who "really believe that they were gonna lose the country if Hillary Clinton won. This is not an idle thought; it's not an exaggeration. They really believe that the country as founded was up for grabs. It was over if Hillary had won, if the Democrats had another four or eight years to do what they do with the judiciary and so forth."[64]

Part of the globalist community that campaigned for Clinton against Trump remains behind, according to Limbaugh, to defeat Trump from within the bureaucracy. It is called "the deep state," an Obama shadow government embedded in the bureaucracy that is working against Trump.[65] This concept will be examined shortly.

Limbaugh said "the deep state" is real. "It's the Democrat Party. It's Hillary. It's Obama. It's all those people who just can't accept that they lost [the 2016 presidential election]." He went on to explain "all they've got is their embeds in the bureaucracy and the judiciary, and they're pulling out all the stops. There's no question." It is "run by Obama and Hillary and the hierarchy in the Democrat Party…is doing everything they can to undermine, to sabotage, and to prevent Trump from implementing his agenda. There's no question about it."[66]

"The deep state" includes the mainstream media and much of the liberal judiciary. Limbaugh said, "Donald Trump has nobody helping him other than the people that voted for him. Obama had the media; Obama had the judiciary; Obama had all kinds of support." He went on to explain that, unlike with Trump, "Obama was never challenged seriously by the media."[67]

The globalists who own and run the media are a cadre for "the deep state," according to Limbaugh. By "media," Limbaugh means: ABC, CBS, NBC, *New York Times*, *Washington Post*, *USA Today*, and *LA [Los*

Angeles] Times. "That cadre. They have a formula, they have a blueprint for destroying Republican political officials they don't like. It's not gonna work on Trump. He doesn't fit that model. They're trying to every day."[68]

Immigration is an issue captured by "the deep state" agenda as well. Limbaugh said:

> Immigration today, if you listen to the left, equals anybody who wants to come into the country should be allowed. That's not what immigration is. That's illegal immigration, and we ought to all oppose it. We are all in favor of immigration that determines who gets in, the quantity of people who get in, whether they assimilate or not. Nobody's opposed to that. But immigration has been defined now [by "the deep state" people] as people flooding the country who are noncitizens.[69]

The globalist-versus-nationalist war is taking place across the world. While globalists seek to destroy national cultures, borders, language, economies, currencies, and national resources in order to create their one-world government under their control, they are opposed by newly awakened people coming to better understand their radical agenda and how that threatens their lives.

EVIDENCE OF NEW COLD WAR

It takes two sides to fight, and recently Western Europe and the U.S. are awakening to the globalist-fostered war. Nationalists across those countries and elsewhere are beginning once again to push back against the twenty-first-century globalists' campaign.

Christopher Lasch and Benjamin Barber chronicle views regarding this new war in their books, *The Revolt of the Elites* and *Jihad vs. McWorld*. Both authors predict the death of democracy thanks to the globalist-inspired war.[70]

Lasch points out the globalists elite betray their own citizens and their allegiance to global initiatives. He addresses the so-called Davos man, the elite transnational who pushes for greater centralization and control, favoring global authorities and values. He anticipates a global takeover thanks to the divergence of the political, corporate, and professional Western elites.[71]

These globalists elite anticipated push-back from the nationalists, given sufficient success and time. Barber as well wrote that the globalists see the surge of nationalistic anti-establishment activity as the "last deep sigh" before what he calls the "yawn of McWorld" is baked in, or the surrender of the nationalists to the inevitable globalist agenda.[72]

Lasch and Barber both realize the siren-song, seductive powers of mass entertainment and cheaply produced fast food for formerly starving and bored non-Westerners. What they failed to foresee was the prolonged exposure to those same things would create a dulled and empty population. That emptiness would eat away at the leading populations of the West, and prove repulsive to the emerging world. They did not see that the appeal of the fruits of multinational corporations would be considered threats to older orders, sparking autoimmune reactions.[73]

These men were blind to how weak the first world had become stewed under a treasonous leadership. They surmised the McWorld has become drugged and softened up to the point the masses no longer pose a threat to the elites. Further, neither author believes the elite would actually seek to destroy their own nations by relishing a flood of foreigners.

The elite idea is to stuff the wealthy nations with enough aliens and minorities to make them so weak that even the nationalists couldn't rally enough backing to fight. But the globalists also failed to anticipate that Western elites would overreach both economically and socially to create some of the contemporary crises, such as the deep recession starting in 2009 across America and Europe.

Lasch and Barber provide indictors of the new cold war and cite some pretty terrific miscalculations on the globalists' behalf, but many more indicators will follow. There is overwhelming evidence the war is just beginning.

Consider some of that evidence.

Globalists want to disarm all citizens.

A major indicator of the globalist-nationalist war is the globalist attempt to encroach on American's Second Amendment rights by persuading the U.S. Congress to pass the UN Small Arms Treaty. Globalists pushed the treaty, which denies civilians the right to own, buy, sell, trade, or transfer all weapons, including handguns as well as most ammunition, as well as "parts and components" of weapons.[74]

Globalists will use their influence to push the U.S. to embrace the treaty. If in fact Congress at some future time passes the Small Arms Treaty, then it must enforce the no buy, sell, trade, or transfer aspects—and that could result in another revolutionary war.

Globalists are pushing more wars.

Globalists want to initiate unprovoked wars of aggression against nationalist leaders. We saw that in Iraq against that country's dictator Saddam Hussein. Granted, he was a terrible leader, but now, more than a decade later, does anyone defend any of the rationale for going to war in 2003? No. That was an unnecessary war and arguably started because of globalist, neoconservative leaders beginning with President George W. Bush.

Much the same can be said of the civil war that mushroomed in Syria. The Syrian war reflects just how highly consequential the globalist's *modus operandi* can be at displacing millions of war refugees and killing hundreds of thousands of people throughout the Northern Levant.

The Libyan civil war is another fiasco that demonstrates how quickly the globalists can ruin a reasonably well-run nation (albeit with a clenched fist) and one that long cooperated with the U.S. Likewise, the Ukraine civil war shows how efficiently the globalists can inflame religious differences, cultural disparities, and nationalist interests to destroy a national economy and split a nation.[75] Yes, we can blame Russia in part for that civil war, but remember: Our push into Moscow's periphery shares some of the blame for poking the Russian bear in the eye and daring him to attack.

Once the war is undertaken, the globalists then seize upon completely legitimate acts of self-defense and spin them as some type of war crime that never occurred. It is virtually always the globalists who are committing the actual war crimes when they do occur, as well as the shocking crimes against humanity in other countries around the world. They then use the many false flag bombings and shootings and assassinations to frame the nationalists. In the aftermath, they invariably ramp up the false media reports which unjustly vilify the nationalists as war criminals when it is the globalists who are really the criminally insane psychopaths.

Globalist create terror groups.

The Islamic State of Iraq and Syria (ISIS) is a creation of the globalists to terrorize the world, and that started with President Bush and especially with President Obama.

Globalists use Islamists to advance their fight. A former Defense Intelligence Agency chief said the Obama administration made a "willful decision" to support al-Qaeda, the Muslim Brotherhood, and other jihadist groups in Syria. Those groups fought Syrian dictator Bashar al-Assad and, as a result, gave rise to the extremist group the Islamic State.[76]

Retired Lt. Gen. Michael Flynn, the former DIA chief and briefly Trump's national security director, responded to an interview that cited a 2012 DIA-produced report that confirms the globalist-backed "revolution" against Assad was a "holy war" being led by al-Qaeda, the Muslim Brotherhood, and other jihadi. The report confirmed that the West and its Sunni Islamic dictator allies were supporting those same forces.

"The West, Gulf countries [regimes of Saudi Arabia, UAE, etc.], and Turkey support the Syrian opposition," the report states. Then it indicates that al-Qaeda and other terrorist groups are the "major forces driving the insurgency" against the Syrian despot.

Flynn confirmed in the interview the Obama administration supported Islamic terror groups, including al-Qaeda, in the fight against the Assad regime. "I don't know that they turned a blind eye, I think it was a decision," the former DIA chief said. "I think it was a willful decision." The report continued: "A willful decision to support an insurgency that had Salafists, al Qaeda and the Muslim Brotherhood?" Flynn replied: "It was a willful decision to do what they're doing."

Harness the power of international organizations.

Globalists love international organizations such as the United Nations that seeks to usurp the sovereign state's rule and replace it with a global government—one-world government. That view is evidenced by the UN leadership.

Former UN Secretary-General Ban Ki-moon said on June 26, 2015: "The United Nations is the hope and home of all humankind. The [UN] charter is our compass." The secretary-general is not unique in his UN idolatry. Millions of people across the world have bought into UN globalism believing that organization is the salvation in every crisis.

The UN has become their "god." No, UN officials and their supporters will deny that they advocate actual worship of the organization and its charter, but UN authorities and their elitist supporters in the media, nongovernmental organizations, and many governments advocate for the UN, as it is said, to "transform the Tower of Babel on the East River [the UN headquarters building on the Hudson River in New York City] into an object of global worship."[77]

Some within the UN community do enthrone the UN as a neopagan, demonic religious force. *The New American* published detailed exposes of the UN's Ark of Hope (a mockery of the Ark of the Covenant), the Earth Charter, the World Curriculum, and more.[78]

Robert Muller, the author of *The World Core Curriculum*, declared the UN would lead to "the apotheosis of human life on Earth." Muller is the friend of the UN's official guru, Indian spiritualist Sri Chinmoy, who conducted meditations for UN staff, ambassadors, and diplomats. Chinmoy said, "No human force will ever be able to destroy the United Nations, for the United Nations is not a mere building or a mere idea; it is not a man-made creation. The United Nations is the vision-light of the Absolute Supreme, which is slowly, steadily and unerringly illumining the ignorance, the night of our human life."[79]

Ban Ki-moon awarded divinity to the UN by labeling it mankind's "compass." That's not surprising when you consider that the idea of the UN was crafted by communist Alger Hiss. After all, a former top communist, Joseph Zach Kornfeder, once said "The UN 'blueprint' is a communist one"—a view backed by former UN Secretary-General U Thant of Burma, a Marxist who once said, "Lenin's ideals of peace and peaceful coexistence among states...are in line with the aims of the UN charter." Of course, it was Lenin who has the blood of millions on his hands thanks to his push for worldwide mass murder, war, persecution, torture, enslavement, and subversion.[80]

Globalists push population control.

Globalists elite and their proxies are enthusiastic about the concept of population reduction. Of course, the globalists elite see themselves as a separate species with superior makeup and destined for global rulership. Ted Turner, the globalist owner of CNN, told *Audubon* magazine, "A total world population of 250–300 million people, a 95 percent decline from present levels, would be ideal."[81]

Just how far might globalists like Turner go with their push for population control? John Holdren, President Obama's science advisor, once said: "A program of sterilizing women after their second or third child, despite the relatively greater difficulty of the operation than vasectomy, might be easier to implement than trying to sterilize men…. The development of a long-term sterilizing capsule that could be implanted under the skin and removed when pregnancy is desired opens additional possibilities for coercive fertility control. The capsule could be implanted at puberty and might be removable, with official permission, for a limited number of births."[82]

This is a radical view and frightening that a top presidential adviser would openly recommend such a policy. Perhaps globalists like Holdren espouse such a view because they are eugenicists believing as did the Nazis and their "final solution" that some people are genetically inferior and should be eliminated. Then there is also the possibility that globalists like Turner want a smaller global population because it is much easier to dominate, their ultimate aim.

One step at a time to one-world government.

Africa could be the first victim of one-world government globalists. It is being unified economically and politically under an EU-style regime known formally as the "African Union." Some say that push is a plot to eliminate national sovereignty. This effort was supported by the Obama administration, the EU, and communist China.

Other regional plots are under way across the world in Latin American, Eurasia, and Europe, Southeast Asia, and the Middle East. Of course, the most advanced is the European Union.

These regional union regimes are being created by globalists who claim they are working for "free trade" although in reality they are building transnational bureaucracies with the intent of bringing all regions into a single global system.

The path for Africa began much as did Europe's to the EU with the establishment of transnational governmental institutions for collective trade, prosperity, and peace. It hasn't happened as yet in Africa because the continent lacks the necessary infrastructure. So, as a preliminary goal to reach continent-wide unity, globalists accepted subregional governments hoping in time they will merge into a single African government.

The subregional approach is illustrated by the creation of the "Tripartite Free Trade Area" (TFTA). The aim of the TFTA is to integrate African regional economic communities (REC) into a free-trade area that encompasses Cape Town, South Africa, to Cairo, Egypt. The bloc will include three subregional areas effectively removing national borders for six hundred million people with more than $1 trillion worth of economic activity.[83]

In time Africa's other subregional areas are expected to join the TFTF, thus realizing a single "economic governance." It is noteworthy that the UN is training African officials on the particulars of trade by mostly Western globalists. Eventually, according to Soamiely Andriamananjara at George Washington University, the plan will require "real political will from regional and national policymakers."

"Indeed, the deal is expected to be the launching pad for the establishment of the even more ambitious continental free trade area that is expected to cover all of Africa. In the process, the launch has demonstrated the possibility of collective action among 26 very heterogeneous nations (e.g., with GDP per capita ranging from the Seychelles' almost $16,000 to Burundi's $270) and shows the feasibility of harmonizing three very different preferential trade regimes into one unified scheme.[84]

Globalists hope to follow a similar plan for the entire world, and this isn't a secret. "The contemporary quest for world order [world government] will require a coherent strategy to establish a concept of order [regional government] within the various regions and to relate these regional orders [governments] to one another," explained globalist Henry Kissinger.[85]

Formation of "deep state."

The formation of a globalist shadow government by the left—or, which some like Rush Limbaugh refer to as "the deep state"—ramps up the new cold war and the seriousness of the ideological conflict ahead, especially in Washington. The "deep state" is a shadow government, a term coined in Turkey, a system composed of elements of the intelligence services, military, judiciary, and organized crime.

Author of *The Party Is Over* Mike Lofgren defines "deep state" as "a hybrid association of key elements of government and parts of top-level finance and industry that is effectively able to govern the United States with only limited reference to the consent of the governed as normally expressed through elections."[86]

The globalists elite certainly fit that definition because they have broad influence over many power centers—government, finance, industry, politics, and much more. Besides, the elite have no respect for the peasant class—that's the rest of us. The widespread suspicions in Washington and across the country about National Security Agency surveillance ignited a national debate about civil liberties and who is spying on whom. But the loss of power is expansive and breathtaking, going far beyond simple wire-tapping of citizens.

Trump supporters were certainly aware of the disproportionate influence of powerful people—read "globalists elite"—over affairs in Washington, which explains why Trump promises to "drain the Washington swamp" resonated. Over decades, there has been a gradual "revolution within the form," a concept championed by the sixteenth-century philosopher Niccolò Machiavelli. While outwardly the institutions of government [the form] appear to remain the same, Lofgren rightly contends that our venerable government institutions "have grown more and more resistant to the popular will as they have become hardwired into a corporate and private network with almost unlimited cash to enforce its will."[87]

The globalist cabal controls much of the power centers in Washington and will do whatever necessary to maintain that position, a necessary step to their new world order.

Other aspects of globalist agenda seen today.

There are many more indictors pointing to the new cold war. For example, there are a variety of global financial crises being created or at least leveraged by globalists. We've seen the U.S. Federal Reserve and the IMF create significant financial distress and others have threatened to manipulate financial markets in Europe, China, and even here in the United States. This manipulation impacts jobs and personal wealth, and creates significant stress for much of the world.

CONCLUSION

The globalist-nationalist cold war is very real and heating up. Unfortunately, much of the world is naïve about the growing conflict and the threat it poses.

CHAPTER FOUR

What the World Public Understands about the Ideological Cold War

Not Much, and Why

Most people are clueless about the globalists elite and the impact they are having for the world—in particular for the lives of virtually every human being. However, the issue of globalized trade and public reaction to it provide some insight about how the public might react to the more nefarious aspects of the ideological fight if, in fact, they ever become aware, and if it's not already too late.

In 2014, Pew Research asked the public across forty-four countries about the impact of globalization for their country and them personally. That survey found four in five people across the world say international trade and global business are good for their country and, by a similar number (74 percent), those same people believe it is beneficial for their economy when foreign companies build in their country.[88] However, there was bad news for the apostles of globalization in the same survey. Specifically, only half (54 percent) believe trade creates local jobs, and less than half (45 percent) believe it increases wages.[89]

Americans are the most skeptical about the benefits of international trade, according to the same survey. Barely 17 percent of Americans think international trade leads to higher wages and only one in five believes it creates new jobs. Slightly more (28 percent) say foreign companies buying American companies is good for the country.[90]

The Pew Research finding was echoed two years later by *The Economist*, a weekly magazine-format newspaper owned by the globalist Economist Group in London. The Economist Group's survey arm reached out to residents in nineteen countries to find that globalization suffered a recent setback—fewer than half support globalization—in countries like the U.S., Britain, and France, where wages are stagnant. On the broader issue of whether globalization is a "force for good" in the world, according to the same survey, only 11 percent of Americans believe the world improved in the past year.[91]

Globalism was hit especially hard in France, where some 52 percent of Frenchmen now believe their economy should not have to rely on imports, and a little more than one in ten (13 percent) reckon immigration has a positive effect on their country. That's good news for France's nationalists, especially groups like the European nationalist parties.[92]

Demographically, globalization is viewed favorably by millennials far more than other groups, according to the survey. In America, 46 percent of those aged 18–34 (the Millennials) believe immigration has a positive effect on their country, compared with 35 percent of those 55 and older. That generational gap is larger in Britain: 53 percent and 22 percent, respectively.[93]

It is not surprising that countries with the fastest-growing economies are far more positive about the effects of globalization. While majorities in the Western countries oppose the idea of foreigners buying indigenous companies, most Asians favor the purchases, believing they are good for their countries and themselves.[94]

Globalization is about much more than trade, as you have come to realize in the earlier chapters. The growing and broad skepticism demonstrated above explains in part the 2016 political eruption in Great Britain and as well as in the United States. Electorates across those countries were awakened at least momentarily to the globalist threat, albeit from trade and the immigration aspects.

How resilient is this rejection of the globalist agenda? It really comes down to whether the broader global public really comes to appreciate the real agenda of the globalists elite.

Tyler Durden wrote an insightful blog for Newstex: "Are Globalists Evil or Just Misunderstood?" The blog profiles four public views about globalists.[95] Durden's analysis is not encouraging if, in fact, it will take a global, concerted reaction to push back on the broader globalists elite.

The public that gives any thought to the globalists do so from at least one of four perspectives, according to Durden. The first group dismisses the allegation that globalists are in fact financial elitists who seek global power. Their skepticism would be hard to overcome without irrefutable evidence, and then it might not even change their behavior.[96]

The second category of public thought about the globalist cabal are those who attribute the globalists' ambitions and collusion to being motivated by greed and profit. This group dismisses the idea the globalists conspire within their circle of like-minded elitists to grasp control of the earth.

The third public group soberly believes the globalists elite are an organized cult, a byproduct of corruption, a reflection of the dire state of mankind, nothing more. They are accused of promoting an "ism"-like agenda: communism, socialism, and totalitarianism. Of course, this group believes these elitist "ism" advocates are interested in promoting their leadership and their ideological "ism" across the world.

The fourth group of public observers is the biblical prophecy sector of the population who believe the globalists elite will in fact usher in the "new world order" quickly followed by the rise of the Antichrist and then the end times. One view among the prophecy watchers is that resisting the globalists is futile because of the influence of the unseen realm, and defiance is not God's will. This is a rather naïve view and inconsistent with Scriptures, because Christians are consistently called to resist the evil and promote the salvation of Christ until His return.

Yet another view among some prophecy watchers is a clear view of the prophecies that remain to be fulfilled, and they feel accountable to God for sounding the alarm and peacefully but strongly resisting what they believe is the evil intent of the globalists. These "watchmen" would invoke Ezekiel 33:1–6 (KJV), which states:

> Again the word of the Lord came unto me, saying, Son of man, speak to the children of thy people, and say unto them, When I bring the sword upon a land, if the people of the land take a man of their coasts, and set him for their watchman:
>
> If when he seeth the sword come upon the land, he blow the trumpet, and warn the people; then whosoever heareth the sound of the trumpet, and taketh not warning; if the sword come, and take him away, his blood shall be upon his own head.
>
> He heard the sound of the trumpet, and took not warning; his blood shall be upon him. But he that taketh warning shall deliver his soul.
>
> But if the watchman see the sword come, and blow not the trumpet, and the people be not warned; if the sword come, and take any person from among them, he is taken away in his iniquity; but his blood will I require at the watchman's hand.

Similarly, these "watchmen" would invoke Matthew 24:42 where Jesus gives a command to Christians to watch for the signs of His return.

Clearly, at least in 2016 we saw plenty of evidence that a segment of Westerners of all stripes are aware of the globalist threat. Likely, they account for the last three groups Durden identifies above and likely many others as well. Specifically, we saw evidence of this in the June 2016 Brexit (a portmanteau of "Britain" and "exit," meaning the British referendum to leave the European Union [EU]) and the November

2016 election of President Trump together evidence an awakening in the West to the globalist threat. The pregnant question is: How long will the awakening last?

Consider an analysis of what prompted the British public to rebuff globalist EU membership.

The British rejection of EU membership is a response to the ruling globalists elite who really don't care for what some refer to as the "ignorant masses" and the things they want like their culture, language, sovereignty and not the least of which their jobs.

The globalists elite were shocked by the outcome of the June 23, 2016 British vote to exit the European Union. This "earthquake" called Brexit literally shocked most of the political class, the media and the master puppeteer globalists.

"Brexit earthquake has happened, and the rubble will take years to clear," wrote Rafael Behr in the U.K.'s *Guardian*, a pro-EU daily. "Politics as practiced for a generation is upended," said Behr, "traditional party allegiances are shredded; the prime minister's authority is bust— and that is just the parochial domestic fallout. A whole continent looks on in trepidation. It was meant to be unthinkable, now the thought has become action. Europe cannot be the same again."[97]

Leading up to the vote the pro-EU British media labeled those who favored Brexit as "project fear," a propaganda campaign. Those criticizing the referendum were globalists such as British Prime Minister David Cameron, German Chancellor Angela Merkel, President Barack Obama, billionaire investor George Soros, the International Monetary Fund, global bankers, the pro-EU political class, elites with the Council on Foreign Relations (CFR), and the British Royal Institute of International Affairs (RIIA), to name the most prominent. This cabal of globalists elite threatened that a British vote to leave the EU would result in an economic crash, loss of jobs and pensions, and worse.

The British people turned out to defy the globalists' predictions to demand their government's departure from the European Union. What does the British decision mean for the global community? It is a shot across the bow of the globalists' aim of the new world order, and in particular, the European Union, which is considered the model for future regional organizations ultimately leading to one world government.

EU skeptics have good reason to push back. The EU morphed from the former six-member 1951 Treaty of Paris establishing the European Coal and Steel Community (ECSC) focused on production of coal and steel into the European economic community, then into the European community and finally into today's EU. Each step meant the members surrendered more sovereignty to the collective bureaucracy in Brussels under the collective thumbs of the Eurocrat elite. British voters saw what happened and wanted no more surrendering of their threadbare sovereignty. They demanded their country back.

The Brexit earthquake was slow in coming. The path leading to that outcome was jammed with an assortment of agreements that incrementally robbed Britain of her sovereignty that began, as outlined above, with the ECSA, but soon became the European Communities Act (1972), the Single European Act (1986), the Schengen Agreement (1990), the Maastricht Treaty (1992), the Amsterdam Treaty (1998), the Treaty of Nice (2000), and the Lisbon Treaty (2007). The worst was arguably the 1957 Treaty of Rome that called for "an ever closer union," that set the stage for the economic and political union across Europe.

This house of cards held, albeit by thin threads until the massive refugee/migrant crisis of 2015 pushed the average British citizen over the edge. Although the Brits opted out of the open-borders 1990 Schengen agreement, they watched in horror as EU states were overrun by 1.5 million mostly Muslim "refugees" from North Africa and the Middle East. Even though the United Kingdom didn't embrace Schengen its pro-immigration Labor government (mostly socialists with globalist views) allowed in hundreds of thousands of migrants.

Brexit was indeed a victory for the average British citizen over the elite classes of big government, the misguided Labor parliamentarians, their media, business, and of course the EU. Predictably, the globalists elite aren't accepting defeat. The elite insist Brexit doesn't mean Britain should exit the EU, because, as the elite insist, the ignorant "leave" voters should be ignored. So much for democracy—but a sure indication of the elite's true agenda.

Globalist Jeremy Shapiro wrote an article titled, "Brexit Was a Rejection of Britain's Governing Elite. Too Bad the Elites Were Right." Shapiro is the director for the European Council on Foreign Relations and a senior fellow at a Washington liberal think-tank, Brookings Institution, and a former Obama adviser at the State Department on topics such as the disastrous "Arab Spring" and the Muslim Brotherhood, the seed organization for Osama bin Laden's al Qaeda that attacked America on September 9, 2001.

Shapiro, like other global elites, attacked the British who favored leaving the EU. Brexit showed, according to Shapiro, that "like turkeys voting for Christmas, the British have opted to weaken their economy, reduce their international standing, and create massive uncertainty at a time when the world really doesn't need it. All in the name of the abstract concepts of 'independence' and sovereignty."

Much like other arrogant globalists elite, Shapiro attacks the British voters' desire to recover independence and sovereignty, which for them are more than "abstract concepts." Shapiro rightly discerned why the vote happened. "It has to do with a growing divide between the governing and the governed."

James Traub joined the elitist attack on British voters in his *Foreign Policy* article, "It's Time for the Elites to Rise Up Against the Ignorant Masses." "The Brexit has laid bare the political schism of our time. It's not about the left vs. the right; it's about the sane vs. the mindlessly angry," wrote Traub.[98]

"The schism we see opening before us is not just about policies, but about reality," Traub argues in *Foreign Policy*. The "ignorant people" won the Brexit vote because they believed the "lying" and "cynical" Brexiteers.

Traub believes "it is necessary to say that people are deluded and that the task of leadership [the elites] is to un-delude them. Is that 'elitist'? Maybe it is; maybe we have become so inclined to celebrate the authenticity of all personal conviction that it is now elitist to believe in reason, expertise, and the lessons of history."[99]

Shapiro and Traub reflect the cabal of elitist denizens who decry the citizen uprising in Great Britain, and collectively they intend to reverse not only the results of the Brexit referendum, but also to stop similar "earthquakes" elsewhere in Europe and unseat Donald Trump as well.[100]

Expect the globalists elite to strike back with a vengeance. Certainly, we've seen that in part in Great Britain's elite rejection of the Brexit decision and much the same regarding President Trump's election. Will the contagion that brought about Brexit and the Trump election end there, or might it spread to defeat the globalists elite?

The organized globalists elite are not about to give up and expect to overcome recent setbacks. Their conspiracy, evil-inspired counters are just beginning to be seen.

Hillarie du Berrier wrote an account of the conspiratorial history of the Common Market/EU and the role of the elitists in the early 1970s. That report, the "Story of the Common Market," outlined the intrigues of elites with the CFR-RIIA-Atlantic Council-Bilderberger-Trilateral Commission.

"The CFR," wrote du Berrier, "saw the Common Market from the first as a regional government to which more and more nations would be added until the world government which [the] UN had failed to bring about would be realized. At a favorable point in the Common Market's development America would be brought in. But the American public had to be softened first and leaders groomed for the change-over."

Brexit was an important shot across the bow, but the battle for sovereignty and genuine representative government, and against plutocratic absolutism, continues—and will intensify.

CONCLUSION

The cold war is brewing and picking up steam. Yet much of the global public is totally unaware of the fight. They see the fight consisting of differences of opinion, politics, left vs. right, rich vs. poor, and Western vs. all others. They see the daily fights over trade and sovereignty. But the general public is far from recognizing that the real goal of the globalists is control—total control over life on the planet to the benefit of the elite. In other words, people tend to see the skirmishes, but fail to see the total campaign picture. And as we shall see, the campaign is controlled by what is unseen in an entirely different invisible realm.

CHAPTER FIVE

Globalism Over the Horizon

Many globalists believe the nation-state is obsolete, national sovereignty is a problem, and mankind must establish a system of global governance. They argue that nation-states are almost always in conflict, and more often than not, that leads to war. Therefore, the only way to prevent future wars, according to globalists, is to eliminate nation-states by placing mankind under a single global authority such that, when disputes do inevitably erupt, a worldwide authority imposes its will to maintain peace.

America has a history of prominent leaders who subscribed to that global peacemaker view and who took direct action to attempt to stand-up such a system of global governance. This chapter will address a few of those leaders, their globalist, new-world-order agenda, their radical modus operandi, and a Christian view of the globalist phenomenon as well as what it means for the coming biblical end times.

Following World War I, U.S. President Woodrow Wilson had the vision to prevent future wars by establishing a system of global governance called the League of Nations, an initiative mentioned earlier in this volume. The League's Covenant included collective security and disarmament and settling disputes, as well as addressing labor conditions, human and drug trafficking, global health, and protecting minorities. However, the League lived but twenty-six years and proved incapable of preventing the Second World War. Fortunately, the U.S. Congress understood Wilson's goal of creating the League as tantamount to the surrender of U.S. sovereignty to an international governance body. Congress refused to ratify (approve) the treaty.

President Franklin D. Roosevelt shared Wilson's vision for global governance. Shortly before his death in 1945, President Roosevelt said, "The structure of world peace cannot be the work of one man, or one party, or one nation…it must be a peace which rests on the cooperative effort of the whole world."[101] That view led President Roosevelt to serve as the principal architect of the United Nations with the purpose of keeping the peace, encouraging respect for human rights, and creating conditions under justice and respect for international laws.

It is clear Roosevelt intended for the U.N. to be a global power, and that organization's history demonstrates that it has become a paper tiger in spite of its lofty aim. Author Stephen Schlesinger wrote in *Act of Creation: The Founding of the U.N.* that Roosevelt "insisted that nations had to abide by the decisions of the [U.N.'s] Security Council. They either obeyed or they quit the U.N." It's also noteworthy that Roosevelt was a supporter of international collective security to the point, according to Schlesinger, that Roosevelt "wanted to quit the [U.S.] presidency and become the U.N.'s first secretary general. This is what he really wanted to be remembered for rather than as an American president."[102]

President Roosevelt's Wilsonian "new world order" passion, vis-à-vis the U.N., was even evident in his decision regarding the American dollar bill, as strange as that might seem. Roosevelt ordered the term "*Novus Ordo Seclorum*" placed on the back of the one-dollar bill, under the pyramid. *Novus* is Latin for "new," *ordo* means "order," and *seclorum* means "secular or world"; thus, the phrase is translated "A New Order of the Ages," which, according to then Secretary of Agriculture Henry

Wallace, who recommended the addition to Roosevelt, meant for him the "New Deal of the Ages."[103]

Wallace explained his recommendation to use the phrase on U.S. currency. At the time "the reverse side of the Seal [of the United States] had never been used [on U.S. currency]." Roosevelt noted, according to Wallace, the nation's Great Seal "was first struck with the representation of the 'All Seeing Eye,' a Masonic representation of The Great Architect of the Universe. Next he was impressed with the idea that the foundation for the new order of the ages had been laid in 1776, but that it would be completed only under the eye of the Great Architect. Roosevelt like myself [Wallace] was a 32nd degree Mason." The new bill, with the term under the pyramid with the "All Seeing Eye," began to be printed in the summer of 1935. But does Wallace's translation, "New Deal of the Ages," really mean "new world order"? Certainly, it could, and was in fact a precursor view later echoed by others.

Wilson and Roosevelt were joined by many other influential American figures over the subsequent decades who share grand new-world-order ambitions for mankind. In 1992, presidential candidate Bill Clinton's future deputy secretary of state, Strobe Talbot, predicted that "within the next hundred years, nationhood as we know it will be obsolete; all states will recognize a single, global authority."[104] The concept of a new world order started slowly, but began to resonate late in the twentieth century, especially among globalists elite.

One size doesn't necessarily fit all when it comes to globalists, however. Not all are focused on total world domination, a new world order. Some actually want the best for all mankind and believe the pathway to that goal is simple: free trade, economic migration, and shared wealth.[105] Many of these same people truly believe that modern man faces a very serious environmental threat—climate change—as well, and that mankind must quickly address that issue before life on earth becomes physically intolerable.

Other globalists who may share those views also seek ends that are far more sinister: Destroy all nations and unite them under one world government, not because of "man-made" climate change or the danger of future war. No, they believe their agenda for the world is best. For example, David Rockefeller, the former chairman of the board of Chase Bank, said as much after he was accused of being "part of a secret cabal working against the best interests of the United States, cauterizing my family and me as 'internationals' and of conspiring with others around the world to build a more integrated global political and economic structure—one world, if you will. If that's the charge, I stand guilty, and I am proud of it."[106]

The new-world-order theory espoused by Rockefeller and his fellow luminaries posited a period of world power realignment in which the earth is ruled by a single, worldwide system of government—something far more powerful and encompassing than Wilson's League of Nations or Roosevelt's United Nations. The empty promise is that this future one world system of government will free the world of wars as well as defeat famine, disease, and political turmoil.

More contemporary figures like Henry Kissinger, the former secretary of state under President Richard Nixon, encouraged President Barack Obama to focus on a new world order much like the other presidents mentioned above. "I think his [Obama's] task will be to develop an overall strategy for America in this period when, really, a new world order can be created. It's a great opportunity; it isn't just a crisis."[107]

This world system, according to globalists like Kissinger, will do away with diverse governments and install a one-world political body that eliminates all borders and differences across cultures, values, faiths, and ideologies; uses a single, worldwide currency; and promotes unity through one language for all people. After all, globalists elite like Kissinger tend to be collectivists because that's the best form of social control. So, they favor giant organizations like the United Nations and totalitarian regimes like the one in China.

The globalists elite come to embrace this view through ideology. They tend to be social Darwinists, which means they subscribe to the self-deluded view that their personal financial success and natural intelligence made them worthy of dominance over the masses. That view leads them to embrace the nineteenth-century view of natural selection and survival of the fittest to human society. This globalist viewpoint has significant implications for practices commonly associated with the globalist agenda, such as population control.

Some globalists like Bill Gates want to reduce the world's population through force such as forced vaccinations and eugenics.[108] Why? One source indicates the globalists elite see a large global population as a threat to their dominance, and especially an intelligent middle class. That's why the globalists elite plan to destroy the middle class and marginalize the balance of the population to prevent them from rebelling. How large is large enough for the globalists? One source (CNN's Ted Turner) suggests the global population should be five hundred million, rather than today's 7.4 billion population.[109] Does that mean that some globalists are predisposed to facilitate measures that shed the world of seven billion souls?

Part of the globalists' agenda is to keep the vast majority of the earth's population uneducated and uninformed through substandard education and media manipulation. Further, they keep the masses in an obedient stupor through fear; violate national sovereignty through executive actions, false debt, rigged banking systems, equity market manipulation, corporate theft, the weaponization of the Internet (cyberwarfare), global pervasive surveillance violating all civil liberties, and much more.[110]

We will explore these so-called globalists elite and their agenda in far more detail in the next section. However, for now, understand the globalists' general aims as well as some of their worst characteristics and how these play out on the world stage.

Andrew Lobaczewski, in his book, *Political Porerology: A Science on the Nature of Evil Adjusted for Political Purposes,* claims that some globalists elite are psychopathic, as are up to 10 percent of the world's overall population.[111] Psychopathy is a personality disorder characterized by persistent antisocial behavior, impaired empathy, and egotistical traits.

Some of the best known psychopaths in history include Ivan the Terrible, Adolf Hitler, and Jack the Ripper.[112]

Globalists elite who may be psychopathic employ their deep pockets and their psychopathic views to capture global centers of power to thus gain more control over the masses. Lobaczewski claims this group has no conscience, as demonstrated by a sheer lust for power, and are capable of anything. They subscribe to a philosophy that says the ends justify the means, and they are not above lying or waging war to reach their objectives.[113]

Evidently, some globalists elite even practice a form of pagan religion "based on the mystery school religions of Sumer and Babylon under which they seek to achieve godhood." They also are accused of using religion to control the masses, which reminds us of Lenin's view that religion is the opioid of the masses.[114]

We will explore the very dark side of the globalists elite community and their secret societies in the next section. However, at least for now it's important to understand some of the tools the globalists elite use to reach their nefarious goals.

GLOBALISM'S MODUS OPERANDI: TOOLS FOR THEIR SINISTER AGENDA

Some globalist proxies resort to violence much like what happened in early 2017 at the University of California Berkeley. On that night at Berkeley, globalist anarchists reported to be George Soros-paid agents attacked free speech, an all-too-common modus operandi of their educational philosophy.

Jon Rappaport, an investigative reporter with thirty years of experience, wrote in February 2017 about the shutting down of free speech at Berkeley because the campus Republicans were to host Milo Yiannopoulos, a British public speaker and former editor for *Breitbart News*, to speak. That evening, the Soros anarchists chanted: "No borders, no nations, [f...] deportations."[115] This was an obvious reference to newly inaugurated President Trump's campaign promise to get tough on illegal immigration.

The violent protests were widely reported by the news media. SFGATE reported, "A protest at UC Berkeley over a scheduled appearance by right-wing provocateur Milo Yiannopoulos turned fiery and violent Wednesday night, prompting police to cancel the event and hustle the Breitbart News editor off campus."[116]

CBS News reported the protest was infiltrated by vandals:

As the gathered crowd got more agitated, masked "black bloc" activists [hired anarchists] began hurling projectiles including bricks, lit fireworks and rocks at the building and police. Some used police barriers as battering rams to attack the doors of the venue, breaching at least one of the doors and entering the venue on the first floor. In addition to fireworks being thrown up onto the second-floor balcony, fires were lit outside the venue, including one that engulfed a gas-powered portable floodlight.[117]

NBC News reported:

"The violence was instigated by a group of about 150 masked agitators who came onto campus and interrupted an otherwise non-violent protest," UC Berkeley said in a statement. Some people were attacked and police treated six people for injuries, the university said.... Berkeley College Republicans said before the protests that a "groupthink phenomenon" has taken hold at the California university that silences conservative speech, and while it doesn't agree with everything Yiannopoulos has said or done "We saw the chance to host Milo as an opportunity that was too good to pass up. He is somebody who stands up for those who are too afraid or intimidated to speak out on campus, and he voraciously defends speech from all sides of the political spectrum", the group said in a statement earlier. After the violence, the group said in a statement: "The Free Speech Movement is dead. Today, the Berkeley College Republicans' constitutional right to free speech was silenced by criminals and thugs seeking to cancel Milo Yiannopoulos' tour."[118]

It's noteworthy that free-speech intolerant globalists allegedly hired those anarchist thugs to shut down someone who evidently agrees with them on many issues. Milo Yiannopoulus, in his past speeches, points out issues that ought to be a concern of leftists, such as what he once said: "Hillary Clinton is funded by people who murder homosexuals." He has said, "Now, some of the most dangerous places for women to be in the world are modern, Western, rich European countries. Why? One reason. Islamic immigration—it's got to stop."[119]

There were reports at the time in Russia's Sputnik News that claim large sums of money were offered to protesters who would disrupt Trump's inauguration and, by association, those who align with his message. Were the ads a hoax? Judge for yourself. The following solicitations for protesters were reported in Sputnik News.[120]

Job advertisements running in 20 cities across the US are offering $2,500 a month for "operatives" willing to protest the upcoming inauguration of US President-elect Donald Trump.

San Francisco-based Demand Protest posted ads on Backpage.com, seeking applicants who would like to "Get paid fighting against Trump!" Along with the monthly $2,500 retainer, the company offers a "standard per-event pay of $50/hr., as long as you participate in at least 6 events a year," and full-time operatives are eligible for vision, dental and health insurance.

Allegedly globalists like George Soros do fund anarchists to trample messages they don't like while other globalists conspire to overturn entire countries, according to author Servando Gonzalez who wrote, *Psychological Warfare and the New World Order: The Secret War Against the American People.*[121]

Mr. Gonzalez outlines a globalist modus operandi that he attributes to the Council on Foreign Relations conspirators. Gonzalez contends there are two traditional ways to illegally grab control of a country: by force through a mass revolt—the communist way—or through a coup d'état—the fascist way. But he claims there is a "third way: by infiltration and brainwashing. That's the Fabian Way."[122]

The Fabian Way is attributed to the Fabian Society, which is "a British socialist organization whose purpose is to advance the principles of democratic socialism via gradualist and reformist effort in democracies, rather than by revolutionary overthrow."[123]

The British Fabian Society was named after the Roman general Fabius Maximus, who practiced a strategy of harassment and attrition rather than head-on battles against the Carthaginian army under the renowned General Hannibal. It is noteworthy that every British Labor prime minister has been a Fabian, and today more than two hundred parliamentarians in London are members of the Fabian Society.[124]

Richard Butrick writes in the *American Thinker* that President Obama practiced the Fabian Way, a "bait-and-switch" way of governing. Obama felt morally justified to give the American public "BigOgov. org," explained Butrick because even though the public is too dense to embrace socialism, Obama knew it is the best for them and "eventually the public will be grateful."[125]

Forbes magazine said Obama might as well be in the Fabian Socialist camp because he was motivated by a sense of moral superiority as were others in the Fabian camp such as Saul Alinsky, a hero of Hillary Clinton, and author of "Rules for Radicals."[126]

Mr. Gonzalez states the CFR employs the "Fabian Way" by infiltrating and taking control of the mainstream press as a tool to brainwash the masses. Next, they infiltrate the political parties and then the public schools, colleges, and universities. Despite CFR's alleged success in America, Gonzalez says there are major obstacles; the first obstacle is the American belief in freedom and liberty. Second, Americans are fully "convinced that the only thing that ultimately guarantees such natural rights is the possession of firearms."[127]

Paul Warburg, son of CFR founder James Warburg, testified before the U.S. Senate Foreign Relations Committee on February 17, 1950, to threaten the senators by stating: "We [CFR] shall have world government whether or not you like it—by conquest or consent." Warburg's obstacle to this "world government" aim appears to be an armed American public. Gonzalez goes on to explain the Bolsheviks, Nazis, Mao of China, and Castro in Cuba took over their countries only after disarming the people, which gives credence to his claim—American globalists elite must first disarm Americans before taking over.[128]

It is worth pointing out the globalist plan to continue their campaign to take over America failed in the 2016 U.S. presidential election. They hoped to elect Hillary Clinton, who would then carry out their radical agenda: open borders, eugenics disguised as a "woman's right to choose," trample on the U.S. Constitution much like President Obama had by fiat, embrace more global governance through organizations like the U.N., a pro-homosexual push to include a transgender move to marginalize sex differences, and of course, whittle away at our Second Amendment rights.

Remember, Clinton was not friendly with the Second Amendment. During the 2016 campaign, she promised: "I do not want to repeal the Second Amendment. I do not want to take anyone's gun away.... I just don't want you to get shot by someone who shouldn't have a gun in the first place." But Clinton's gun-control platform went far beyond her promise and in fact would have disarmed a lot of Americans.[129]

Shortly after the June 2016 Orlando night club mass shooting, Ms. Clinton reiterated her call for a new national ban on assault weapons, and during her 2000 Senate campaign, she openly supported a national registry for all handgun owners. Had Clinton been elected in 2016, she would have appointed an anti-Second Amendment Supreme Court justice to replace the pro-gun and pro-Constitution late conservative jurist Antonin Scalia. She also favors higher taxes on firearms and making gun makers and sellers liable for guns that end up involved in crimes.[130]

Donald Trump's campaign, which promised to do just the opposite of the globalists', drew popular support that fortunately defeated Clinton. However, and perhaps only momentarily, enough Americans believed that Clinton would continue to carry out the radical Fabian agenda begun by Obama.

No doubt the 2016 presidential election was a watershed election and certainly the most ideological in America's recent political history. Trump won because of what many voters perceived as a globalist agenda pushed by Clinton and her party: dismantling the Second Amendment, outsourcing American jobs, destroying our industrial base, perpetuating a dismal economy, contributing to increasing unemployment, fostering a growing police state, promoting rampant political correctness, pursuing wrongheaded foreign policy, demonstrating disrespect for the Constitution and endorsing the ideological push for a radical new world order.[131]

Of course, it's obvious that Clinton and the CFR are allied with the Trilateral Commission, which pushes a similar agenda using many of the same tools. The Commission was founded in 1972 by David Rockefeller, who created the elite association composed of government officials, bankers, and Western industrial leaders. "Trilateral" refers to the triangle of power brokers in North America, Europe, and Japan. "The commission had as its purpose nothing less modest than the creation of transnational elite with a shared consciousness," said Richard Barnet, a scholar-activist who cofounded the Institute for Policy Studies. The commission's goal, explained Barnet, is "the coordinated management of the increasingly interdependent market economies of north America, Europe, and Japan."[132]

The Commission was united around Western world national economic and political self-interests. "The industrial nations had to cooperate because their economies were inextricably linked," Barnet said. "The most fundamental message of trilateralism was interdependence." It worked and grew in its influence to include capturing much of the U.S. government.

As previously mentioned (in chapter 1). former 1964 presidential candidate and Arizona U.S. Senator Barry Goldwater exposed the Trilateral Commission in his book, *With No Apologies*. Goldwater said the Commission "represents a skillful, coordinated effort to seize control and consolidate the four centers of power—political, monetary, intellectual and ecclesiastical. What the Trilateral Commission intends is to create a worldwide economic power superior to the political governments of the nation-states involved. As managers and creators of the system, they will rule the future." That's what they tried to accomplish.

Zbigniew Brzezinski was the Trilateral Commission's first director and one of the early members was then Georgia Governor Jimmy Carter. It's not surprising that once Carter became president, he recruited fellow commission members such as Brzezinski, who brought to the national security staff his "one world global strategy." This view is supported by the book *Trilateralism*, edited by Holly Sklar, that claims the commission promotes a new era of the corporate empire: "Trilateralism is the creed of an international ruling class whose locus of power is the global corporation. The owners and managers of global corporations view the entire world as their factory, farm, supermarket, and playground. The trilateral commission is seeking to strengthen and rationalize the world economy in their interests."[133]

The next section will explore in far more detail the globalists elite community, past and present, their various secret associations (CFR, Trilateral Commission, and others) and expand on their agenda. What's clear at this point is these globalists elite have great influence and employ a variety of "tools" to leverage authority across the world.

How should the Christian respond to globalization and globalists elite?

CHRISTIAN VIEW OF GLOBALISM AND END TIMES

Globalization is a process that could bring every aspect of human life under a central authority forcing all humanity to share in common everything like language and culture. Globalists promise such an outcome is desirable for reasons outlined earlier, but the modern Christian must be skeptical of those claims and consider biblical truth in light of those globalist promises.

King Solomon wrote in the book of Ecclesiastics 1:9 (NIV), "What has been will be again, what has been done will be done again; there is nothing new under the sun." That's true of globalists and their agenda because they and their ilk have been a thorn in mankind's side throughout history, and their basic philosophy isn't new.

Military conquests from the earliest times were launched by globalist-minded leaders who sought to bring the known world under a central authority's control. Beginning in the twenty-fifth century B.C., the ancient Assyrians conquered surrounding territories and eventually controlled the area that includes modern-day Iraq, Turkey, and down through Egypt. The Assyrians were murderous task masters who used the worst kind of torture and enslaved the conquered peoples to include the Israelis (2 Kings 17).

The Assyrians weren't the first to seek a one-world government. Even before the Assyrians came on the scene, man tried to globalize control by constructing the Tower of Babel (Genesis 9:1) under the rule of the earth's first monarch, Nimrod. But God rejected that effort by confusing their languages and scattering them widely across the face of the earth (Genesis 11:8–9).

Other empires and psychopathic leaders tried to conquer the entire known world besides the Assyrians (the Mede and Persians led by Cyrus, the Greeks led by Alexander the Great, and the Roman Caesars who sought a utopia called "Pax Romana"), but in each case, those ambitious tyrants' efforts failed. That's because God has other plans, and we get an indication of those plans in Daniel 2—specifically, from King Nebuchadnezzar's vision of the fifth and final world empire.

Nebuchadnezzar saw in his vision of the future, which was interpreted by Daniel, a series of empires. His vision was of a large statue—"an enormous, dazzling statue" with the head of pure gold, its chest and arms of silver, its belly and thighs of bronze, and its legs of iron and clay. Daniel explained that the image represented a succession of major kingdoms (Medo-Persia [silver], Greece [brass], Rome [iron]) that would culminate with a peaceful kingdom of God. His mighty Babylon would fail, and so would three successive empires. The last would break into many separate nations.

Daniel 7:23 (KJV) also speaks of the fourth beast "which shall be diverse from all kingdoms, and shall devour the whole earth, and shall tread it down, and break it in pieces." This is a reference to the Antichrist, the "beast" that rises out of the sea having seven heads and ten horns (Revelation 13:1), who will rule just before Christ's return. A couple of verses later, Daniel writes that the world government will continue until the return of Christ.

The final empire that Nebuchadnezzar envisioned is ruled by the Antichrist, the "beast" and the lawless one, being followed by and receiving worship from "all the world" as outlined in Revelation 13:3–4. Clearly the Antichrist is the last globalist who will have "authority over every tribe, people, language and nation" (Revelation 13:7). He will control all wealth and religions, and anyone who refuses to worship him will face a certain death (Revelation 14:9–11).

Modern man has sought to establish that elusive one-world government (Napoleon, Stalin, Hitler, Mao), but each failed. Even President Wilson's League of Nations and Roosevelt's United Nations failed to bring the world under one umbrella, much less deliver the promised peace, prosperity, and hope.

So, is the view expressed in Daniel and Revelation some sort of joke, and will there ever be universal peace and equality? That outcome won't occur this side of heaven, but there is a coming time and perhaps very soon when most of mankind will unite under one leader.

The Antichrist is that leader who will rule over a one-world future government. But how does such an enterprise come about, given the current world of diverse systems of government? What might compel them to willingly subjugate themselves to a single ruler? Perhaps that outcome happens as a result of disasters described in Revelation that happen after the rise of the Antichrist and then the seal and trumpet judgments create such a monumental global crisis that people seek relief in anyone willing to help.

At some point in the future, the "beast" (Antichrist), with the power of Satan supporting him, will establish absolute control over the whole earth, outcomes prophesied in Isaiah 14:12–14. This absolute control will seem to work, because the Antichrist will control all commerce using a one-world currency that requires the satanic mark of the beast to buy and sell (Revelation 13:16–17).[134]

How close are we, and how does this fit with the globalist agenda? I interviewed Dr. Manfred Steger, the renounced globalist, author, and professor of sociology at the University of Hawaii. Dr. Steger, an Austrian transplant, described to me two possible future outcomes of the current world over the next fifty years. One outcome, according to Professor Steger, is rosy, whereby mankind moves to a more transnational setting and finds new forms of cooperation. However, his alternative view fits well with the scriptural interpretation above.

Dr. Steger believes we could see much of the globe turning to fascism, whereby more authority over the masses becomes something like past imperial powers while maintaining the façade of democratic institutions but diminishing democratic liberties. Security issues increase with conflict and destruction, and meanwhile, the earth faces a climate-change crisis of rising temperatures, lack of adequate rainfall, and rising sea levels.[135]

One event that Steger did not mention that will surely be a key to the formation of a one-world government is the Rapture of the Church. That's when Christ comes for believers, both living and dead (1 Thessalonians 4:13–17). The Rapture will occur prior to the identification of the Antichrist and his rise to world leadership. With perhaps billions of people suddenly vanishing in the Rapture, the world will be clamoring for a leader with the answers. The satanically directed Antichrist will be the man with the plan, and he will be greeted as the savior.

How does mankind respond to such global crises? Steger believes the only way out of these global crises is to turn to global leadership and, by extension, a one-world government.

Of course, every past effort to globalize to date has turned bad, and not surprisingly, because the "world is a prisoner of sin," man is corrupted, and even his best intentions aside from God are folly. Only God's plan for genuine "globalization" under Jesus Christ will work.

Human government consistently fails to provide the hope and peace men seek, and as a result, bitterness and resentment blossom. Globalists will promise utopia but deliver only suffering, discontent, and death. The new world order is a false heaven.[136]

Yes, the true heaven is coming, as it says in Daniel 2:44 (KJV), "and in the days of these kings shall the God of heaven set up a kingdom, which shall never be destroyed: and the kingdom shall not be left to other people, but it shall break in pieces and consume all these kingdoms, and it shall stand for ever."

The great event in Daniel 2 is the coming of Jesus Christ to establish His kingdom on earth, "the blessed hope" (Titus 2:11–13, KJV), which says:

For the grace of God that bringeth salvation hath appeared to all men, Teaching us that, denying ungodliness and worldly lusts, we should live soberly, righteously, and godly, in this present world; Looking for that blessed hope, and the glorious appearing of the great God and our Savior Jesus Christ.

CONCLUSION

Human globalism is a bankrupt idea when taken to its logical conclusion. God settled that at the Tower of Babel, but it is His plan to bring about a spiritual globalism called heaven, which is man's only true hope for eternal hope and peace.

In the next section of this volume, we will dig much deeper into the globalists elite—past and present, their secret societies, their growing success at true global domination of power centers, and then their harnessing of the unseen spiritual domain.

GLOBALISTS ELITE

INTRODUCTION

The globalists elite who lead today's campaign to transform the world into their vision are a very influential superclass that govern from secret societies that control most of the world's centers of power. These globalists are instruments of the unseen world and in perhaps a few years will lead humankind to the biblical end times.

This section of six chapters begins with a "Globalism: A Globalized Progressive Ideology," which sets the stage by taking a deep dive into the marriage between modern globalism and the progressive movement, how they came to share the same ideology, and what that means for the modern world.

The second chapter, "History and the Fathers of Modern Globalism," reviews globalism's history, some of the factors that contributed to those labeled as the fathers of modern globalism, and the views they nurtured that carried over into the present times.

The third chapter, "Current Globalists and Their Tribal Influence," explores the modern tribe of globalist luminaries who claim to "know best" and aren't afraid of imposing their will on the rest of us.

The fourth chapter, "Globalist Secret Societies," examines the closed associations of the global elite, why they meet secretly, what they do at those meetings, and the likely outcome of their weighty efforts.

The fifth chapter, "Globalist Power Centers," outlines how the globalists elite are taking much of the world captive and how they intend to employ earth's power centers to carry out their agenda.

Finally, the sixth chapter in this section, "Globalism v. Religion," explores the significant spiritual dimension of the global fight that will lead to the end times.

CHAPTER SIX

Globalism

A Globalized Progressive Ideology

President Barack Obama distinguished the key difference between competing ideologies—globalism and nationalism—in a July 2016 speech to ambassadors at the White House. His statement also links his established progressive thinking with contemporary globalism:

> I think we have to step back [from the Nice, France, terrorist truck attack on July 14, 2016] and reflect on what we are doing to eliminate this kind of chronic violence. It's been a difficult several weeks in the United States. But the divide...is between people who recognize the common humanity of all people and are willing to build [international] institutions that promote that common humanity, and those who do not—those who would suggest that somebody is less than them because of their tribe, or their ethnicity, or their faith, or their color. And those impulses [for solidarity] exist in all our countries. And those impulses, when we do not speak out against them and build strong institutions to protect people from those impulses, they can take over, they can be unleashed—so that all of us [international leaders] have responsibilities.[137]

Marc Clausen points out in his *Bereans at the Gate* article that Obama's July 2016 speech demonstrates a clear ideological distinction between competing ideologically driven groups. On one hand, progressive leader Obama sympathetically said he "recognize[s] the common humanity of all people and are willing to build [international] institutions that promote that common humanity." The other group, which he demonizes, doesn't want to build those institutions "that promote that common humanity."[138]

Obama denigrates this second group, which he implies are sovereignty-loving nationalist bigots, by stating they "would suggest that somebody is less than them because of their tribe…ethnicity…faith… or color." Not surprisingly, Obama's criticism of this group is the same rhetoric spewed by many like-minded progressives who attacked Mr. Trump and his supporters in the 2016 election campaign.

The 2016 self-professed progressive presidential candidate Hillary Clinton attacked Trump voters, calling them "deplorables," and accused Mr. Trump of building "his campaign largely on prejudice and paranoia and giving national platform to hateful views and voices."[139] As you will see in this and the next chapter, Clinton's characterization of Trump followers is a typical retort from the progressives for more than a century.

Obama's statement comparing the two groups illustrates not only the ideological gap between the progressives and the Trump nationalists/ populists, but it also demonstrates that what we have come to understand as globalism in this volume is interchangeable with the better understood political ideology known as progressivism.

Earlier, we examined Professor Steger's three types of globalist ideologies: market, justice, and religious. Now in this chapter, I will elaborate on that ideology and its link to progressivism, or simply put, contemporary globalism has "globalized" what has come to be known as progressivism.

Television personality Glenn Beck wrote a book about progressives, *Liars: How Progressives Exploit Our Fears for Power and Control*. In it, Beck profiled progressive goals as "the insatiable thirst for control and betterment of others; the determination to build a massive, all-controlling welfare state that holds the rest of us hostage to its preferences and whims; and the flirtation with totalitarianism masked by the guise of political correctness. Progressives regularly espouse ideas and support causes that openly involve the subjugation, murder, or mutilation of their fellow human beings, always in the name of a better world for all."[140]

A nineteenth-century German by the name of Georg Wilhelm Friedrich Hegel is the father of the progressive movement. He believed that the history of mankind was the rational evolution of mankind to "perfect" humanity, but that process required a government to tame man's raw impulses. Further, Hegel's "philosophy of history" can be understood as man becoming god on earth.[141] That view explains the basis for progressive foreign policy as well, which is built on two central ideas from nineteenth-century German philosophy: ethical idealism and historical evolution.

Ethical idealism, according to Christopher Burkett, an associate professor of political science at Ashland University, "is any action motivated by a concern for one's own happiness, welfare, or interest is not moral, and accordingly, the only moral action is one undertaken purely to promote the good of others." The state's proper role, explained Burkett, is to "discourage individualistic pursuit of private interests, promoting instead cooperative moral actions that contribute to the good of the whole."[142]

Historical evolution, the second tenet of progressivism, asserts that human societies evolve from primitive origins and over time they become "more civilized, more ethical, and more democratic culminating in the emergence of the state." The culmination of that evolutionary process is freedom, which comes only when "a people become civilized, ethical, and democratic under the tutelage of the state."

These progressive tenets are in stark contrast to the theory of our founders, who believed the laws of nature, human nature, and natural rights did not evolve; they are God given. Further, our founders rejected the progressive notion that all self-interested actions were immoral.

Burkett concluded, "Accepting human nature for what it is, they [the founders] believed that the primary purpose of government was to allow individuals to exercise their liberty in pursuit of their own happiness."

The progressive movement from its early days in America was always a microcosm of globalism, which was predicated on the idea of elites who "knew better" than ordinary people—that's the rest of us. They (the elite) know what is best for us, which gives them the moral authority to take over more functions and establish centralized government with large bureaucracies run by "unbiased experts."

President Woodrow Wilson, a familiar globalist to the reader, was an early American progressive with global aspirations. In 1917, Wilson told Congress, "The world must be made safe for democracy," seemingly his justification for entering the country into the First World War. But Wilson's call to spread democracy "was more urgent and pressing, more obligatory," wrote Christopher Burkett.[143] That call, according to Burkett, was for a more active role in the world. It was meant to spread freedom and democracy, an ideological call for action, a new progressive foreign policy.

Wilson's foreign policy beliefs were widely shared among progressives and in stark opposition to that of our founders. After all, Wilson was not a fan of the American Constitution.

In a 1912 campaign speech, Wilson outlined a progressive's approach to our Constitution: "All the progressives ask or desire is permission [in an] era when 'development,' 'evolution,' is the scientific word, [to] interpret the Constitution according to the Darwinian principle; all they ask is recognition of the fact that a nation is a living thing and not a machine." That view compelled his progressive view that we should use force abroad to promote freedom and welfare of other peoples, while our founders endorsed the use of force abroad first and foremost, according to Burkett, "for the sake of securing the lives and liberty of America's own citizens."

President Roosevelt was very much a progressive as well. He is remembered for many statements, but perhaps the best is: "The only thing we have to fear is fear itself—nameless, unreasoning, unjustified terror." He masterfully played on public fear to move America closer to his progressive control. Consider Roosevelt's word play in the following statement:

> You're scared silly. You're afraid of losing your jobs, your savings, your homes. You're scared of empty pots and starving children. I will save you from hunger. I will save you from bankers. I will save you from the saber-toothed cat! Just hand over your gold and your future income, and let me plan your retirement for you.[144]

The progressive's answer to your problems is to give them more power, and that's what happened to Roosevelt. His New Deal was about big government, more regulations, more taxes, and ultimately far less freedom.

Americans were divided throughout the balance of the twentieth century regarding the appropriate foreign policy—focus on being the world's big brother versus what the founders had in mind of focusing on American security. This conflict was very much in play even as recently as the 2003 Iraq war, Operation Iraqi Freedom. Should we fight to defend our interests or to bring freedom to the Iraqi people?

Burkett warned about the long-term effect of such a progressive foreign policy. He explained that "over time American leaders and politicians have become hesitant, unwilling, and sometimes even apologetic for doing those things necessary for the defense of our nation and interests."[145]

John Fonte and John Yoo with the Hudson Institute elaborated on the ideological divide in this country created by progressives. Fonte and Yoo argue the U.S. is today at a decisive fork in the road, and that choice is between "preserving our constitution system and embracing transnational progressivism."[146]

"Transnational progressivism" is ideological globalism as previously defined. For example, one significant and telling aspect of Obama's "transnational progressivism" was his effort to ignore constitutional requirements by surrendering U.S. sovereignty to international oversight. Obama's sinister use of the Comprehensive Test Ban Treaty (CTBT) illustrates the point.

The CTBT bans all nuclear tests and 183 countries have signed the treaty, but that does not include the United States. That treaty will not come into force until the U.S. and several other countries ratify it.

The Obama administration supported the treaty but lacked the two-thirds vote in the U.S. Senate for ratification. So, the Obama administration sought a United Nations Security Council resolution to "circumvent the constitutional treaty process and greatly harm our ability to deter nuclear armed-adversaries," according to Senator Tom Cotton (R-Ark.).[147]

Obama threatened to circumvent the U.S. Senate's constitutional obligation to approve treaties by asking the United Nations to pass a resolution that made any testing of nuclear weapons by a treaty signatory (including the U.S.), which would essentially "defeat the object and purpose of the CTBT." Passage of that resolution would then bind the U.S. by international law not to conduct further tests, assessed Fonte and Yoo.

Obama's intention to try an end-run around Congress rankled many in the Senate, who rightly complained the administration cannot ignore the Constitution to achieve its policy goals. But that ideological (read "progressive") approach was a common practice for Obama. After all, globalists elite or "transnational progressives" like Obama promote the concept that "global problems [like CTBT] require global solutions" and, therefore, "the need for ever expanding global governance [like the United Nations]."[148]

Republican senators went on to accuse Obama of using the same constitutional dodging trick to reach a broad U.N. deal on climate change. Sen. John Barrasso (R-Wyoming), chairman of a Foreign Relations Committee subpanel, said, "Just like the Kyoto Protocol and the

United Nations' framework convention on climate change, any agreement that commits our nation to targets or timetables must go through the process established by the founders in our Constitution. It must be submitted to the United States Senate for its advice and consent."

A State Department spokesman responded to Barrasso: "The president has made clear that he doesn't see it that way, as was the case with the Iranian nuclear deal."[149]

Former U.S. Ambassador to United Nations John Bolton explained the "vast disparities" between what he described as "globalists" and "Americanists." Bolton wisely explained that globalists favor transferring decision-making from nation-states to international authorities (a progressive agenda item outlined above) when so-called "global-solutions" are required. Meanwhile, "Americanists," understand them as nationalists, believe political decision-making should remain within our constitutional system.[150]

Bolton warns that globalists are making major gains while Americanists sleep. He concludes his *Chicago Journal of International Law* article by claiming that the current conflict with globalists is "the decisive issue facing the United States internationally."[151]

The international aspect of the progressive agenda becomes pretty evident upon close examination. Two authors with the Council on Foreign Relations (CFR), a known globalism advocate organization, argue that building progressivism requires the "forging [of] transnational democratic progressive alliances." Further, the CFR advocates an international regulatory regime: "solving the cascade of emerging global problems, perhaps most notably climate change, will depend on the globalization of regulatory state capacities."[152]

"Regulatory state capacities" for the progressive is the concept of "global rule of law," meaning U.S. courts must cede judicial authority to supranational courts. The 1998 Rome statute that created the International Criminal Court (ICC) is a classic example of ceding authority, a favorite of progressives.[153]

The ICC is a permanent global court to deal with war crimes, crimes against humanity, genocide, and crimes of aggression. It claims jurisdiction over all nations to include the U.S., even though the U.S. Senate has not ratified the treaty. Further, the ICC claims jurisdiction even if a nation-state is "unwilling" to try its own citizens for alleged crimes.

Part of the problem for nationalists is that the ICC is not accountable to democratic authority such as our Constitution, but a darling to transnational progressives like Hillary Clinton, who told a Kenyan audience in 2009 that it is "a great regret" the U.S. has not submitted to the ICC.[154]

Clinton surrounded herself at the State Department with ideological transnational progressives such as Princeton professor Anne-Marie Slaughter, who advocates global governance through the "coercive power of vertical [government] networks" that make "it possible for [a] supranational court [read ICC], regulatory entity, or parliament to create a relationship with its national counterparts to make those rules directly enforceable."[155]

Global governance as promoted by Obama, Clinton, and their many progressive advisers demands the transfer of authority to transnational institutions to provide "global solutions" without regard for national or constitutional interests.

The American constitutional system of government is in stark opposition to the infringements of international governance like the ICC. American power is invested with her people, and any government that tries to usurp that authority risks removal. Further, there is no provision in our Constitution to surrender sovereign authority outside of this country which explains why progressives like Obama and Clinton ignore this principle and try to circumvent our system. Besides, to date, the Supreme Court has wisely reaffirmed the Constitution, not globalist organizations, has the final say in all matters of law.

Obama's progressive ideological use of international obligations, whether about missiles or nuclear programs like the 2015 Iran agreement or the Paris accords on environmental regulations, violate a core constitutional principle: federalism.[156] Our Founding Fathers purposely limited federal government powers. However, granting global governance through universal regulations violate the Constitution's restrictions on federal regulation.

CONCLUSION

The new cold war being fought between globalists/transnational progressives and Bolton's "Americanists"/nationalists is just beginning to really heat up, as demonstrated in the first section of this volume. However, there are many elites networked across the globe who manipulate centers of power to advance their radical globalist agenda. They will continue to promote global governance while trashing our constitutional framework and spouting the mantra that "global problems require global solutions."[157] But before exploring these people in detail, it is essential to first explore the origins of globalism and the views embraced by globalists that influence the contemporary world.

CHAPTER SEVEN

History and the Fathers of Globalism

Just how did we arrive at the present world governed by transnational progressives who evidence the ideology outlined in the previous chapter? I will attempt to answer that question through a brief historical overview of the incremental globalization of the world across millennia, and then offer a few concise biographies of nineteenth- and twentieth-century leaders—the fathers of modern globalism—who seeded our world with thinking that contributed to the current globalist ideology. In the next chapter, we will then examine contemporary globalists who carry the mantle of their progressive forefathers.

Remember, globalization, as you have seen previously in this volume, is the physical expansion of the geographical domain by the interconnectivity across great distances linking localities to one another in terms of trade, communication, migration, culture, and much more. Although that linking process spanned many hundreds of years, it was especially evident during the eighteenth and nineteenth centuries' Industrial Revolution in terms of trade and, by association, the blending of migrating peoples and ideas. Over those centuries, and especially in the past half-century, thanks to the acceleration of technology, the world has become truly interconnected.

Globalist scholar, Professor Manfred Steger, divides the history of the globalization process into five periods "that are separated from each other by significant accelerations in the pace of social exchanges as well as a widening of their geographical scope."[158] Those social exchanges accompanied by new technologies incrementally made the world seem physically smaller, but also had the simultaneous effect of marrying diverse cultures, and in time emerged the progressive ideology that gave us the contemporary transnational progressivism, the modern era's globalism.

First, the prehistoric period dates back twelve thousand years, according to Steger, when bands of hunters and gatherers dispersed across the earth's five continents. This nomadic type of life transitioned to producing food, especially in areas such as the Fertile Crescent, North-Central China, and North Africa. Their food production successes led to centralized healthy and growing patriarchal social structures with expanded populations.

These agrarian societies, once sufficiently productive, morphed to create other occupations not directly involved in food production, such as craftsmen who invented new technologies to improve the quality of life including iron products, pottery, and buildings. A second group of non-agrarians became public servants, bureaucrats, and soldiers who oversaw broad societal interests such as managing wealth, establishing trade, exploring new lands, and defending the citizenry.

Steger characterized this phase of globalization as the "divergence—people and social connections stemming from a single origin but moving and diversifying greatly over time and space."

Second, the premodern period (3500 BCE–1500 CE) saw the invention of writing in Mesopotamia, Egypt, and China, as well as the invention of the wheel. These advances helped to expand man's reach to more distant places. Specifically, the wheel resulted in infrastructure innovations such as the cart, which required roads, while writing advanced man's social interactions and both innovations helped facilitate the rise of many empires such as the Egyptian, Persian, Macedonian, Aztecs, Incas, Roman, Indian, Byzantine, Islamic, Holy Roman, various

African, and the Ottoman. Each empire extended the reach of mankind and the exchange of culture and goods.

The ancient Chinese empire was arguably the most innovative and enduring, which spanned seventeen hundred years. It touched much of the known world with its science, art, technology, agricultural achievements, and civil society institutions that included laws, road networks, and extensive trade. The most famous Chinese road, mentioned in the previous section, the Silk Road, linked for the first time Asia and Europe. Also, Chinese sea-going vessels crossed the vast Indian Ocean, pushing trade to Eastern Africa.

This period also saw the militarization of the seas, thanks to people like Vasco da Gama, who forced rulers in Indian Ocean ports to pay tribute and used military force to settle Portuguese along the sea lanes whereby colonialists engaged in trade, acquired local lands, and established a network of imperial authority over a growing swath of the world. These measures inevitably produced competition for access to ports and trade routes among mostly Europeans seeking new horizons.

By the end of the premodern period, trade networks connected population centers in Eurasia and northeastern Africa as well as the civilizations of the South American Aztecs and Incas. These networks triggered migration to urban centers, which meshed cultures and religions, often resulting in conflict.

Third, the early modern period (1500–1750) is essentially the European Enlightenment era known for major social development and the rise of European metropolitan centers and their merchant classes who expanded trade. The emerging capitalist world system provided the trading nations the means to explore the new worlds and to establish trading firms such as the Dutch and British East India companies.

By the eighteenth century, these European trading firms enjoyed government protection as they traveled to East Asia and returned with cargo that generated considerable profits for investors and significant revenues in the form of taxation for their nation-states. Those same European nations also controlled the Atlantic economy, which took advantage of forced labor in the silver mines of Peru as well as the transportation of slaves to the Americas, providing labor for the plantation economy in coastal America.[159]

As these government-supported enterprises grew, they brought regulation to economic transactions and, as a result, established colonial governments that introduced foreign administration and culture. Globalization was still in its infancy at this point, but it was clearly linking cultures and all that implies.

Fourth, the modern period saw the south Asian region incorporated into Europe's trade and colonial network. It was during this period (1750–1980), according to Steger, that Western capitalists gained stature and imposed their so-called virtues of the free market.[160] European expansion accelerated with the help of nation-state military power to advance national interests abroad as the capitalists used that force to accumulate more wealth. For example, many of the state-chartered companies became monopolies that helped nation-states expand control of territories across the world, a phenomenon known as "economic imperialism."

Structural changes in the evolving global economy began to reshape in the late eighteenth century. The European control of the Americas was lost while capitalists jealously forced their political constituents to fight independence movements such as in the United States (the American Revolution of 1763 to 1787).

The reshaping of the global economy contributed to dramatic social shifts. Steger explains that German political radicals like Karl Marx and Friedrich Engels outlined for the first time the "qualitative shift in social relations that pushed globalization to a new level during the modern period."[161]

The discovery of America prepared the way for mighty industry and its creation of a truly global market. The latter greatly expanded trade, navigation, and communication by land. These developments, in turn, caused the further expansion of industry. The growth of industry, trade, navigation, and railroads also went hand in hand with the rise of the bourgeoisie and capital, which pushed to the background the old social classes of the Middle Ages…Chased around the globe by its burning desire for ever-expanding markets for its products, the bourgeoisie has no choice but settle everywhere; cultivate everywhere; establish connections everywhere…Rapidly improving the instruments of production, the bourgeoisie utilizes the incessantly easing modes of communication to pull all nations into civilization—even the most barbarian ones…In a nutshell, it creates the world in its own image.[162]

Marx and Engels correctly assessed the dramatic impact of globalization during their era. The bourgeoisie built banking enterprises, expanded the flow of goods internationally, and pushed the free use of British and Dutch currency worldwide. Soon, international trade accounted for a significant 12 percent of total trade for the industrialized West, and commodity trade exploded as well. Western manufactured goods like Coca-Cola, Campbell Soup, Singer sewing machines, and Remington typewriters became household names.

Global trade happened thanks to rapid advances in technology during the late nineteenth and early twentieth centuries, not due to the bourgeoisies' expertise, as Marx and Engels explained. Thanks to railways, motorized ships, and the airplane, international trade came to full blossom, removing the limitations associated with moving goods long distances. Those innovations were complemented by similarly earth-shaking communication advances; first, the telegraph, then the telephone, wireless radio, and eventually the entire rainbow of mass media and global communications technologies known today such as the World Wide Web.

Another explosion of sorts took place in tandem with the technological revolution, the rapid population growth. The world's population grew a sobering five-fold from 760 million in 1750 to 3.7 billion by 1970. (Today the global population is 7.5+ billion.[163]) That rapid increase in humanity, coupled with international trade, accelerated social change across the earth, to a large part because of disparities in wealth.

The uneven distribution of wealth, especially in the urbanizing, industrial West led to the creation of labor movements and fostered new ideologies and "interstate rivalries intensified at the outset of the twentieth century," according to Steger, because "of mass migration, urbanization, colonial competition, and the excessive liberalization of world trade." That scenario of interactions spurred the rise of extreme nationalism that contributed to two world wars and economic depression.

Finally, Steger's fifth era, the contemporary period, which he labels the "latest globalization wave," is the modern period that experienced the most dramatic acceleration of global exchange, especially since the early 1980s. It's breathtaking to reflect on the global changes in just the past few decades: the end of the East-West Cold War, the deregulation of national economies, the Information and Communication Technology Revolution that connects localities globally through the Internet and much more.

Steger explains that this "globalization wave" is a "convergence," and defines it as "different and widely spaced people and social connections coming together more rapidly than ever before." Then he warns, "globalization is not a single process but a set of processes that operate simultaneously and unevenly on several levels and in various dimensions." Clearly, contemporary globalization impacts the modern world across many domains: economic, political, cultural, ecological, and ideological.

The aforementioned emergence of globalization through the millennia is interesting. However, the ideological impact of this process is the focus of the balance of this chapter and the more important aspect of the phenomenon for this volume. Perhaps the best way to understand how globalization has and will impact mankind in the future is to examine the lives and thinking of some of globalization's fathers, with emphasis on their philosophies.

From a biblical perspective, the original father of globalization was Nimrod, the architect of the Tower of Babel, someone introduced in a previous chapter.

God instructed man to disperse and "replenish the earth" in Genesis 9 after the Flood, but King Nimrod thought he had a better idea

(Genesis 11). King Nimrod ordered his followers to build a city and a tall tower to reach the heavens. God was displeased with Nimrod's primitive version of globalism, and as a result, "the Lord scattered them from there all over the earth, and they stopped building the city. That is why it was called Babel—because there the Lord confused the language of the whole world. From there the Lord scattered them over the face of the whole earth" (Genesis 11:8–9, NIV).

Nimrod's globalization experiment—one language, one culture, one government—failed because it was contrary to God's plan. Therefore, God's punishment was to confuse their language so they could no longer work together and no longer be a unified global body.

There are a host of other historical figures who compete for the title of father of globalization, such as Alexander the Great and a number of Roman Caesars. Perhaps one of the most successful ancient globalists was the Mongolian warrior Chiniggis Khann, aka Genghis Khan. He was one of history's most barbaric and genocidal conquerors. His empire was vast—stretching from Asia to the Middle East—and his administration skills were brilliant. He facilitated international trade, used passports and credit cards, created a public school system, and a primitive postal service.[164]

Genghis Khan left a major impression on the world stage, but his influence is anecdotal as compared to more contemporary globalization "fathers." The true ideological fathers of modern globalization are likely those who influenced the contemporary globalists the most, and they are a rather small cabal of personalities who lived in the mid-nineteenth through the mid-twentieth centuries.

We will examine four such men and their influence on the modern globalist movement: Darwin, Hegel, Wilson, and Rockefeller. The world they knew was rapidly changing at their time, and it was in this cauldron of human cultures being mixed from across the globe and combined with advancing technologies that influenced their thinking about mankind and the future. They are the fathers of modern transnational progressivism, aka globalism, and their views about life are evident today.

CHARLES DARWIN (1809–1882)

Darwin was an English naturalist best known for the theory of evolution in his book, *The Origin of Species*, wherein he theorized that plants and animals evolve and develop without the aid of an intelligent creator (God) through a process of natural selection, which ensures the "survival of the fittest." That work sought to disabuse his readers of the view that humans possess an exalted position as a creation of God.[165]

It is noteworthy that Darwin was not the first to write about evolution. In fact, Darwin cites twenty-four other naturalists in his well-known work, *On the Origin of Species,* that shared his views. However, his work caught global attention and the concept of evolution was subsequently identified with him. Yet, many today might be surprised to learn that Darwin studied to be a minister at Cambridge University, and he consistently kept any reference to God or a Creator out of his work until the final edition of *Origin*.

Only in the sixth and final edition of the *Origin* was the word "evolution" mentioned. Meanwhile, in that edition, he used the word "Creator" nine times and the word "God" twice. Further, Darwin at no time claimed evolution was godless or directionless. The second page of the sixth edition of *Origin* states: "To conclude, therefore, let no man out of a weak conceit of sobriety, or an ill-applied moderation, think or maintain, that a man can search too far or be too well studied in the book of God's word, or in the book of God's works; divinity or philosophy; but rather let men endeavour an endless progress or proficience in both."[166]

Darwin's biology-based views were extrapolated by others and applied to man's intellectual life and more broadly to his origins. Meanwhile, much of Darwin's views about man, such as his racist and sexist sentiments, are ignored by his proponents. After all, the complete title of his much-cited liminal work is *On the Origin of Species by Means of Natural Selection or, the Preservation of Favoured Races in the Struggle for Life*. Clearly, racist Darwin favored the white race and he taught that women were biologically inferior to men, a distinction presumably due to natural selection. In a further denigrating comment about women, Darwin wrote in his autobiography that "the average mental power in man must be above that of women."[167]

The world ignored those bigoted views to embrace Darwin's theory of evolution. Progressive businessman John D. Rockefeller (the father of one of the contemporary globalists profiled in the next chapter, David Rockefeller) fawned over Darwin's views to justify his business tactics. "The growth of large business is merely a survival of the fittest…. This is not an evil tendency in business," said Rockefeller. "It is merely the working out of a law of nature and a law of God."[168] Luminary and fellow billionaire Andrew Carnegie echoed a similar pro-Darwin sentiment, stating, "Light came in as a flood and all was clear. Not only had I got rid of theology and the supernatural, but I found the truth of evolution."[169]

The father of atheistic communism was also a Darwin enthusiast. Karl Marx said Darwin's *Origin* served as "a basis in natural science for the class struggle in history." Marx's students—Vladimir Lenin and Joseph Stalin—justified revolution and genocide thanks to Darwin's corrupted views of man.

Progressive philosopher John Dewey said Darwin's theory of evolution created a revolution in the social sciences. Dewey wrote:

> Prior to Darwin the impact of the new scientific method upon life, mind, and politics, had been arrested, because between these ideal or moral interests and the inorganic world intervened the kingdom of plants and animals. The gates of the garden of life were barred to the new ideas; and only through this garden was there access to mind and politics. The influence of Darwin upon philosophy resides in his having conquered the phenomena of life for the principle of transition, and thereby freed the new logic for application to mind and morals and life.[170]

Social Darwinism, Dewey's extrapolated Darwinian notion that social institutions must evolve to survive, just as species do in nature, became entrenched in Western government and education and was used to promote racism, fascism, and totalitarianism. Even Adolf Hitler, the genocidal German dictator who plunged the globe into World War II, attributed the genocide of the Jews to Darwin's theory. "The German fuhrer [Hitler]," anthropologist Arthur Keith wrote, "consciously sought to make the practice of Germany conform to the theory of evolution." Hitler's desire to create a master race led to the Jewish Holocaust.[171]

GEORG WILHELM FRIEDRICH HEGEL (1770–1831)

Hegel was a German philosopher and university professor known as an important figure of German idealism. Evidently, he studied Jakob Bohme, a German Christian mystic, who saw the Fall of Man at the Garden of Eden as necessary so man could evolve to eventually achieve perfect knowledge, which Hegel called a dialectic: "a progression in which each successive movement emerges as a solution to the contradictions inherent in the preceding movement."[172]

Hegel's favorite term was *zeitgeist*, the spirit of the time, by which he meant the process in which man's spirit develops gradually—like Darwin's evolution—into its purest form. For Hegel, every nation that exists within the continuum of history is the product of all the previous. He explained "world history is thus the unfolding of spirit in time, as nature is the unfolding of the Idea in space."[173]

Thus Hegel came to believe the history of man was the process of his "achieving consciousness," and eventually perfect humanity (god on earth)—the seed for progressivism—a metamorphoses that happens only through the taming influence of state government. Hegel warns that once man achieves his peak of history, then he will lapse back into irrationality, barbarism. The point here is that attaining rationality is very difficult and comes at a cost of suffering and hard work.[174]

His theology was that god is spirit and that "spirit is ultimately the human mind." Hegel believed Christianity was true at least metaphorically for the human condition—god becomes man. The human mind becomes increasingly "rational until finally at the end of history, it becomes purely and perfectly rational."[175]

The emergence of the rational man as the true god, or what is referred to as the apotheosis of man, turning man into a god, attracted a lot of followers. One such follower was the progressive John Burgess, a Columbia University political scientist. Burgess is regarded as having been "the most influential political scientist of the period" (late nineteenth and early twentieth centuries). He was also a bigot. Darwin "agreed with the scholarly consensus that blacks were inferior," and wrote that "black skin means membership in a race of men which has never of itself succeeded in subjecting passion to reason, [and] has never, therefore, created any civilization of any kind."[176]

Hegelian theology was embraced by adherents of the social gospel movement in America. In fact, progressive theologian Richard Ely, an economics professor at the University of Wisconsin, interpreted Hegelian apotheosis of man to mean we (Americans) need to perfect ourselves and our government needs to help that process and then we can go help others to perfect themselves.

Hegel was critical of granting too much freedom for individual property rights and making money. Naturally, American progressives at the time like Burgess latched on to Hegel's idea that there was something wrong with a country that allows the individual too much self-reliance and self-indulgence in private passions instead of communal dedication to the higher things.

It is understandable why Hegel, given Burgess' view, is celebrated as the father of early American progressivism. But Hegel would not recognize modern American progressivism because his idea of freedom meant you are respectful of other people's rights, you are patriotic and support your community, and you believe in marriage as an institution. These Hegelian precepts and others were part of American progressivism until the 1960s.

Hegel may have shared some of Darwin's racist views in that he believed some societies progressed faster than others because of genes. Evidently, according to Hegel, Germans had superior genes, and thus "were the first to attain the consciousness that man, as man, is free."[177] It could also mean the Germanic peoples were the vehicle of reason in Hegel's world, but it didn't mean being born German necessarily meant one was going to be smarter than those born elsewhere or of another race. Rather, he may have meant given his view of history that the German nation happened at the time to have achieved the greatest fulfillment of rationality in their political and social order.

Hegel's influence was considerable, both in Europe and the United States. He certainly influenced Karl Marx who ran with Hegel's idea that history is about the movement from irrationality to rationality. Although Marx's *Communist Manifesto* was not true Hegelian progressivism, it was ideologically rooted in Hegel's idea that mankind would evolve.

WOODROW WILSON (1856–1924)

Wilson is often ranked among the top ten presidents and led the pack of presidents for displaying the most contempt for our Constitution, perhaps with the exception of President Obama. He was also known for his progressive ideology and his disdain for women and minorities.

Wilson was the son of a Presbyterian minister from the South and a lifelong churchgoer. His Christian roots haven't protected him from significant criticism about his failed leadership, however. Political scientist Ronald Pestritto, the author of *Woodrow Wilson and the Roots of Modern Liberalism,* said Wilson's leadership "is not as democratic as it seems, but instead amounts to elite governance under a veneer of democratic rhetoric."[178] Others like Glenn Beck are less charitable. Beck called Wilson an "S.O.B." and charged him with perverting Christianity—and even ranked him the worst on his "top ten bastards of all times" list behind Adolf Hitler and Pontius Pilate. Of course, Beck is vulnerable to similar criticism for his beliefs in a religious system that is considered by most denominations as apostate.

He was the "most" academic of any president. Wilson spent his entire adult life in the classroom: North Carolina's Davidson College, Princeton, University of Virginia Law School, Johns Hopkins University, Cornell, Bryn Mawr, Wesleyan, and finally back to Princeton. He only left academia for politics when he lost an argument about selecting the location of a new residential college, which demonstrates Wilson's pettiness.

The story is told by Pulitzer Prize-winning columnist George Will that Woodrow Wilson, then Princeton University's president, insisted that a new residential college be built on the main campus, but the university's trustees and donors chose a more secluded location adjoining a golf course. "When Wilson lost," Will said, "he had one of his characteristic tantrums, went into politics and ruined the twentieth century."[179]

Decades in academia prepared Wilson to seed radical changes in the U.S. government. At Johns Hopkins, he came under the influence of progressive economist Richard Ely, and he studied Darwinism to embrace the need to evolve centralized government. He was passionate, ambitious, and arrogant. While serving as a Bryn Mawr professor, he wrote, "All the country needs is a new and sincere body of thought in politics." Toward the end of his long academic career, he wrote "A New Theory of the Presidency and of the Whole Political System."

Wilson left Princeton to become the democratic governor of New Jersey in 1912, and then seemly almost overnight he became the president of the United States in 1913. The new president wasted no time pushing his progressive policies both at home and abroad.

Wilson is roundly criticized for creating the Federal Reserve System and implementing a progressive income tax. He was criticized by the left for his bigotry in sanctioning official segregation in Washington, D.C., and for using the country's entry into World War I as the rationale for crushing civil liberties.

Wilson believed the American government he inherited was ill prepared for modern times. It embodied Newtonian, mechanical ideas, and institutions that stood in the way of progress. After all, the founders designed it for a small, sparsely populated country, but the intervening century radically changed and the government had to adapt. To Wilson, the American Constitution should be "modified by its environment" because it must be a "living and breathing constitution," a Darwinian view.

He wrote a progressive treatise for a modern constitution: "All that progressives ask or desire is permission [in an] era when 'development,' 'evolution,' is the scientific word, [to] interpret the Constitution according to the Darwinian principle; all they ask is recognition of the fact that a nation is a living thing and not a machine."[180]

The Hegelian Wilson embraced the view the state existed only in the context of history, a process—Hegel's dialectic, it must embrace change in order to stay on the right side of history. Of course, the self-righteous Wilson believed governance demanded an elite class educated in historical intelligence. As fellow progressive John Dewey wrote, only "intelligent administration" can remove the blockages to historical progress.

"Intelligent administration" meant that only elite progressives know how to run government, a Hegelian concept. He advocated for public over private rights, stating: "Communities are supreme over men as individuals."[181]

Wilson was a racist much like Darwin. While serving as president of Princeton, he said the "whole temper and tradition of [Princeton] are such that no Negro has ever applied for admission, and it seems unlikely that the question will ever assume practical form." He continued his racist ways as governor of New Jersey and later as president when he resegregated parts of the federal workforce.[182]

He presided over America's entrance into World War I and, by association, our entrance onto the international stage. Although Wilson promised in his inaugural address, "We stand firm in armed neutrality,"[183] after only five weeks in office, President Wilson asked for and got a declaration of war. He quickly mobilized millions of young Americans and paid a high price in our blood to vanquish the Germans alongside our allies.

The end of the war gave him the opportunity to push his progressivism abroad by advancing the idea of the League of Nations, a global governing body to prevent future conflicts, and a step closer to the progressive goal of a one-world government. But Wilson couldn't sell the treaty to a Republican-controlled Senate in spite of his public attacks against opponents, "blind and little provincial people" with "pygmy minds" and his barnstorming cross-country speaking tour to appeal for support.[184]

President Wilson is the American father of globalism, a distinction recognized by none other than fellow progressive Hillary Clinton. In 2012, the Wilson Center bestowed on Ms. Clinton its Award for Public Service at a gala that included a video tribute featuring interviews with former secretaries of state led by fellow progressive Henry Kissinger.[185] Unfortunately, the at the time soon-to-be Democrat nominee for presiden, made no statement to distance herself from either the Wilson Center or the organization's namesake who, as columnist George Will said, "ruined the twentieth century."[186]

FRANKLIN D. ROOSEVELT (1882–1945)

President Roosevelt was a progressive with globalist ambitions who shared much in common with Hegel and Wilson: big government ruled by elites, public over private rights, a malleable U.S. Constitution, and deference to international government.

Arguably, Roosevelt's main historical legacy is the establishment of the American welfare state thanks to his New Deal, the vast expansion of government thanks in part to the opportunity created by the Great Depression, a crisis caused by progressive policies.

Presidential candidate Roosevelt campaigned in 1932 on his promise of a New Deal to deliver the country from the Great Depression. It did eventually lead the country out of the economic crisis, but in its place, it created an American welfare state and out-of-control deficit spending, a legacy the U.S. grapples with today.

His critics argued the Depression was the byproduct of a monetary system run amok, which dated back to the mid-nineteenthentury. But Colonel Edward House, a key Roosevelt advisor and the Council on Foreign Relations founder, said, "The real truth of the matter is, as you and I know, that a financial element in the larger centers has owned the government ever since the days of Andrew Jackson.... The country is going through a repetition of Jackson's fight with the Bank of the United States—only on a far bigger and broader basis."[187]

There was more to the Depression's underbelly than big banks and a failed monetary system. Progressives had previously imposed on American government antitrust laws, income taxes, increased business regulation, minimum wage laws, the Federal Reserve System, and much more. They also gave America a problem with the truth; progressives married the public press, and the media then flacked for big progressive government long before Roosevelt came to office.

Upton Sinclair's book, *The Jungle*, illustrates the relationship between journalism and big progressive government at the time. Sinclair greatly exaggerated the conditions at Chicago meat-packing plants in his book, which he later explained was an attempt to persuade Americans that socialism was their best hope. Sinclair said he aimed to change the "American heart," and he was successful, because his efforts directly contributed to the establishment of the Pure Food and Drug Act of 1906.[188]

President Roosevelt's New Deal fed the progressive hunger for big government, and Congress complied by granting the new administration great latitude. In just the first of three terms, Roosevelt worked with

Congress to create numerous new government entities: Unemployment Relief Act, which created the Civilian Conservation Corps; the Agricultural Adjustment Act; the Tennessee Valley Authority Act; the Federal Emergency Relief Act; and the National Industrial Recovery Act. Roosevelt also won passage of twelve other major laws, including the Glass-Steagall Banking Bill as well as the Home Owners' Loan Act. Collectively, that avalanche of big-government programs failed to reverse the impact of the Great Depression—unemployment persisted and people demanded more of government. So, in the spring of 1935, Roosevelt launched what he called the Second New Deal, which further expanded government. He created the Works Progress Administration (to build post offices, bridges, schools, highways, and parks); the National Labor Relations Board to supervise unions and protect workers from business abuses; and then, in 1935, he signed the Social Security Act, which guaranteed pensions for millions and a system for unemployment insurance to care for dependent children and the disabled.

The Second World War, like the Great Depression, was Roosevelt's excuse for expanding his power in other areas. Francis Biddle, Roosevelt's attorney general during the war, wrote, "The constitution has never greatly bothered any wartime president." For example, Roosevelt decided to evacuate Japanese-Americans from the Pacific Coast and place them in internment camps.[189] The 1942 relocation of these people was, in Roosevelt's view, a necessary national security act. But Roosevelt's decision was not necessary based on the testimony of the military chiefs at the time that dismissed concerns about a Japanese invasion or sabotage by Japanese-Americans to justify the act.[190]

President Roosevelt also used the excuse of the nation at war to centralize more power under the executive to ignore tariffs, to order the military to seize land, and create draconian labor regulations to keep the war industry operating at a high speed.

Running Roosevelt's rapidly expanding government required Hegelian elite leadership. That meant Roosevelt's bloated New Deal big political government would be led by elite experts who would replace the invisible hand of the marketplace, replacing federalism as the founders intended with big government's welfare state.

Former Roosevelt Brain Trust member Raymond Moley wrote in his 1952 book, *How to Keep Our Liberty*, that some of Roosevelt's so-called elite had ulterior motives.[191]

> It was no secret that a great number of … reformers [in Roosevelt's bureaucracy] were admirers of the "great soviet experiment." And some…were secret agents of communism.
>
> In my opinion, there is a greater danger in collectivists than in the betrayal of our secrets to foreign powers. The danger lies in what can be done to a nation by public officials who do not believe in a free economy. In Roosevelt's day there were many people working for the government who regarded his reforms as a mere prelude to revolution.
>
> America has been fortunate to avoid such a fate so far, but Roosevelt's revolution not only accomplished more than Wilson and the other progressives who came before him had ever dreamed possible, but it also set the stage for what was to come next.

A New Deal and a second Bill of Rights were terrific starts, but what America really needed was someone who could pull all of the disparate pieces together. Someone who could appeal to all races and creeds and make Americans believe that they could achieve what no one before them had, that it was their duty to work together something bigger than themselves, something he called a great society.

Yes, for many reasons Roosevelt's New Deal was a major disappointment. Henry Morgenthau Jr., a close Roosevelt friend, secretary of the Treasury, and key New Deal architect, testified on May 9, 1939: "I say after eight years of this Administration we have just as much unemployment as when we started.… and an enormous debt to boot!"[192]

Historian Burton W. Folsom Jr. called Morgenthau's statement a "startling confession." "In these words, Morgenthau summarized a decade of disaster, especially during the years Roosevelt was in power. Indeed average unemployment for the whole year in 1939 would be higher than that in 1931, the year before Roosevelt captured the presidency from Herbert Hoover," Folsom writes in his book, *New Deal or Raw Deal?: How FDR's Economic Legacy Has Damaged America.*[193]

On another important issue, Roosevelt's progressive colors were in full bloom as they relate to the U.S. Constitution. While campaigning for the presidency in 1932, Roosevelt called for "a reappraisal of values," specifically America's original constitutional order needed to adapt to the times, a Hegelian concept. He used the U.S. Declaration of Independence at the time to justify his view for making the constitution a "living" adjustable document.[194]

"The Declaration of Independence discusses the problem of government in terms of contract…under such a contract rulers were accorded power, and the people consented to that power on consideration that they be accorded certain rights," Roosevelt said. Then he applied a progressive interpretation to that view: "The task of statesmanship has always been the redefinition of these rights in terms of a changing and growing social order."[195]

That interpretation is contrary to what the founders had in mind. President Abraham Lincoln said our founders gave us a constitutional order in conformity with the eternal cause of civil liberty and natural rights. He warned about the likes of Wilson and Roosevelt who believe in so-called progress in government.[196]

Progressives reject Lincoln's fixed principle-based Constitution and went about the process of amending the document during the progressive era. They passed the 16th, 17th, 18th and 19th Amendments to alter the political landscape to fit their goals. For example, the 16th Amendment, the creation of an income tax, reflected the Hegelian view of public over private, and it placed more power in the hands of the centralized government.

Roosevelt was a globalist at the core as well. His seminal role on the international stage was the formulation of the blueprint for the United Nations. He played the role of global statesman by starting early, before the Second War ended, to establish an international venue for nations to resolve their differences without resorting to war. This idea wasn't new; after all, President Wilson's failed League of Nations after World War I had the same aim as Roosevelt's UN. Wilson's effort failed in part because he tried to bully the Republican-controlled Senate, but also because Americans at the time were generally isolationists.

Years earlier as the Democratic vice-presidential nominee, Roosevelt had made hundreds of speeches in support of Wilson's League of Nations. He argued for the "practical necessity" for the organization, telling his audiences that if the U.S. failed to join, it "would degenerate into a new Holy Alliance" among European states.[197]

Roosevelt learned from Wilson's failure to gain congressional support for the League of Nations. To prevent such a reoccurrence, he included many administration members and elected officials in the effort to create the United Nations. Those efforts included consultations with Congress and a congressional resolution declaring its support for the U.N. as well as its intention to join.[198] Six months prior to his death, the U.N. officially came into existence with the signatures of China, France, the Soviet Union, the United Kingdom, and the United States. And just prior to his death, as previously cited, Roosevelt, according to author Stephen Schlesinger, "wanted to quit the [U.S.] presidency and become the U.N's first secretary general. This is what he really wanted to be remembered for."[199]

CONCLUSION

The sweep of history demonstrates how globalization has changed mankind's interconnectivity and especially over the past century—plus, the world has become seemingly smaller and more homogenized. Progressive thinkers like Darwin, Hegel, Wilson, and Roosevelt helped shape progressive globalist thinking, and it is now being played out across the world stage. We shall examine the new tribe of globalists—our peers—in the next chapter, taking a look at their impact and how they are pressing in every direction for a very new kind of future world.

CHAPTER EIGHT

Modern Globalists Elite

The modern globalists elite are a dangerous tribe—and not just because they embrace the progressive ideologies of Darwin, Hegel, Wilson, and Roosevelt. They are a racially diverse, wealthy group as well, "eager to assimilate the fun-seeming bits of foreign cultures—food, a touch of exotic spirituality," explains *New York Times* columnist Ross Douthat. They pretend that they earned their elite status by merit, and they tend to think globally and self-righteously progressively, but "think and act as members of a tribe."[200]

Their tribe has a distinctive worldview, according to Douthat, who cites a social psychologist's label for their elite worldview as WEIRD—for Western, Educated, Industrialized, Rich, and Democratic. They seek comfort and familiarity in each Western "global city"; wherever these "citizens of the world" travel they feel at home, "which is why the age of empire made cosmopolitans as well as chauvinists—sometimes out of the same people."

Their global tribalism defines their behavior, grants identity and values, and motivates. They can be positive but dangerously divisive, prejudiced, and small-minded. They tend to engage in groupthink around their often radical progressive politics, arrogantly believing they know better than you and me. Their agenda tends to be anti-God, and they want to abolish all religions (especially Christianity) and destroy private property rights, except regarding their own elite assets.

Most members of the global elitist tribe are wealthy, which protects them from the rigors of normal life, like paying a mortgage, affording quality healthcare, and funding a good education for their children. Many use their riches to impose their views, which are most often progressive like Ted Turner, owner of Times Warner and CNN, who funds organizations focused on reducing world population (read "abortion on demand") and Microsoft's Bill Gates, who campaigns to vaccinate the world while also advocating for population control. These self-righteous elite speak about globalism in religious tones much like climate alarmists passionately threaten global Armageddon due to "man-made global-warming."

The modus operandi of the globalists elite tribe goes something like the following: There are four interconnected groups of globalists elite who feed on one another. There are the globalist corporate elite who are especially wealthy, like David Rockefeller, who creates global trading and/or finance goals which are then justified by the second group, the heavily endowed academic elite at Ivy League colleges who draft studies and white papers to support their corporate sponsors' aims. Those documents are given to the third elite group, the corporate-funded politicians in Washington who use the academic-produced arguments to persuade the public via the ideological progressive media (like Ted Turner's CNN and progressive entertainers like Barbra Streisand), or they (the political class) pass laws to satisfy their donors' corporate goals (read Obama's green energy initiatives). Finally, nonprofit organizations—some of which are corporate-funded "think tanks" filled with "elite" former government people or so-called secret, exclusive societies like the Bilderbergers or Council on Foreign Relations with close ties to serving political figures—and others such as organized religious groups promote the progressive corporate globalist agenda and all its salient appendages.

Now consider this rather cynical although accurate view of the globalists elite as applied to famous contemporary representatives from each of the four groups: corporate, academic, government, and non-profit. Members of this conspiring cabal share many of the characteristics outlined above and certainly demonstrate interconnectedness, which gives this cynical view credibility. In a couple of chapters, we will consider the spiritual implications of this circus of horrors as well. However, for now, consider biographical sketches of representatives from each of the four groups and how they are indeed are playing us all for fools.

CORPORATE ELITES: DAVID ROCKEFELLER

What names come to mind when you think about corporate elite? One source identified sixty American families from the early twentieth century that held near monopolies over the worldwide banking system, entertainment industry, food industry, energy industry, transportation, and many more.[201] Through this domination, they pulled the strings of the U.S. and many other governments across the world.

Author Ferdinand Lundberg painted a dire picture those wealthy elite:

> The United States is owned and dominated today by a hierarchy of its sixty richest families, buttressed by no more than ninety families of lesser wealth.... These families are the living center of the modern industrial oligarchy which dominates the United States, functioning discreetly under a de jure democratic form of government behind which a de facto government, absolutist and plutocratic in its lineaments, has gradually taken form since the Civil War. This de facto government is actually the government of the United States—informal, invisible, shadowy. It is the government of money in a dollar democracy.[202]

The Rockefeller family is among America's elite ruling class (families) and our contemporary was David Rockefeller, the youngest son of John D. Rockefeller Jr., who was a prominent figure in the world of finance, foreign relations, public service, and philanthropic pursuits. Even though he died in early 2017, his influence will continue for many years.

His long public life (101 years) demonstrates like few others who leveraged their wealth to manipulate the academic, government, and nonprofit elites to promote a globalization and socially progressive agenda. "He spent his life in the club of the ruling class and was loyal to members of the club, no matter what they did," wrote *New York Times* columnist David Brooks.[203] He was the crème de la crème of the elite.

David Rockefeller was educated at philosopher John Dewey's Experimental Lincoln School in Manhattan before attending Harvard and the London School of Economics. Finally he earned a Ph.D. in economics from the University of Chicago before launching into his career as a banker. It is noteworthy that, as an international bankcr, he was credited with opening the first Western banking operations in the former Soviet Union and communist China.[204]

Banking was not his passion, however. He was best known for his philanthropic pursuits and his unofficial foreign relations work. He gave away some $2 billion to various causes, including medicine, science, urban development, and education. He helped many worthy causes across his ten decades of life, but also raised many eyebrows by his largess to others, as did his family's long-standing foundation.

The Rockefeller philanthropies included so-called family planning initiatives ostensibly to "solve pervasive social ills, including poverty and crime." That generosity included a grant to eugenics activist Margaret Sanger's American Birth Control League to "research contraception." The foundation also sponsored research that included the abortifacient "Norplant which has been widely used in the developing world."[205] A study cited by the Population Research Institute found a "staggering 86% [of women using Norplant] reported suffering ovarian cysts...

breast lumps…increased blood…pressure…insomnia…headaches…
temporary visual disturbances and more."[206]

David Rockefeller personally endorsed the agenda of "population
control." His 1994 address to the New York City-based Annual Ambassadors' Dinner drew attention to his support for the United Nation's
"stabilizing the population" work. That is code for a phalanx of activities
to stop population growth: sterilization, vaccinations, abortions, using
food as a weapons, and disease as a means of correcting overpopulation.
There is also Obama's Global Health Initiative, another population-con-
trol scheme, supported by Rockefeller's Good Club, along with other
elites like George Soros, Ted Turner, Bill Gates, and Oprah Winfrey.[207]

Before Rockefeller's time at the helm of the family dynasty, the Rockefeller Foundation funded Alfred Kinsey through the National Research
Council's Committee for Research in the Problems of Sex. Kinsey is
the author of *Sexual Behavior in the Human Male*. Kinsey's research was
controversial to say the least.[208]

Robert Knight, a current columnist with the *Washington Times* and
formerly with Concerned Women for America, said: "Alfred C. Kinsey's
studies have had a profoundly negative impact on American women
and children, weakening legal protection from sexual abuse and falsely
portraying 'sexual liberation' as an unalloyed good, despite astronomic
increases in divorce, abortion, sexually transmitted diseases and physical
abuse of women and children."[209]

In 2014, the Rockefeller Foundation hosted a LGBT (lesbian, gay,
bisexual, transsexual) Pride Month event for the Diversity & Inclusion
Ambassador Group. The event hosted two speakers, Fabrice Houdart
with the World Bank and Carrie Davis with a New York City LGBT
Community Center. The event was designed to help promote and normalize homosexuality both at home and overseas. This is yet another
example of radical values passing from one generation of Rockefellers to
the next.[210]

Put aside the social issues and consider domestic and international
politics, an area that captured Rockefeller's interest even though he never

held public office. On the domestic front, he pushed progressive policies that moved America toward bigger, more intrusive, and costly centralized government. His doctoral thesis at the University of Chicago showed his progressive views when he wrote that he was "inclined to agree with the New Deal [President Roosevelt] that deficit financing during depressions, other things being equal, is a help to recovery."[211]

The Rockefellers in general and David in particular had a reputation for pushing the nation in a globalist direction. The family foundation played a key role in the shift from "isolationism" to "globalism" in U.S. foreign policy between 1939 and 1945, according to a study by Interject Parmar, a senior lecturer in government at the University of Manchester, United Kingdom. Parmar wrote, "The foundation [Rockefeller] utilized its considerable financial resources in a conscious and systematic attempt to assist official policymakers and academics to build a new globalist consensus within the state and public opinion.'"[212]

David Rockefeller's foreign policy interloper actions tended to leverage his status as a founding member of the Council on Foreign Relations (CRF), the Trilateral Commission and the Bilderberger Group. For example, he worked with former secretary of state Henry Kissinger, a well-known progressive, to persuade President Jimmy Carter, another progressive, to admit the deposed shah of Iran into the United States. That move enraged Islamic radicals in Tehran who seized the U.S. Embassy on November 4, 1979, and held our diplomats and embassy employees 444 days until just after President Ronald Reagan was sworn into office.

Rockefeller's globalist views were evident by his association with other leaders of the CFR, an organization he chaired from 1970 to 1985. Richard Haass, the current CFR president, famously endorses a "more integrated global political and economic structure." That view was expressed in CFR's report, "Building a North American Community," which "openly called for dissolving the borders between Canada, the United States, and Mexico and establishing 'regional governance.'"[213]

Haass and CFR's membership by association not only favor eliminating borders but "rethinking" national sovereignty. Haass wrote that "the time has come to rethink the notion of national sovereignty." He calls for "new mechanisms...for regional and global governance that include actors other than states." These "actors" include transnational corporations and nongovernmental organizations (NGOs). "States," he said, "must be prepared to cede some sovereignty to world bodies if the international system is to function. This is already taking place in the trade realm."[214]

CFR's Haass is a globalist like Rockefeller who encourages acceding our sovereignty. "Globalization," Haass said, "implies that sovereignty is not only becoming weaker in reality, but that it needs to become weaker. States would be wise to weaken sovereignty in order to protect themselves, because they cannot insulate themselves from what goes on elsewhere. Sovereignty is no longer a sanctuary."[215]

David Rockefeller likely full-heartedly endorses Haass and shares his views about sovereignty. Rockefeller has always been especially keen for international activities, many of which were unassociated with his somewhat unorthodox banking activities, including befriending foreign dictators to help expand his bank's overseas presence.

Rockefeller's club associations such as with the CFR were significant in his free-wielding style. He even took great pride in those associations when he stated in his memoirs:

> Some even believe we (the Rockefeller family) are part of a secret cabal working against the best interests of the United States, characterizing my family and me as "internationalists" and of conspiring with others around the world to build a more integrated global political and economic structure—one world, if you will. If that's the charge, I stand guilty, and I am proud of it.[216]

He wasn't shy about his wealth and the associated power, nor about using it to get his way. A 2016 report illustrates just how effective Rockefeller manipulated the other three elite groups (academic, political, and

NGO) to promote his globalist agenda. Specifically, Rockefeller worked with the other elites and elitist groups "as a means to expand their [Rockefeller's] empire over the past three decades," according to a December 2016 report by the Washington, D.C.-based Energy and Environment Legal (E & E Legal) Institute entitled "The Rockefeller Way: The Family's Covert 'Climate Change' Plan."[217]

One example of throwing his considerable influence is illustrated by the climate change debate. Alex Newman reported on the "climate" scam for the *New American*, stating "under the guise of fighting alleged 'man-made global-warming,' the Rockefeller family and its billions have been bankrolling everything from 'climate' journalism (propaganda) efforts, politicians, and 'academia' to politically motivated 'investigations' of energy companies 'investigations' of energy companies and nonprofit organizations by government officials."[218]

The billionaire's goal was "to crush the oil and gas industry, using government power as the weapon of choice, to ultimately gain greater control over the energy sector once again." Yes, the family holds a lot of renewable energy stock and using dirty business tricks is an old family recipe.[219]

David's grandfather, John D. Rockefeller Sr., had a well-deserved reputation for shady tactics through which he gained a virtual monopoly over the nineteenth-century U.S. energy enterprise. Today's efforts by the late David Rockefeller to capture the energy market were more nefarious.

The cast of characters in Rockefeller's scam includes New York attorney general Eric Schneiderman, who evidently took the bait provided by Rockefeller-funded media reports alleging energy giant ExxonMobile knew man-made "global warming" was a real threat. AG Schneiderman and other state AGs launched the "AGs United for Clean Power." Newman indicates that campaign-targeted nonprofit groups opposed the climate alarmists.

E & E Legal's report indicates that Rockefeller-funded climate-alarmists had planned their assault in 2012, when they met in California to craft a strategy to target ExxonMobile through the criminal justice system and the media. Next, Rockefeller brought the climate alarmists together with the political class, a meeting reported by the *Washington Free Beacon*. Their agenda: Wage war on the oil companies.[220]

The Rockefeller clan used its elite globalist cabal to advance the climate-change agenda for its own benefit. The E & E Legal report found that "through their financial influence, it is posited that the Rockefellers planned, coordinated, and subsidized the combined efforts of the Columbia journalism school and New York attorney general Eric Schneidman's investigation into ExxonMobil."[221]

E & E Legal concluded that the Rockefeller's ambitions go well beyond green energy. They "are intent on controlling nearly every major institution in America using philanthropy as a means of increasing their influence on the world stage under the guise of advancing various social causes."[222]

ACADEMIC ELITES: HENRY KISSINGER

Dr. Henry Kissinger's life illustrates the role played by elite academics in the interplay among the four categories of elite globalists.

Kissinger is the godfather of the one world order, a man who immigrated to this country with his parents from Nazi Germany in 1938. He served with the U.S. Army in World War II and later the globalist Rockefeller Foundation helped finance his Harvard education, which, after he earned a Ph.D., became his employer. He remained on the Harvard faculty until 1969. While serving as a Harvard professor, Kissinger joined the elitist Council on Foreign Relations, and by the mid-1960s he had become a close associate with Nelson Rockefeller, the forty-first vice president of the U.S., a CFR member, and the elder brother of David Rockefeller.

Kissinger's globalist views were evident in his 1960 book, *Necessity for Choice*. In that volume, Kissinger wrote: "The self-sufficient nation-state is breaking down," and he urged the U.S. to take the lead in "creating federal institutions comprising the entire north Atlantic community" as part of a new global order. His idea at the time for dealing with the Soviet Union was to "summon the initiative and imagination to show the way to a new international order."[223]

Kissinger's CFR associations, according to Admiral Chester Ward and Phyllis Schlafly, advanced Kissinger's rise in order to "bring about the surrender of the sovereignty and independence of the United States."

"The elitist cliques calculate that such a posture would provide an irresistible incentive for us to join a global government before we were forced to surrender," Ward and Schlafly wrote.[224]

Kissinger left Harvard to serve as assistant to the president for National Security Affairs beginning in January 1969 and then became the fifty-sixth secretary of state in September 1973, serving until January 1977. His views about a new world order were front and center, even during his government time.

In October 1975, Dr. Kissinger addressed the General Assembly of the United Nations as the serving secretary of state, stating:

> My country's history, Mr. President, tells us that it is possible to fashion unity while cherishing diversity that common action is possible despite the variety of races, interests, and beliefs we see here in this chamber. Progress and peace and justice are attainable. So we say to all peoples and governments: Let us fashion together a new world order.[225]

He continued to serve in a variety of foreign policy roles even after leaving the State Department. He was appointed by President Reagan to chair the National Bipartisan Commission on Central America and as a member of the President's Foreign Intelligence Advisory Board until 1990.

Dr. Kissinger's service earned him many honors, to include the Nobel Peace Prize in 1973. However, his critics claim he has a lot of blood on his foreign policy hands.

Dr. Greg Grandin, a history professor at New York University, summarized Kissinger's bloody legacy in an article about his new book, *Kissinger's Shadow: The Long Reach of America's Most Controversial Statesman.*

> Let's consider some of Kissinger's achievements during his tenure as Richard Nixon's top foreign policy-maker. He (1) prolonged the Vietnam War for five pointless years; (2) illegally bombed Cambodia and Laos; (3) goaded Nixon to wiretap staffers and journalists; (4) bore responsibility for three genocides in Cambodia, East Timor, and Bangladesh; (5) urged Nixon to go after Daniel Ellsberg for having released the Pentagon Papers, which set off a chain of events that brought down the Nixon White House; (6) pumped up Pakistan's ISI [inter-services intelligence], and encouraged it to use political Islam to destabilize Afghanistan; (7) began the U.S.'s arms-for-petrodollars dependency with Saudi Arabia and pre-revolutionary Iran; (8) accelerated needless civil wars in southern Africa that, in the name of supporting white supremacy, left millions dead; (9) supported coups and death squads throughout Latin America; and (10) ingratiated himself with the first-generation neocons, such as Dick Cheney and Paul Wolfowitz, who would take American militarism to its next calamitous level.[226]

Others blame the former diplomat under President Nixon of engineering the U.S. defeat that delivered South Vietnam to communist control and, Mark Sauter and Jim Sanders in their book, *The Men We Left Behind: Henry Kissinger, the Politics of Deceit and The Tragic Fate of POWs after the Vietnam War*, blame Kissinger for abandoning our men. "From the earliest years of U.S.-Vietnamese negotiations, the only real issue was how, not whether, the U.S. would pull out of Vietnam and leave Saigon to fend for itself," wrote Sauter and Sanders. "The other basic fact was that while the U.S. wanted to withdraw with as few entanglements as possible, Hanoi wanted reparations.... As Vernon Walters, a senior soldier-diplomat in the Nixon administration, later put it: 'Reparations were sine qua non for peace, [for the] return [of] the prisoners, for everything.'"[227]

The deal was never struck because Kissinger never told Congress about the promise of reparations (a ransom). So, when Congress rejected any economic aid to Hanoi, they unbeknownst to all but a few wrote the death sentence for those Americans left behind.

Dr. Kissinger also profited from our enemies, and in particular, the role Western elites played in building Iraq's military, according to William Norman Grigg in a *New American* article. Evidently, according to Grigg's references, the Kissinger Associates, a consulting agency "for-hire" created with the help of Brent Scowcroft and Lawrence Eagleburger (fellow CFR members), counseled "an exclusive group of multinational corporations and banks that paid them huge fees."[228]

More recently, Dr. Kissinger has kept some notable "friends." Russian President Vladimir Putin identified Kissinger as a trusted foreign policy adviser in his book, *First Person*. Putin gave Kissinger an "honorary doctorate" in "diplomacy," explaining "you have not simply been doing diplomatic service or similar activities; you have been a global politician for almost your whole life." Putin continued, "You have many friends in Russia, both among our foreign policy veterans and among other people as well."[229]

Kissinger is also closely aligned with the Clintons. During the 2016 presidential campaign, Hillary Clinton called Kissinger "a friend," praised his "astute observations," and said she "relied on his counsel" during her time at the State Department. Both Hillary and the former president have regularly socialized with Kissinger, to include spending their winter holidays with them in the Dominican Republic.[230]

Recently, Dr. Kissinger earned attention for his latest book, *World Order*. However, he fails to define the term "world order" in the volume. The political science world easily associates "order" with "government," but Kissinger avoids the term "world government" even though most of us know what he means.

Recent interviews with Dr. Kissinger demonstrate that his globalist views are very much on his mind. "The economic system has become global, while the political structure of the world remains based on the nation-state," Kissinger explained. "The international order thus faces a paradox: its prosperity is dependent on the success of globalization, but the process produces a political reaction that often works counter to its aspirations." His solution is to globalize the political system.[231]

Kissinger told the *Atlantic* magazine that to deal with the world's chaos, we must create a "coherent world order based on agreed-upon principles that are necessary for the operation of the entire system." Once again, the father of American progressivism and author of "world order" is obliquely making reference to the need for world government, the necessary custodian for world order.[232]

POLITICAL ELITES: HILLARY CLINTON

Hillary Clinton's life illustrates the potential adverse consequences of becoming an elite globalist. It didn't have to end up this way, but the Clinton family enriched themselves while advancing the globalist agenda at our expense.

Ms. Clinton is a woman with significant accomplishments and influence. Her resume is very impressive: a graduate of the elite Wellesley College and Yale Law School, faculty member with the School of Law at the University of Arkansas, a law firm partner, member of many prestigious boards of directors, wife of the Arkansas governor, first lady of the United States, U.S. senator from New York, and secretary of state. Her capstone accomplishment is certainly winning the 2016 Democrat party's nomination for the presidency.

What makes such an accomplished lady revert to unethical and in some cases criminal conduct? Further, why would she abandon her conservative Middle America roots to become a dyed-in-the-wool globalist willing to sell out her country? Perhaps, as pointed out earlier in this volume, she is counted among the psychopathic part of the human race that willingly does whatever necessary to acquire power.

She came to her progressive, globalist views after arriving at Wellesley, a private women's liberal arts college west of Boston in the town of Wellesley, Massachusetts. Hillary Diane Rodham (Clinton) grew up in a Republican family in Park Ridge, Illinois, a Chicago suburb. Once at Wellesley, she was elected president of the College Republicans, and she even attended early in her college career a "big meeting of Massachusetts Republicans," a self-acknowledged turning point experience for her. She said after that meeting:

> I remember walking around [at that meeting], talking to a lot of people, and I began to see more clearly what a movement to a radical version of republicanism actually meant. So I got back to college and it was more emotional and intuitive, I just went to see one of my good friends, who was a vice president of the College Republicans and said: "I don't know what I am right now, but I know I can't be the president of the College Republicans."[233]

After leaving her Republican post, she remembers "sitting in the reserve room of the Wellesley library, hour upon hour, reading everything I could find about what was happening in the world." Then she was introduced to some key figures such as Henry Kissinger.[234]

Dr. Kissinger came to "Wellesley to speak and we all crowded in to hear him speak…about the future of Europe." She recalls asking Dr. Kissinger: "You didn't say very much about Germany's future. What did the future of Europe have to do with the resolving policy in Vietnam?"[235]

The Vietnam War was on the mind of most Americans in the mid- to late-1960s, and Hillary was no exception. She said:

> I was just very interested in all of that [the Vietnam War]. So I just spent a couple of years searching for my own sense of

politics, carrying with me some of my sort of bedrock beliefs in promoting individual responsibility and promoting the kind of conservatism in which you do try to sustain institutions like families and communities against the onslaught of change, so that there can be some anchoring for people as they go through the past part of the twentieth century.[236]

Her introspective search "for my own sense of politics" led her to investigate some interesting people like Saul Alinsky. His most famous book, the 1971 *Rules for Radicals: A Pragmatic Primer for Realistic Radicals*, includes a dedication to "the first radical known to man who rebelled against the establishment and did it so effectively that he at least won his own kingdom—Lucifer."[237]

Ms. Rodham was interested in Alinsky's work, especially regarding his efforts "trying to organize people on the grassroots level, something in opposition to the programs of the Great Society that were trying to help them." She read Alinsky's work, and says, "I met him, and I talked to people about him, and I wrote a senior thesis in which I basically argued that he was right." She admitted, "I really enjoyed getting to meet him [Alinsky] because he was a real character, he was a radical."[238]

There's no doubt the grown-up Ms. Clinton is a very intelligent, deep thinker with significant knowledge and experience. She will be remembered as a towering figure among twenty-first-century progressives and feminists, influenced by a rich tapestry of people like Kissinger and Alinsky.

Her work and associations over the past decade (2008–2017) have been especially noteworthy, an outcome that doesn't surprise anyone who has followed her career. Even *Esquire* magazine once identified Ms. Clinton as among "the best of the new generation, men and women under forty who are changing America." She has indeed helped to change America—and unfortunately for the worse.[239]

Her political life began as a young lawyer fresh from Yale working with the chief counsel of the House Judiciary Committee during the

Watergate inquiry that began in 1973. She was a young staffer drafting Articles of Impeachment of the President of the United States. Ms. Rodham (soon to be Clinton) had a front-row seat observing the collapse of the highest office in the land because of President Richard Nixon's obsession with privacy, a scenario that played out in Clinton's life more than four decades later.

In 1975, Hillary married Bill Clinton in the living room of their home in Fayetteville, Arkansas. At the time, Mr. Clinton was a law professor at the University of Arkansas, which provided him a platform first to unsuccessfully run for Congress and then in 1976 to win the office for Arkansas Attorney General. That launched his political career that, a few short years later, landed him in the state's governor's office (1979–1981) and again as the forty-second governor from 1983 to 1992.

Hillary leveraged her husband's political fortunes in Arkansas to win spots on many boards and to become a partner at the prestigious Rose Law Firm. The power couple went on to defy most political prognosticators to win the U.S. presidency in 1992. Their meteoric rise and notoriety placed Hillary dead-center among the four groups of societal elites who helped mold her views and behaviors.

She was a passionate progressive globalist by the time she started running for the White House in 2008, views that were seeded while still at Wellesley. She came to favor a future world system ruled by international norms and an all-powerful, one-world government. Milo Beckman wrote that Clinton evidenced this vision in her firm commitment to international agreements as well as a strong interventionist ideology; the U.S. must not shirk its international responsibilities, she often expressed.[240]

She came to envision the world like a small town without governance. In such a world, all parties are best served by a formal body—government—that draws up rules of engagement and deters defection by consistently punishing defectors. She would co-opt today's institutions to create a pluralist, democratic, peaceful, human rights-enforcing international order. Until that utopia becomes a reality, the U.S. must leverage its position as the biggest and strongest guy in town to punish extreme defectors.

Ms. Clinton's lust for power resulted in relationships with a host of unsavory people and led her into criminal behavior. In fact, *The Hill*, a Washington, D.C.-based magazine, reported that former assistant FBI director James Kallstrom said in an interview: "The Clintons, that's a crime family, basically. It's like organized crime. I mean the Clinton Foundation is a cesspool.... God forbid we put someone like that [Clinton] in the White House."[241]

The Clintons used three platforms to fuel their "crime family." Their political roles provided them significant leverage and notoriety, which generated income from speeches. The British magazine *The Economist* estimates the couple gave 728 speeches since the former president left office, making $154 million in fees, and $49 million of that was made while Ms. Clinton served as the secretary of state and much of that money came from aboard.[242]

The Clinton Foundation is a big money winner as well. Originally, it was formed to raise funds for Mr. Clinton's presidential library, but soon it exploded in size and encompassed global activities. In 2014, the Foundation had twelve divisions with activities across the world, with revenues from donations and grants exceeding $338 million and a staff of two thousand.[243]

Meanwhile, the Clintons' association with other elites illustrates their climb into criminality. They have close ties with billionaire financier and radical progressive globalist George Soros, who, as you will see in the next section of this chapter, is a globalist who funds radical and perhaps illegal activities. Soros has been especially generous to the Clintons, who used their political platforms to advance radical globalist policies.

WikiLeaks released hacked e-mails that showed communications between Soros and Clinton confidants' John Podesta, Robby Mook, and Hillary's personal aide Huma Abedin. In 2014, Abedin wrote an e-mail to Mook stating that Hillary "is having dinner with George Soros tonight," and Soros intends to ask Hillary whether she will attend a fundraising dinner at his [Soros'] home for America Votes, a progressive coalition effort he funds. Hillary's condition: "I would only do this for political reasons."[244]

Soros and his sons poured million into Clinton's political campaigns and foundation expecting a quid pro quo. The payoff came in many forms, such as supporting Soros' radical immigration views. The Clintons supported German Chancellor Angela Merkel's failed immigrant plan for Europe, which is credited to a Soros agent. At the time, sensing a regional emergency, Hungary and Poland reimposed border controls as a tsunami of migrants flooded into Western Europe, a move attacked by Bill Clinton. Evidently, the Hungarian prime minister was aware of Soros' hand in the failing immigration plan and said, "Although the mouth belongs to Clinton, the voice belongs to Soros."[245]

The Clintons' progressive support for open borders goes beyond the failed Soros-pushed approach in Western Europe. WikiLeaks revealed a speech Hillary gave to Latin American bankers in which she said: "My dream is a hemispheric common market, with open trade and open borders."[246]

The Clintons' questionable elite political maneuvers demonstrate just how depraved power can corrupt even "our best and brightest." Further, their actions advance a globalist agenda of weakening sovereign states to establish international institutions and the elite who control them.

Most readers will recall that Ms. Clinton, while serving as the secretary of state, operated a private e-mail server out of her New York home. Thousands of her e-mails were hacked and later released by WikiLeaks, revealing she frequently violated federal law (Title 18 U.S. Code 798) by disclosing classified information such as war plans in Iraq. One widely reported classified Clinton e-mail revealed an intelligence report that states, "The governments of Qatar and Saudi Arabia...are providing clandestine financial and logistic support to ISIL [the terror group Islamic State] and other radical Sunni groups in the region."[247]

Her cavalier attitude about protecting state secrets continued even though Clinton left the State Department in 2013. She and her staff continued to access top-secret materials for years, according to Fox News. Ostensibly the purpose for the access was to research work on Hillary's future memoir, and that access continued even after she announced her second White House bid in April 2015. Senator Chuck Grassley (R.—Iowa) said, "Any other government workers who engaged in such serious offenses [leaking highly classified information] would, at a minimum, have their clearances suspended pending an investigation. The failure to do so has given the public the impression that Secretary Clinton and her associates received special treatment."[248]

Hillary also evidently used her official position at the State Department to run a pay-for-play front for the Clinton Foundation. In 2011, John Podesta, Bill Clinton's former chief of staff wrote an e-mail to Doug Band, head of the consultancy firm Teneo used as a pass-through vehicle for purchasing influence from the Clintons: "I'm also starting to worry that if this story [pay-to-play] gets out, we are screwed."

A review of Associated Press reports found that more than half of all private individuals with whom Hillary Clinton met while serving as secretary of state had donated to the Clinton Foundation. That's 85 of the 154 people outside of government. What did these meetings harvest for the Clintons?[249]

Band reported in a leaked memo entitled "Leveraging Teneo for the Foundation" all the donations he solicited from Teneo "clients" for the Clinton Foundation. They amounted to $14 million, with the largest contributors being Coca-Cola, Barclays, the Rockefeller Foundation, and Laureate International Universities.[250]

Hillary's willingness to sell out her country is evidenced by the abuse of her secretary of state decision-making power on the Committee for Foreign Investment in the United States (CFIUS). She used that influence to approve the Russian government's purchase of the majority control of Uranium One, a uranium mining company headquartered in Toronto, Canada. Evidently the Clintons and their Foundation received reportedly $130 million from investors for arranging the deal worth at the time $1.3 billion, which means that our enemy Vladimir Putin now controls at least 20 percent of our strategic uranium assets.[251]

The Clintons illustrate better than any other American political couple how to milk their elitist status. They served in the White House, State Department, and U.S. Senate, and then milked many domestic and international elites seeking special access and influence into the U.S. government.

This example of elite politicians demonstrates the danger of crooked globalists and how the transnational community manipulates sovereign governments like the United States. Like others who came before them, the Clintons retired from government to enrich themselves at our expense and to promote a progressive globalist agenda.

NONPROFIT ELITE: GEORGE SOROS

Mr. George Soros' deep pockets and progressive ideas have been used to manipulate the other elite groups (corporate, academic, and political) to promote his globalist views. Mr. Soros arguably impacts world politics and culture more profoundly than any other living person, and besides, he admits to fantasies about being a god.

"I admit that I have always harbored an exaggerated view of self-importance—to put it bluntly, I fancied myself as some kind of god," Soros wrote in his 1987 book, *The Alchemy of Finance*. That self-image hasn't changed much over the past decades; in fact, he has grown more megalomaniacal. Then, of course, he admits, "Next to my fantasies about being god, I also have very strong fantasies of being mad," which evidently might be a genetic issue. He told a British audience: "In fact, my grandfather was actually paranoid. I have a lot of madness in my family. So far I have escaped it."[252]

Soros was born in Budapest, Hungary, to Jewish parents who survived the 1944 Nazi invasion by hiding and running from the Germans and their collaborators. This period of his life significantly contributed to the formulation of his worldview. Soros said:

> [My] view of the world, I would say, was formed very much in the traumatic experience in the Second World War when Hungary was occupied by Nazi Germany and they were deporting Jews to Auschwitz. I was lucky enough to have a father who understood that this is not normalcy. This is far from equilibrium. And if you go by the rules that you normally go by, you're going to die. I learned from a grand master in the Second World War, and I basically applied this view of the world to the financial markets and also to my political vision.[253]

In 1947, Soros fled Hungary for England and later to the United States. While in England, he earned a bachelor of science in philosophy degree from the London School of Economics and a doctorate in philosophy at the same school in 1954, which over the years he successfully leveraged into a fortune thanks to hedge funds. He hides his money in the Netherlands Antilles, a self-governing federation of five Caribbean islands known as a "transshipment point for South American drugs bound for the U.S. and Europe and as a money-laundering center."[254]

Over the years, his financial wheeling and dealing has earned him considerable attention—some from law enforcement. He was convicted in France of insider trading and is known as the man who broke the Bank of England. Soros also signed a consent decree in U.S. District Court, in a Securities and Exchange Commission case involving stock manipulation for which he was fined for holding positions "in excess of speculative limits."[255]

His success at making money, albeit in some cases under suspicious circumstances, is matched in enthusiasm by his use of that money to promote his progressive globalist views. He successfully leverages politicians, nongovernment organizations, and the media to manipulate entire countries and arguably much of the world in order to advance his radical globalist interests.

His level of influence belies the imagination. He has funded numerous color revolutions, the Arab Spring and other political uprisings, seeded controversial groups in the U.S. such as Black Lives Matter, the planning behind the mass migration of Muslims into Europe, and much more.

He is considered one of the deep pockets behind efforts to undermine President Trump. In fact, it appears that Soros launched a new "color revolution" here in America to defeat Mr. Trump. This "soft coup" is what Russian President Vladimir Putin said is an attempt to "delegitimize" the U.S. president using the "Maidan-style" methods previously used in Ukraine. In 2014, Ukrainian President Viktor Yanukovych was ousted following a violent coup, which some believe was carried out with the help of American intelligence operatives.[256]

Attributing such an anti-Trump conspiracy to Soros isn't too far-fetched. He tried the same in Russia because it became a threat to his globalist new world order.

Evidently after the collapse of the Soviet Union in 1989, Soros helped Russian oligarchs to control the production of various industries. His agenda was to push for more globalism using the remnants of the former United Soviet Socialist Republic, but Russian leaders fought back. Meanwhile, Soros sent his Open Society Foundation (OSF) into Russia to destabilize that country. That created a backlash by Russian nationalists, who clamped down on NGOs like the OSF and essentially kicked them out of the country.[257]

The U.S. experienced similar disruptions in this country during the 2016 presidential campaign, but much of the blame was put on Russia. President Obama and his Democrat party minions were quick to "blame Russia" because of leaked Democrat operative e-mails allegedly attributed to Russian-owned or associated media outlets. But likely others such as Soros' OSF and its proxy NGOs stirred up trouble to sideline Trump, whom he called "a would-be dictator."[258]

It's unfortunately not too far-flung to attribute some of the disruption in the U.S. 2016 election an the disarray in Western Europe and Russia to the likes of Soros. After all, the business magnet and globalist manipulator has been blamed as the mastermind behind Asian financial crises that ruined the Malaysian economy; as well, he is known for meddling in politics across Europe, North America, and Asia.

Soros has a radical progressive worldview that includes virtually every left-wing issue: drug legalization, abortion on demand, normalizing homosexuality, climate change, wiping out national borders for unfettered migration, one-world government, and much more. He doesn't hesitate to throw millions of his own dollars at these issues.

He is even blamed for Europe's 2015–2016 migration crisis, which brought more than a million illegal migrants to Western Europe.

Hungarian Prime Minister Vicktor Orban said, "This invasion is driven, on the one hand, by people smugglers, and on the other by those (human rights) activists who support everything that weakens the nation-state.... This Western mindset and this activist network is perhaps best represented by George Soros."[259]

Soros responded to Orban's allegation with an e-mail to *Bloomberg Business* stating that his foundation helps "uphold European values," while Orban's action "treats the protection of national borders as the objective and the refugees as an obstacle."

"Our plan treats the protection of refugees as the objective and national borders as the obstacle," Soros said.

Soros' statement clearly illustrates a key difference in ideology—globalism versus nationalism. Orban accused Soros and other pro-immigration globalists of "drawing a living from the immigration crisis." He reminded the world that Soros funds groups that support transnational bodies like the European Union and the United Nations—part of his globalist agenda.

Soros is widely known to be associated with true radicals and progressive politicians as well.

Through NGO proxies, he has funded people like Linda Evans, the lady President Bill Clinton pardoned for her involvement in the Weather Underground, a terrorist group involved in the 1981 Brinks robbery, in which three murders were committed. He also funded Bernardino Dohrn, another Weather Underground member who expressed solidarity with mass murderer Charles Manson.[260]

The list of Soros-sponsored radicals is long and ncludes a good number of political figures.

His progressive political associates are significant as well. He gave to Barack Obama's run for the senate in Illinois, long before much of the country knew about the man. He was also a big contributor to Obama's two presidential campaigns.

Soros was a significant contributor to Hillary Clinton's 2016 presidential campaign. He gave millions to Clinton's leading super PACuPriorites and various pro-Clinton groups. This is in addition to the money Soros gave to the Clinton Foundation.

Soros earned allegiance from like-minded political progressives. Strobe Talbott, U.S. deputy secretary of state from 1994 to 2001, a well-known one-world government type, said, "Whenever George Soros called and asked to meet, I would move heaven and earth to do so. I treated him like the foreign minister of another country because of all that he had done."[261]

Much of Soros' promotion of his globalist agenda comes through NGOs and especially his Open Society Foundation (OSF).

The progressive billionaire reportedly spent more than $12 billion funding the OSF, the face of Soros' efforts to impose his globalist agenda on much of the world. Here in the U.S. Soros funnels money through the OSF to dozens of 501(c) (3) and (c) (4) charities involved in so-called civil rights activities as well as to progressive politicians like Clinton and Obama.[262]

Some of Soros' support for U.S. political activities comes in the form of sponsoring litigation attacking election integrity measures, such as voter -dentification efforts. His money has been used to attack state voter-identification laws in places such as Wisconsin, North Carolina, and Virginia. In 2016, Soros-funded litigation won an appeals court suspension of the North Carolinian election integrity laws.

Soros funded the League of Women Voters' effort "to catalyze greater participation from black and Latino youth in advocacy both before and after elections." That effort was intended to stop states like Kansas, Georgia, and Alabama from verifying that only citizens are registering to vote.[263]

Soros-tied nonprofits have also launched attacks against President Trump. One such group is the Emergent Fund, which fights "immediate threats" to "immigrants, women, Muslim and Arab-American communities, black people, LGBTQ communities, and all people of color." That organization, which started in 2016, fights Republicans and gives to groups such as Black Lives Matter.[264]

A Soros-funded nonprofit even tried to soil Pope Francis' two-day stop in Philadelphia in September 2015. OSF gave $650,000 to a Catholic-led interfaith organization called PICO (Pacific Institute for Community Organization) national network to host a "faith matters in America" summit featuring clergymen involved with Black Lives Matter.[265]

Soros' money is behind much of the organized racial and civil chaos in American cities over the past several years. Street theater performed by Black Lives Matter, MoveOn.org, International Action Center, and other far-left groups receive funding from OSF to spew their anti-police actions and, of course, attack Mr. Trump.

Mr. Soros was especially generous during the 2016 election cycle to the tune of $19.5 million in political contributions. Much of that money went to "527 Groups," which raise funds for political campaigns. His Democracy Alliance NGO tapped dozens of wealthy people to provide cash for his candidates and causes.[266]

Soros-funded NGOs are not enough for the globalist billionaire. He needs a mouthpiece to advance his agenda as well.

There is compelling evidence that Mr. Soros' OSF is linked to mainstream American media organizations that are used to manipulate public opinion. No doubt his use of the media, according to Soros, in *The Life and Times of a Messianic Billionaire*, is linked to his fascination as a child with "history and journalism or some form of writing." Soros even served as "editor-in-chief, publisher, and news vendor of" his own paper, *The Lupa News*.[267]

He strategically targeted American journalist education to seed his radical views and for manipulation. American Media Research Center reports:

> The Soros dream to control mass media naturally started with Columbia University's School of Journalism. Columbia is headed by President Lee Bollinger, who also sits on the Pulitzer Prize board and the board of directors of the *Washington Post*. Bollinger, like some of Soros' other funding recipients, is pushing for journalism to find a new sugar daddy or at least an uncle—Uncle Sam. Bollinger wrote in his book *Uninhibited, Robust, and Wide-Open: A Free Press for a New Century* that government should fund media. A 2009 study by Columbia's journalism program came to the same conclusion, calling for ""a national fund for local news." Conveniently, Len Downie, the lead author of that piece, is on both the Post's board and the board of the Center for Investigative Reporting, also funded by Soros.[268]

America's Media Watchdog indicates that "the Open Society Institute is one of several foundations funding the Investigative News Network (INN); a collaboration of 32 non-profit news organizations producing what they claim is 'non-partisan investigative news.'" That network includes the liberal *Huffington Post*, which merged with the leftist Center for Public Integrity.[269]

American news outlets impact the world community, part of Soros' intention. Certainly, the Washington-based International Center for Journalists (ICFJ), which is backed by Knight International Journalism

Fellowships and funded by Soros, push the globalist agenda across the world. Even our State Department's journalism exchange program is run by the ICFJ.

Udo Ulfkotte, a German political scientist, wrote about the corruption of journalism by the left. He wrote in "Purchased Journalists" how politicians sway the German media to spin their reporting. Ulfkotte is quoted in an interview about that corruption:

> When you fly to the US again and again and never have to pay for anything there, and you're invited to interview American politicians, you're moving closer and closer to the circles of power. And you want to remain within this circle of the elite, so you write to please them. Everyone wants to be a celebrity journalist who gets exclusive access to famous politicians. But one wrong sentence and your career as a celebrity journalist is over. Everyone knows it. And everyone's in on it.[270]

Soros' use of the media, NGOs, and politicians is manipulating America—and by association, the world community. He aims to undermine populist movements such as Mr. Trump's 2016 campaign by using some of the very same tactics seen in the color revolutions that transformed countries like the Republic of Georgia to ultimately benefit his one-world government, globalist goal.

CONCLUSION

The globalist agenda is pushed by a phalanx of elites like Rockefeller, Kissinger, Clinton, and Soros, who promote and feed upon one another. They are a dangerous tribe that wields great influence, in part because they are networked in public and secret societies, the topic of the next chapter.

CHAPTER NINE

Globalist Secret Societies

There are plenty of secret societies today, and some have roots dating back thousands of years. Does their existence really impact our lives in a serious way? Further, do the globalists elite profiled in the previous chapters join secret societies? If so, do such associations advance their radical goals?

Secret societies are part of our daily lives, but we seldom give them notice—that is, until they are in the news. Many readers who follow national news will recall that on February 13, 2016, former Supreme Court Justice Antonin Scalia died of "natural causes" while participating in a West Texas event hosted by a secret society of elite hunters. The secret group, the International Order of St. Hubertus, is an Austrian society that dates back to the 1600s and is named in honor of Hubert, the patron saint for hunters and fisherman.[271]

Members of the exclusive order are all male and wear dark-green robes emblazoned with a large cross, and the motto *Deum Diligite Animalia Diligentes*, which means "Honoring God by honoring His creatures," according to the Washington Post. Some group leaders hold titles such as Grand Master, Prior, and Knight Grand Officer.

The society's U.S. chapter began in 1966 at the Bohemiam Club in San Francisco, according to the *Post*. That club is associated with the Bohemian Grove—another secret society for the elite (addressed in Appendix B to this volume). The Bohemian Grove is a 2,700-acre virgin redwood grove in Northern California, where the elite visit with each other the last two weeks of July "to camp."[272]

The St. Hubertus society sounds like a pretty innocuous group of old men who like to hunt, fish, and enjoy being outside. We can dismiss the robes and titles as eccentric. However, what if there is a nefarious aspect to this group or other secret societies, such as globalists elite meeting to conspire to create circumstances that result in a one-world government? Outlandish? Demonic?

Most people at least in the U.S. likely haven't seriously considered these so-called secret societies, and if they gave them any thought, more than likely they dismissed them as quaint gatherings or something like the grown-up version of the fraternity-partying scene on college campuses. Others may laugh at such associations, labeling them full of wacko conspirators from the extremes of the political spectrum. After all, no rational, intelligent person, it may be said, really gives any credibility to such groups. Right? Not so fast!

The reasoning goes that the average American is focused on doing his or her job and raising their family to give two seconds of consideration to such wacko groups. Let them do silly stuff, just leave me alone, some might say. After all, there's no harm from a bunch of old men meeting for comradery over a meal and drinks to discuss politics or sports.

I wish that was the end of the story. Unfortunately, there is more to some of these secret societies than just good fun. Some actually meet for serious business purposes, and a few are charting our future—whether or not we are aware or even care.

This chapter will explore the general parameters of so-called secret societies and the influence and beliefs of such associations, and offer some serious analysis of a few of those secret societies that attract the globalists elite.

Let's begin our exploration of these associations with the more inno-
cent examples.

It is understandable why some people associate secret societies with
college campuses and adolescent behavior in adult skin making excuses
for misbehavior. Many college campuses, and not just the Ivy League
schools, host so-called secret societies. Their purposes and methods vary;
some keep their members' identities secret while others maintain the
mystery around their activities and proceedings.

Most of these groups are truly silly adolescent associations. Consider
a few contemporary campus-based "secret societies."

The Flat Hat Club at the College of William & Mary, Williams-
burg, Virginia, is allegedly the first collegiate society in the U.S., reportedly formed in 1750. One of the first members was founder and early
nineteenth-century U.S. President Thomas Jefferson. At the time, the
club had a secret handshake and met to discuss current issues, but it dis-
banded during the American Revolution only to reemerge in the early
twentieth century.[273]

The University of Virginia in Charlottesville has numerous secret
societies, which range from service-oriented to the bizarre. One such
group, the Rotunda Peers, allegedly exists for its members to urinate on
the campus rotunda at night. Another closed group is the Seven Society, which reportedly started when a group of eight "men" agreed to
meet for cards, but only seven showed up. Their identities are unmasked
only after a member's death, which is announced by the appearance of a
wreath of black magnolias at his grave.[274]

These secret societies are characteristically clubs whose activities and
inner workings are kept secret from those who are not members. Silly
or more professional, secret societies tend to have a few things in common, such as membership qualifications, secret rituals or ceremonies,
and close—usually life-long—connections among members.

Secret society membership is often dictated by the nature of the
association; those on college campuses tend to be localized. Other societies with global interests tend to attract people with senior positions

in government, the wealthy, media moguls, or corporation giants—the elite.

Bonnie Erickson writes in the *Journal of Social Forces* to define such groups as a social network with "a persisting pattern of relationships which directly or indirectly links the participants in related secret activities. There must be some secret activities in order to have a secret society; there must be a persistent pattern of relationships among participants in order to have a secret society."[275]

Another study of secret societies suggests these groups all share some of the same characteristics. First, they display arrogant pride. They "parlay a sense that they are above and superior to others, an elite class, specifically are chosen because of their innate and rare knowledge of the 'truth' while the rest of the world are mere peons." This analysis fits with earlier descriptions of the globalists elite.[276]

Second, they "behave one way when they're with their fellow members and then put on a front for others when out in public." That is a natural and a common human characteristic whereby we all tend to be more relaxed when in familiar settings but more guarded when in unfamiliar situations.

Third, they "prize teaching their ways to new members but doing so only in small bits of information at a time until that member meets the requirements to be part of the upper echelon in the organization." That's true of groups like the Freemasons, whereas only the very top leaders know all the group's teachings and dark secrets.

Fourth, they tend to claim man is "inherently good and should be told the secrets through membership, providing the potential initiate meets the criteria to be considered worthy enough to be a society fellow." Of course, that view is contrary to Scripture, which says of mankind, "The human heart is the most deceitful of all things, and desperately wicked. Who really knows how bad it is (Jeremiah 17:9, NLT)?"

Allegedly the oldest secret society was the Brotherhood of the Snake, aka the Brotherhood of the Dragon, which is devoted to guarding the "secrets of the ages" and recognizes Lucifer as the true god. That Brotherhood was dedicated to the dissemination of spiritual knowledge and the attainment of spiritual freedom, opposed the enslavement of spiritual beings, and sought to liberate the human race from custodial bondage.[277]

The Brotherhood allegedly imparts scientific knowledge to include physical healing through spiritual means. In fact, the use of the term "snake" has come to universally symbolize physical healing, which is featured on the logo of the American Medical Association and traceable to the account of the Israelites being bitten by poisonous snakes and God directing Moses to form a bronze snake and put it on a pole; anyone bitten who looked upon the pole would be healed.[278]

Secret societies mirror many facets of ordinary life like health. After all, the exclusivity associated with membership in a group is found in all human endeavors, even those that are not secret, such as sports teams. This exclusivity of membership is actually one of the secret societies' most powerful weapons, as are the use of signs, passwords, and other tools.

America has a rich history of secret societies, and many of those groups are focused on political issues. One such group formed immediately following the American Civil War (1861–65), a period marked by deep bitterness on both sides—and in some ways the war never ended.

Resentful Southerners tried to put African Americans back into their previous place in the post-war Southern society, and when that failed, some resorted to violence and terror to affect political control. They also banned together in a "secret society." Those circumstances saw the emergence of the Ku Klux Klan (KKK), which was formed to reverse the changes imposed on the South and return Southern society to its pre-war, white supremacy era.

Tradition indicates the Klan formed in the summer of 1866 in Pulaski, Tennessee, in the law office of Judge Thomas M. Jones. The group's name comes from the Greek word *kyklos*, translated "circle" or "band," with "clan" spelled with a "K." The group borrowed from the Greeks some of the rituals and titles, such as grand cyclops and grand magi.[279]

Very soon after forming, the Klan became a vigilante "society" perpetrating crime, especially against African American freedmen. The KKK donned costumes and invaded black homes allegedly to protect the public.[280]

"The Klan became in effect a terrorist arm of the Democratic Party, whether the party leaders as a whole liked it or not," wrote Allen W. Trelease in *White Terror: The Ku Klux Klan Conspiracy and Southern Reconstruction*. The KKK's popularity drew membership across the South, and stories emerged of its violence such as beatings, lynchings, assassinations, rape, and destruction of property.[281]

The Klan was never centrally controlled, and although it started with a well-heeled membership, it quickly morphed into a swath of white people that included disaffected Confederate soldiers and others holding grudges.

Unfortunately, the number of potentially dangerous secret societies, like the KKK, has grown, and today they likely number in the thousands across the world.

Contemporary secret societies, according to Jim Marrs, the author of *Rule by Secrecy*, argues that "Secret societies not only exist…they have played an important role in national and international events right up to this day."[282]

Marrs dismisses the popular retort regarding claims about the threats posed by secret societies as the work of conspirators. "The concept of conspiracy has long been anathema to most Americans who have been conditioned by the mass media to believe that conspiracies against the public only exist in banana republics or communist nations," he explained. He continued, "This simplistic view, encouraged by a media devoted to maintaining a squeaky clean image of the status quo, fails to take into account human history or the subtleties of the word conspiracy."

Then he illustrates with historic examples how some secret societies made their members wealthy on wars they promoted and alleged "every person indoctrinated by establishment textbooks believes that historical events are the result of accident—not the carefully laid stratagems of men who make money on wars—men with connections to secret societies and the politics of the occult."[283]

Marrs also addressed secret societies in the globalist camp: "The question of whether or not a plan for one world government is a sinister conspiracy to subjugate the population or simply an attempt to facilitate a natural evolutionary step is a matter still to be decided, apparently with little or no help from the media."[284]

He rightly states based on significant evidence that some elite-dominated secret societies do in fact promote one-world government at the expense of sovereign nation-states. "But one thing is absolutely clear," Marrs states. "It is apparent that globalization or one world government or the new world order is not simply the imaginings of conspiracy theorists or paranoids, but the articulated goal of the secret brotherhoods, organizations and groups, all of which carry the imprint of the orders of Freemasonry, the Round Table Group the Illuminati."[285]

Marrs concludes with "the single most important question: If they [secret societies] do create a centralized one-world government, what's to prevent some Hitler-like tyrant from taking control?" That's a scary proposition.

A more compelling question is: Will the coming one-world government's Hitler be the prophesied Antichrist?

Below are profiles of three elite-dominated secret societies that push a globalist agenda.

BILDERBERGERS: THE HIGH PRIESTS OF GLOBALIZATION

The Bilderbergers represent the top levels of the globalist cabal, which annually gathers the faithful from other secret societies such as the Council on Foreign Relations and the Trilateral Commission. British journalist Will Hutton labeled the Bilderbergers "the high priests of globalization."[286]

The Bilderberg Conference, an annual invitation-only meeting of the world's globalist luminaries that started in 1954, is very secretive. The first such meeting took place in Oosterbeek, Netherlands, at the Bilderberg Hotel, from which the group took its name. The guest list included eighty of the world's most powerful people (the members), and the balance of the participants were invited because of their special knowledge of relevant topics. The annual participant list is unpublished, the meeting place is off-limits to outsiders, and the facility is heavily guarded with physical barriers to keep spectators and the press at a distance. Further, the participants are required to adhere strictly to a blanket gag order and follow Chatham House Rules, which, according to a *New York Times* reporter, means attendees can be candid inside the "conference," but must "understand that they do not talk" about what transpires outside the meetings.[287]

Daniel Estulin investigated and then wrote a book about the group, *The True Story of the Bilderberg Group,* which was published in 2005. In that volume, Estulin describes the cabal as a "shadow world government"—a "private club where presidents, prime ministers, international bankers and generals rub shoulders, where gracious royal chaperones ensure everyone gets along, and where the people running the wars, markets, and Europe [and America] say what they never dare say in public."[288]

In 2016, the late Phyllis Schlafly, an American constitutional lawyer and conservative activist, identified the Bilderbergers as "globalists who sought to undermine the sovereignty of America through a 'bipartisan' foreign policy aligned to the interests of transnational corporations." They are "kingmakers" who recruit aspiring politicians willing to do their bidding, according to Schlafly.[289]

Ms. Schlafly wrote a press release statement after the March 2016 Bilderberger "kingmakers" met off the coast of Georgia. Rich and powerful Americans were among those invited to the conference: CEOs of Apple and Google, media titans Arthur Sulzberger and William Kristol, and top political leaders, including House Speaker Paul Ryan and Senate

Majority Leader Mitch McConnell. Their goal, according to Schlafly, "was to stop Donald Trump from obtaining the Republican presidential nomination" and, as is always the case, "to take power away from 'we the people' and to be kingmakers once again."[290]

The Bilderbergers' Conference guests are always globalists elite— a litmus for attending—who represent government, politics, finance, industry, labor, education, and communications (media). But those meetings, according to a Bilderberger press release, have "no desired outcome, no resolutions are proposed, no votes are taken, and no policy statements are issued." However, there are very tangible outcomes from those conferences.[291]

Wiley Claes, a former NATO boss and two-time Bilderberg Conference attendee, explained there are two such results from these meetings. "The participants are then obviously considered to use this report [the conference discussions] in setting their policies in the environments in which they affect." The conference message is simple: Attendees meet in secret to chart our collective future, a one-world agenda.

Etienne Davignon, a former European Union commissar and Belgian minister of state, told an online program that in fact the Bilderberger summits "helped create" the euro currency imposed on seventeen formerly sovereign nations." That's certainly a tangible outcome of a conference supposedly focused "just on talk." Will Hutton, a former British newspaper editor and pro-EU extremist, confirmed that the Bilderberger meetings provide a backdrop "against which policy is made worldwide."[292]

Evidently, those meetings are also about kingmaking, as Schlafly alleged. The globalists elite gather and take virtually unknown figures whom they enlisted to the "Club" and then foist them onto the world stage.

Bill Clinton was an obscure governor from Arkansas before he was recruited to the Bilderberger "Club," then he rocketed to the U.S. presidency. In 1991, according to the *New York Times*, Clinton accepted an invitation to attend the Bilderberger Conference meeting held at Baden

Baden, Germany. At that meeting, Clinton was, according to the *Times*, "schooled by influential economists and 'free trade' strategists about the desirability of NAFTA [North American Free Trade Agreement] and why he should join them in promoting its aims and working toward its implementation."[293]

Much the same happened with Barack Obama, a relatively unknown junior U.S. senator before he was plucked up, made the rounds at a Bilderberger Conference, and then quickly found his way to the White House. He fulfilled the Bilderberg's aim: advancing the globalist agenda through eight years of arguably America's most progressively radical presidency.

How effective has the Bilderberger's influence been on American policy? The *New York Times* wrote, "some argue...that the first intimations of American determination to wage war in Iraq came from a Bilderberger gathering in 2002." And, yes, there were Bush administration members at that confab, and after him, Obama was an obedient Bilderberger—and had Hillary Clinton been elected to the presidency, she too would have carried water for the globalist Bilderbergers.

The same phenomenon occurred for future presidents of the European Commission. Obscure persons were selected to attend Bilderberger meetings, and before long they were on the world stage leading the globalist charge transferring political power away from sovereign nations and to unaccountable supranational groups.

This is no coincidence and it is evidence of a conspiracy by globalist power brokers. Former British Chancellor of the Exchequer and Bilderberger participant Denis Healey said that conclusion might be a little "exaggerated, but not wholly unfair." He readily admits Bilderberger's goal is global government, an aim shared by those selected to attend the annual meetings.[294]

Healey explained the Bilderberger's rational for global government: "Those of us in Bilderberger felt we couldn't go on forever fighting one another for nothing and killing people and rendering millions homeless. So we felt that a single community throughout the world would be a good thing."[295]

This elite forum is clearly making decisions on the future direction of the world and we, the subjects of their decisions, ought to have a voice, or at least the opportunity to listen in on their discussions.

British parliamentarian Michael Meacher called for an end to the Bilderbergers' secrecy. "These are really big decision makers who have come to concert their plans over the future of capitalism. That is going to affect us, the 99.99 percent, very extensively," Meacher protested. "In a democratic system we have a right to know what they're talking about, what conclusions they reached and ask some questions."[296]

Here in the U.S., such meetings may be illegal for government servants. When top foreign and domestic leaders secretly plot our future with U.S. government officials, those federal agents are violating the Logan Act, which states American officials can't work on policy with any agent of a foreign government without prior approval.[297]

Look at the list of those who attend Bilderberg meetings and you'll find a cross section of civil sector and government people from across the world. Clearly, as outlined above, the outcome of those meetings impacts policy, which may be an illegal act, and they circumvent the people to select elite-favoring future leaders.

Yes, the Bilderberger Conference is a secret society that seeks one-world government overseen by globalists elite, which means they actively seek the demise of sovereign nation-states like the United States.

COUNCIL ON FOREIGN RELATIONS: AMERICA'S RULING ELITE

The Council on Foreign Relations (CFR) claims it is not a secret society. CFR's website tries to convince the reader it isn't a secret society by stating that it "publishes the results of its scholars' research and independent task forces, its annual report, the audio, video, and transcripts of its on-the-record meetings, numerous blogs, as well as information about the organization's initiatives. News and analysis is also shared with CFR's Twitter followers, Facebook fans, and YouTube channel subscribers."[298]

The facts in this claim may be true, and still CFR can be categorized as a classic secret society. How? It is a secret society by stealth which is incredibly successful and dangerous. It seeds its members across the government and then rules by fiat.

CFR was officially founded in 1921, when it spun off a gathering of 150 scholars known as "The Inquiry," who briefed President Woodrow Wilson as he prepared for post-World War I negotiations. That group included Wilson's trusted aide and group director Edward M. House, as well as Walter Lippmann, a 28-year-old Harvard graduate who recruited for "The Inquiry." "What we are on the lookout for is genius—sheer, startling genius, and nothing else will do," Lippmann explained.[299]

The Inquiry helped draw the borders of post-World War I Central Europe and advised President Wilson at the Paris Peace Conference of 1919. Twenty-one members of The Inquiry were on the sidelines of that conference, but were very much a part of the American Commission to Negotiate Peace. Further, the Inquiry scholars made lasting relationships with their European counterparts, especially the British, during those negotiations. In fact, on May 30, 1919, U.S. and British diplomats and Inquiry scholars met at the Hotel Majestic in Paris to discuss how to sustain their relationship and the peace. The outcome was the Anglo-American Institute of International Affairs, with branches in London and New York.[300]

The American delegation returned home to find no appetite for the ideals of Wilson's globalist proposal, the League of Nations, a byproduct of the Paris Peace Conference. However, a loose association of idealistic Americans had already established a League of Free Nations in early 1918. That group and President Wilson's extensive advocacy efforts failed to convince the U.S. Senate to embrace the League of Nations or the Versailles Treaty.

The U.S. Senate refused to ratify Wilson's proposal for America to join the League of Nations, primarily due to objections over Article X of the Covenant, a mutual-defense provision. Two Republican politicians, Henry Cabot Lodge and William Borah, led the opposition, "believing that it was best not to become involved in international conflicts."[301]

Prior to the 1919 Paris Peace Conference, a club of New York financiers and international lawyers was organized by Elihu Root, President Wilson's secretary of state. The New York group of 108 called themselves the "Council on Foreign Relations" and their purpose "was to convene dinner meetings, to make contact with distinguished foreign visitors under conditions congenial to future commerce."[302] Not surprisingly, this group soon attracted the attention of members of the Inquiry, who had returned from the Paris Peace Conference.

The modern Council formed when the two groups—the American Institute of International Affairs established at the Hotel Majestic and the New York men of law and banking—prepared a certificate of incorporation on July 29, 1921, and the new and permanent Council on Foreign Relations came into being.

The CFR quickly became the front organization for America's ruling elite. Almost from its inception, the CFR effectively controlled our federal government and major corporations; promoted world government through its influence over the major media; leveraged massive foundation grants to promote globalism and a significant part of the educational establishment that influenced future politicians and diplomats; shaped contemporary issues; and used its deep pockets *vis-à-vis* its current four thousand-plus members, which included the likes of billionaire David Rockefeller, to promote the "new world order."

CFR's agenda has always been strictly transnationally progressive—globalism. Although today it claims to be a dispassionate source of foreign relations, the facts indicate it is pushing an agenda that includes global governance, open borders, big government, surrendering sovereignty, attacking self-government, and more of the well-established progressive agenda.

That agenda is clearly outlined by CFR's April 1974 edition of *Foreign*

Affairs in an article by Richard Gardner, former deputy assistant secretary of state. "In short, the 'house of world order' will have to be built from the bottom up rather than from the top down," Gardner wrote. "An end run around national sovereignty, eroding it piece by piece, will accomplish much more than the old fashioned assault."[303] The CFR's flagship magazine regularly promotes regional government like the European Union and attacks national sovereignty.

CFR members have dominated the administrations of every president since Franklin Roosevelt, at the cabinet level all the way through to Barack Obama's administration.[304]

The CFR's real power base rests especially with the money establishment. Edith Kermit Roosevelt, granddaughter of President Teddy Roosevelt, wrote: "The word 'establishment' is a general term for the power elite in international finance, business, the professions and government, largely from the northeast, who wield most of the power regardless of who is in the White House. Most people are unaware of the existence of this 'legitimate mafia.'"[305]

There is no doubt about the American "mafia's" influence. CFR founder and globalist elite banker David Rockefeller proudly flaunted that status. As I indicated earlier in this volume, Rockefeller boasted in his book, *Memoirs*:[306]

> For more than a century ideological extremists at either end of the political spectrum have seized upon well-publicized incidents such as my encounter with Castro to attack the Rockefeller family for the inordinate influence they claim we wield over American political and economic institutions. Some even believe we are part of a secret cabal working against the best interests of the United States, characterizing my family and me as "internationalists" and of conspiring with others around the world to build a more integrated global political and economic structure — one world, if you will. If that's the charge, I stand guilty, and I am proud of it.

The CFR leverages government through its tight reign over the major political parties by strategically placing CFR cadre into the most important cabinet positions: defense, foreign policy, and finance. It uses that cadre to push its globalist, anti-nationalist agenda.

Admiral Chester Ward, a former judge advocate for the U.S. Navy and former CFR member, said, "The main purpose of the Council on Foreign Relations is promoting the disarmament of U.S. sovereignty and national independence, and submergence into an all-powerful one-world government." That explains the CFR push for the formation of the United Nations.[307]

The United Nations was conceived by a group of CFR members at the State Department called the Advisory Committee on Postwar Foreign Policy (ACPFP), a secretive group created by progressive President Roosevelt to prepare recommendations for post-World War II foreign policy. They served much the same role played by the Inquiry under President Wilson. The ACPFP pushed for the creation of the U.N. which was Roosevelt's and, by association, the CFR's progressive dream, which prepared the political landscape at home by working closely with Congress to preclude happening to the U.N. what defeated Wilson's League of Nations.[308]

The U.N.'s founding meeting in San Francisco in 1945 included forty-seven American CFR members. John Foster Dulles, one of those CFR members and a future secretary of state, acknowledged: "The United Nations represents not a final stage in the development of world order, but only a primitive stage. Therefore its primary task is to create the conditions which will make possible a more highly developed organization."[309]

One of those conditions is to shape the international financial marketplace. Therefore, "Two other postwar institutions, the World Bank and International Monetary Fund [IMF]," according to James Perloff writing in *The New American*, were created thanks to a CFR economic and finance group, which was part of the Council's Wartime War and Peace Studies Project. The World Bank and IMF are important to globalists because they dictate the conditions for country bailouts, "thus giving the bankers a measure of political control over indebted nations."[310]

Even the famed Marshall Plan to help Europe recover from World War II was a CFR product, according to Perloff. General George Marshall announced the plan at the 1947 Harvard commencement, but that plan was based on a CFR study overseen by progressive David Rockefeller, and it was only named after Marshall as a ploy to fool people into believing it was politically neutral. Once executed, the Marshall Plan landed in the progressive hands of Jean Monnet, the founder of the Common Market, a mini-world government organization.[311]

Even the Vietnam War was prolonged by CFR members, according to Perloff. He attributes prolonging the war to three CFR members: William Bundy, the author of the Tonkin Gulf Resolution and foreign affairs advisor to presidents John Kennedy and Lyndon Johnson; Bundy's father-in-law, Dean Acheson, one of "the wise men" who persuaded President Johnson to escalate the war; and Secretary of Defense Robert McNamara, the author of the war's misguided "rules of engagement." Perloff points out that Bundy moved on from government to edit CFR's journal, *Foreign Affairs,* and McNamara became the president of the World Bank, both CFR and globalist perches.[312]

It is worth mentioning that CFR member Bundy's Gulf of Tonkin Resolution gave President Johnson the authority to assist any Southeast Asian country whose government was considered to be jeopardized by "communist aggression." That was a green light for Johnson to massively increase the American war in Vietnam and to expand it to include Laos and Cambodia as well.

What was the CFR's agenda for the Vietnam War? One view is that the CFR agenda was to use the war in Vietnam "as a smokescreen to conceal a coordinated effort to move America and her people towards socialism." It certainly served as a smokescreen for President Johnson, who pushed his socialist "Great Society" program through while American soldiers were dying in the rice paddies in Southeast Asia and the media was consumed with violent internal opposition to that war.[313]

Hopefully, the election of Donald Trump put an end to CFR's radical use of government to advance its globalist agenda. It does appear that only a few CFR globalists are members of the Trump administration. However, there are some noteworthy exceptions. Lieutenant General H. R. McMaster, the national security adviser, and Judge Neil Gorsuch, the newest associate Supreme Court justice, are both CFR members.[314]

General McMaster may be a great soldier and officer with a lot of medals on his chest, but he is a CFR member with some noteworthy globalist baggage. Specifically, he joined the globalist International Institute for Strategic Studies (IISS) in London as a "senior research associate." IISS describes McMaster's mandate while there as "conducting research to identify opportunities for improved multi-national cooperation and political-military integration in the areas of counterinsurgency, counter-terrorism, and state building."[315]

Working with globalists inevitably impacts one's thinking, and IISS is such a crock pot for brewing one-world government thinking. Further, McMaster has the support of globalists like Senator John McCain (R.—Ariz.), who praised President Trump's selection of the general.[316]

President Trump's secretary of state Rex Tillerson, the former CEO of Exxon-Mobil, isn't an official CFR member, but he boasted in 2007 at a CFR event: "Like the council's founders, I believe we must choose the course of greater international engagements." Does that make him a globalist willing to sacrifice national sovereignty?[317] That's to be determined.

Other CFR members on Trump's staff include Robert Lighthizer, the U.S. trade representative, and Transportation Secretary Elaine Chao, the wife of U.S. Senate Majority Leader Mitchell McConnell. It is noteworthy that Mr. Trump did promise while campaigning for the presidency that members of his cabinet must agree to his "America First" agenda. Time will tell if the CFR nose is under the Trump tent and continuing to use the levers of government to promote a globalist agenda.

What's clear is the CFR is the promotional arm of America's globalist ruling elite. Its membership represents influential politicians, academics, and media personalities, many of whom promote a globalist agenda that attacks American sovereignty. CFR academics advance "scholarly" articles in many print and broadcast forums that advance the globalist message, and CFR politicians push that agenda inside government and to sympathetic media which echo that agenda as the opiate for the masses.

The CFR's efforts are undermining our Constitution and American sovereignty. This has been noted by many Americans for decades, such as Felix Frankfurter, justice of the Supreme Court (1939–1962), who said: "The real rulers in Washington are invisible and exercise power from behind the scenes." President Franklin Roosevelt echoed that view in 1933: "The real truth of the matter is, as you and I know, that a financial element in the large centers has owned the government ever since the days of Andrew Jackson." Further, U.S. Senator William Jenner warned in a 1954 speech: "Outwardly we have a Constitutional government. We have operating within our government and political system, another body representing another form of government, a bureaucratic elite which believes our Constitution is outmoded."[318]

TRILATERAL COMMISSION: GLOBALIST KINGMAKER

The Trilateral Commission is an offshoot of the Council on Foreign Relations and David Rockefeller's dream to form a profitable link among the nations in Japan, North America, and Western Europe—a tariff-free, one economy, but with a much more expansive globalist ambition.

Richard Brookhiser, who wrote for the *National Review* in 1981, interviewed David Rockefeller about founding the Trilateral Commission. Rockefeller explained that as the chairman of the board for Chase Manhattan Bank, he hosted annual international financial forums "to promote Chase's business." In 1972, Rockefeller explained, he was concerned over the world situation. "Governments were faced with an accelerating pace of change" and an "increasing number of crises. They didn't have time to think," Rockefeller explained. They were losing, and as a consequence, the "world outlook" was bleak. Rockefeller was particularly concerned about the industrial democracies—America, Japan and Western Europe.[319]

So Mr. Rockefeller called for the creation of a "well-informed, diversified" association of opinion-makers to "form themselves into a little group and get papers written." That call was repeated at the 1972 Bilderberg Society Conference in Belgium. A number of scholars read Rockefeller's Bilderberger speech to include Zbigniew Brzezinski, a Polish-born Columbia University professor who was known as the architect of the "New World Order," a "Grey Cardinal," and the evil spirit behind five U.S. presidents.[320]

Brzezinski liked what Rockefeller proposed, an idea Brzezinski had similarly proposed in his 1970 book, *Between Two Ages*. Specifically, Brzezinski's proposal called for a "high-level consultative council…linking the U.S., Japan, and Western Europe." Soon, Brzezinski and Rockefeller met to discuss their ideas, which led to another discussion with McGeorge Bundy, the president of the Ford Foundation who expressed his willingness to fund such a project. That, according to Rockefeller, was the seed that grew into the Trilateral Commission in 1973, a non-governmental, nonpartisan discussion group to foster substantive political and economic dialogue among North America, Western Europe, and Japan.[321]

At the first Trilateral Commission meeting in Tokyo, the sparse membership issued a telling and founding declaration: "Growing interdependence is a fact of life of the contemporary world. It transcends and influences national systems. It requires new and more intensive forms of international cooperation to realize its benefits and to counteract economic and political nationalism."[322]

Second, the declaration states the three regions (Japan, North America, and western Europe) will "consult and cooperate more closely, on the basis of quality, to develop and carry out coordinated policies on matters affecting their common interests."[323]

Third, the commission will "play a creative role as a channel of free exchange of opinions." The three-part declaration sounds pretty innocuous on the surface, but behind the scenes, it is far more sinister.[324]

Rockefeller addressed the issue of Trilateral Commission members in the *National Review* interview. "Clearly, if you're going to have a group of this kind function, you have to have knowledgeable people," said Rockefeller. He continued, saying that there must be a "broad spectrum of what you'd call rational forces of opinion." That led the *National Review* reporter to ask how Jimmy Carter came to join the Commission.[325]

Rockefeller had ties to the Atlanta political and economic elite. In addition, he owned investment property in Georgia, according to David Horowitz, coauthor of, "Atlanta Is Rockefeller Center South." Sometime in 1971, Rockefeller invited Carter to dine with him at the Chase Manhattan Bank in New York City, just prior to Carter serving as governor.[326]

Evidently, Carter impressed Rockefeller and then Trilateral Commission director Brzezinski, because "Carter had opened up trade offices for the state of Georgia in Brussels and Tokyo. That seemed to fit perfectly into the concept of the Trilateral." That's when Brzezinski brought Carter into the Commission.[327]

Carter attended every Trilateral Commission meeting, according to Rockefeller. "He treated it as a kind of graduate seminar in international affairs, and read all the working papers studiously." He paid special attention to Brzezinski, who began to tutor the Georgia governor for a White House run in 1976.[328]

Former senator Barry Goldwater explained the commission's push for Carter:

David Rockefeller and Zbigniew Brzezinski found Jimmy Carter to be their ideal candidate. They helped him win the nomination, and the presidency. To accomplish this purpose, they mobilized the money power of the Wall Street bankers, the intellectual influence of the academic community—which is subservient to the wealth of the great tax-free foundations—

and the media controllers represented in the membership of the CFR, and the Trilateral.[329]

Laurence H. Shoup, a San Francisco-based political journalist, who wrote *The Carter Presidency and Beyond*, maintains that politicians and political parties matter very little. Shoup argues that the corporate ruling class—big business executives, financiers, media titans, and influential private citizens are the power brokers that matter. Shoup devotes a chapter to how the Trilateral Commission elite like Rockefeller used its media leverage to promote Carter's presidential candidacy.[330]

Once Carter was elected president, he appointed two dozen members of the Trilateral Commission to key positions in his cabinet, including Brzezinski for his national security advisor; Harold Brown, secretary of defense; Warren Christopher, deputy secretary of state; Walter Mondale, vice president, Cyrus Vance, Carter's secretary of state; and others. Carter also appointed David Rockefeller's friend, Paul Volcker, as chairman of the Federal Reserve Board. Twenty-eight percent of the Commission's membership at the time served in the Carter administration.[331]

The Carter administration was a disaster on so many fronts and, to a large degree, thanks to the influence of his Trilateralist cabinet. Carter made some very bad decisions for America.[332]

President Carter failed to control inflation and unemployment during his administration. He inherited an economy that was emerging from a recession, and during the campaign, he severely criticized former President Ford for his economic failures, but after four years in office, Carter made things worse. During his tenure, inflation rose each year, hovering around 12 percent at the time of the 1980 election. Although he pledged to eliminate federal deficits, the deficit rapidly expanded to $59 billion by Election Day 1980. Further, he left office with eight million people out of work, with a nationwide unemployment rate at 7.7 percent.[333]

Carter's foreign policy was as bad, if not worse, than his economic policies. He made the decision to surrender the Panama Canal. In 1988, he signed the Panama Canal treaty that transferred the American-built Panama Canal to the nation of Panama, which at the time was run by a corrupt, Third-World military dictator and would eventually be controlled by the Chinese, mostly the Chinese Peoples' Liberation Army.

America's worst president (Carter) also terminated the Russian wheat deal, which was a severe blow for American farmers.

Carter's dealings with the Shah of Iran were the worst. That led to the Iran hostage crisis—fifty-four Americans were held hostage until Carter left office, which paved the way for the rise of radical Islam to threaten the free world through the likes of Tehran's terror proxy Hezbollah and its nuclear and ballistic missile programs.

We should lay much of the blame for Carter's disastrous presidency at the doorstep of the Trilateral Commission and, in particular, David Rockefeller.

Brookhiser asked Rockefeller to identify the commission's accomplishments up to that point in 1980. Rockefeller gave two responses: First, he said, the Japanese came "to feel part of the group…it's been terribly important for them and for us. It has given them a sense of self-confidence."[334]

Second, Rockefeller said the commission was effective because "people in [U.S.] administrations did what we hoped" and "they read" Commission publications, which were intended "to enlighten government and public opinion…if you want to understand what's going on in the world, you need to understand other people's opinions." It is an "educational body—nothing less, nothing more."[335]

Brookhiser asked, "What does the Commission do?" Rockefeller said, "Nothing." The Commission is "a medium…an agent of enlightenment and a forum for discussion." The billionaire banker insisted the Commission produce "the synthesized points of view of a collective of people, who are well informed on a given subject that has importance at a moment in time."[336]

Republican Senator Barry Goldwater disagreed with Rockefeller's explanation. The Trilateral Commission is "a skillful, coordinated effort to seize control and consolidate the four centers of power: political, monetary, intellectual, and ecclesiastical…[in] the creation of a worldwide economic power superior to the political governments of the nation-states involved…. As managers and creators of the system they will rule the future."[337]

Years later, the future U.S. senator and libertarian from Kentucky, Ron Paul, expressed a similar view. Paul said during a C-Span interview in which a caller asked him to comment on the "treasonous, Marxist, alcoholic dictators that pull the strings in our country," the Trilateral Commission and the Council on Foreign Relations. Paul said:

> You referred to who really pulls the strings. For years now, it's been claimed by many, and there's pretty good evidence, that those who are involved in the Trilateral Commission and the Council on Foreign Relations usually end up in positions of power. And I believe this is true. If you look at the Federal Reserve, if you look at key positions at the World Bank or the IMF, they all come from these groups. If you have national television on, you might see a big debate about the Far East crisis, and you have Brzezinski and Kissinger talking about how to do it. One says don't invade today, invade tomorrow. And the other says, invade immediately. That's the only difference you find between the Rockefeller Trilateralists.[338]

Just how has the Trilateral Commission been able to keep its true nature hidden? At the June 1991 Bilderberg Group meeting, David Rockefeller acknowledged the role played by the media in covering up his one-world agenda.

"We are grateful to the *Washington Post*, the *New York Times*, *Time* magazine, and other great publications whose directors have attended our meetings and respected their promises of discretion for almost forty years," he stated. "It would have been impossible for us to develop our plan for the world," he continued, "if we had been subjected to the lights of publicity during those years. But, the world is more sophisticated and prepared to march towards a world government. The supranational sovereignty of an intellectual elite and world bankers is surely preferable to the national auto determination practiced in past centuries."[339]

The Commission's one-world agenda was certainly opaque from the beginning. At the first Trilateral meeting, held in Tokyo in October 1973, the executive committee made their primary motive clear: "It transcends and influences national systems. It requires new and more intensive forms of international cooperation to realize its benefits and to counteract economic and political nationalism." This was a direct assault on national sovereignty, which the Trilateral Commission intended to usurp in order to advance regional, global prerogatives.[340]

The Commission's solution was "to develop greater cooperation" among the countries of the world "in view of their great weight in the world economy." They said dealing with "the challenge of interdependence cannot be managed separately."

No wonder the Commission continues to focus on international organizations like the United Nations. The Commission promotes such global organizations in order to seek international political power supposedly to stabilize the global investment climate, which often ran contrary to national interests. This meant as well they promoted big trade umbrellas like the Trans-Pacific Partnership (TPP).

The TPP was negotiated by Michael Froman, a former Trilateralist, and Obama's U.S. Trade Representative.[341] The TPP is a twelve-nation deal negotiated by President Obama and pushed by the Trilateral Commission in order to slash tariffs as well as consolidate and centralize economic and political power.

The Trilateralists like treaties such as the TPP and President Clinton's NAFTA (North Atlantic Free Trade Agreement) because they let mega corporations roam free. Corporations can ship goods anywhere without paying tariffs, and for them, national borders don't matter it's all about the global village.

It was certainly a shock to the Trilateralists when, on January 23, 2017, President Trump formally withdrew the U.S. from the TPP.[342] Of course, Trump campaigned against Hillary Clinton and her Trilateral Commission supporters because he promised to kick globalism down the road, stop the excesses of free trade, and bring back stolen jobs. Does going against the Commission make him vulnerable?

A prior president went against the Trilateral Commission's "free trade" agenda and lost his job. President Richard Nixon was a David Rockefeller man, but he went off the reservation when he began erecting tariffs on a range of goods imported into the U.S. to protect U.S. companies form foreign competition. Tariffs undermined Rockefeller's masterplan, "the entire global program to install 'free trade' and mega-corporate emperors on their thrones for a thousand years could crash and burn." Nixon had to go, which investigative journalist Jon Rappoport believes is the real motivation behind the Watergate impeachment scenario. Evidently, Rockefeller and his cadre sought revenge on Nixon for going off the script. So they unleashed the *Washington Post*, owned by Katharine Graham, a close Rockefeller friend but no friend of Nixon.[343]

The Watergate break-in was the backstory. Bob Woodward, who worked for the Navy in intelligence, and Carl Bernstein were given the story. Rappoport says it was a conspiracy by the *Post's* managing editor Ben Bradlee and Graham, who knew a great deal from the beginning and possibly spoon fed information to the two unsuspecting reporters.

Mr. Rappoport says the so-called "deep throat" informant, the man in the parking garage with all the secrets on the break-in, didn't really matter. Bradlee already had it in his pocket. Deep Throat was merely a contrivance to allow the story to expand and grow by steps. The man behind the curtain was David Rockefeller.

After the whole scandal had been exposed and Nixon had flown away, in disgrace, from the White House for the last time, Rockefeller addressed a meeting of the Chamber of Commerce of the European Community (October 1975). He was there to allay their fears about Nixon's betrayal of the new economic world order. There was really very little he needed to say. Rockefeller had already created (in 1973) the elite free-trade Trilateral Commission's new puppet, Gerald Ford, who was in the White House. Ford dutifully appointed David's brother, Nelson Rockefeller, as his vice president.

Rockefeller told his European Trilateralist members, "Fortunately, there are no signs that these anti-[free] trade measures [of Nixon] are supported by the [Ford] Administration." No wonder; the fix was in, with Nelson firmly inside the White House decision-making loop.

The pregnant question for the future is whether President Trump will face the same type of opposition from the Trilateralists who faced Nixon. Just how far will the globalists go to oppose Trump's decisions such as removing the U.S. from the TPP and possibly NAFTA?

Does the Trilateral Commission still have that sort of influence? Likely it does.

It certainly recruited Jimmy Carter, made him president, stacked his administration with Trilateralists, and then ran the administration like a franchise. Time hasn't changed that approach.

Trilateralists have continued to occupy significant positions of power in all our governments for decades. Even though President Ronald Reagan attacked Trilateralists, some crept into positions in his administration. The same was true with George Bush, and Bill Clinton was a card-carrying member himself, which explains his policies.

President Obama appointed eleven members of the Trilateral Commission to top-level administration positions within his first ten days in office. No wonder Obama pushed a globalist agenda.

Finally, to remove all doubt about the Trilateral Commission's globalization agenda, consider their promotion of the United Nations.

Some of the U.N.'s long-term goals were outlined in a 1992 document known as Agenda 21, a non-binding action plan that takes aim at achieving global "sustainable development."

The U.S. Congress never approved America's participation in Agenda 21, but Presidents Clinton, Bush, and Obama each signed executive orders implementing it.

The U.N. bypassed national governments using Agenda 21's International Council of Local Environmental Initiatives (ICLEI) to make agreements directly with more than six hundred cities, towns, and counties in the United States.[344]

Some critics like Tom DeWeese with the American Policy Center claim Agenda 21 is a "blueprint to turn your community into a little soviet," and "it all means locking away land, resources, higher prices, sacrifice and shortages and is based on the age old socialist scheme of redistribution of wealth."[345]

DeWeese perhaps reads too much into Agenda 21. After all, both former Secretary of State Colin Powell and President George Bush endorsed the agenda. Neither man, according to one conservative writer, would ever embrace a "worldwide plot to deprive Americans of their constitutional rights to rape the land, foul the air, dirty the water, and sprawl development."[346]

Conspiracy allegations may be understandable, but really are not fair, because the ICLEI does its work in the open and with the endorsement of current and past U.S. presidents. The ICLEI convinces local U.S. governments to embrace socialist and extreme environmentalist programs with the funds and encouragement of globalists like billionaire George Soros' Open Society.[347] Where is the opposition to U.N. agents taking their extreme ideas into American communities?

The seven-hundred-page Agenda 21 is divided into four sections that illustrate the type of issues the U.N. aims to attack. Those issues include: social and economic dimensions (poverty, health, sustainable population); conservation and management of resources for development (atmospheric protection, combating deforestation, protecting fragile environments); strengthening the role of major groups (children, women, nongovernment organizations, business and industry, workers, farmers); and means of implementation (science, technology transfer, education, international institutions, and financial mechanisms).

That sounds as if there is nothing outside Agenda 21's purview.

Although this is a voluntary agenda for U.N. members, virtually all nations signed up to participate.

Agenda 21 claims to promote "sustainability," a nuanced word for "environmentalism." That means the U.N. will promote vis-à-vis the ICELEI socialist goals that erode our liberties in order to push to reduce fossil fuel consumption in the name of protecting the environment. Perhaps the best way of thinking of the threat is to envision Obama's Environmental Protection Agency's agenda for America that seeks to reduce private property ownership and private car ownership and put in place population control and Obama's "social justice" reforms, which include calls for redistribution of wealth.

The ultimate threat of Agenda 21, according to a columnist in *Townhall,* is "using government to heavy-handedly accomplish vague goals of caring for the earth" which "goes contrary to our free market capitalism."

What is the evidence the Trilateral Commission supports Agenda 21? A 1978 interview with Commission members by reporter Jeremiah Novak makes the backing clear.

Novak asked, "Why doesn't President Carter come out with it and tell the American people that [U.S.] economic and political power is being coordinated by a [Trilateral Commission] committee made up of Henry Owen and six others? After all, if [U.S.] policy is being made on a multinational level, the people should know."[348]

Richard Cooper (Trilateral Commission member): "President Carter and Secretary of State Vance have constantly alluded to this in their speeches."

Karl Kaiser ([Trilateral Commission member): "It just hasn't become an issue."

It should be an issue because the Trilateral Commission has a clear globalist agenda, it is a kingmaker, and continues to undermine America's sovereignty.

CONCLUSION

I began this chapter asking two questions. Do secret societies really impact our lives? Hopefully, the profile of three of the many "secret societies" in this chapter provides sufficient information to compel the reader to at least be skeptical about their influence on our lives.

Secondly, do these associations advance their radical goals? I believe the answer is yes.

CHAPTER TEN

Globalists Taking Over the World's Power Centers

The elite globalists like those profiled in a previous chapter—Rockefeller, Kissinger, Clinton, and Soros—in the name of equality intend to turn us, the "unwashed masses" of society, into livestock to be exploited. They seek to accomplish that outcome by transforming each of us into an economic unit without identity—job, appearance, and beliefs. How? That is simple. They will harness "globalization," which will reduce barriers among countries by encouraging closer economic, political, and social/cultural interaction, the major centers of world power they intend to control for their personal benefit and to our disadvantage, that is, for those of us who are good enough to survive their coming reign of terror._

Most globalists, as you have seen earlier in this volume, are infected with the religion of progressivism, which drives them to selfishly seek to control the world. They really believe they are genetically superior to the rest of us and truly are certain they know what's best for the world. Consider the evidence of their religious furor.

According to a blog by Wordpress.com, the "Church of Progressivism" is a real religious ideology for the globalists elite. It is replete with all the trappings of traditional religion:

...a holy mission (social 'justice' and climate change), prophets (like Marx [as well as Hegel and Wilson]), saints (like FDR, JFK, LBJ, Gore [Kissinger and Rockefeller]), martyrs (the Rosenbergs...), scripture (the New York Times, CNN, MSNBC, NPR), original sin (our past prosperity and exceptionalism), a messiah (Obama [and/or Clinton]) and a self-righteous worldview that discounts from consideration all counter theories and reviles those who question the complete moral authority of their ecclesiastical body (the Democratic Party)...and that's just the denomination that operates in the United States...the most delusional of the "ultra-orthodox" zealots have been in control of Western Europe since the 60s and Eastern Europe since 1917.[349]

These progressive zealots are driven by their religious ideology to control three primary centers of world power—economics, politics, and culture—which once attained, will enable them to reach their ultimate one-world government goal: total control of mankind and the earth. In this chapter, we will examine each center of power and then answer the questions: Why are these centers significant for the globalists and how are the elite taking them captive?

What if the globalists are actually successful? What might our world look like under the heel of the self-righteous globalists elite? These questions too warrant close scrutiny and possible answers for the good of all mankind.

WORLD'S ECONOMIC POWER CENTER

Consider what greats and near-greats said about those who run our economy:

- "Let me issue and control a nation's money and I care not who writes the laws." —Mayer Amschel Rothschild (1744–1812), founder of the House of Rothschild[350]

- "History records that the money changers have used every form of abuse, intrigue, deceit, and violent means possible to maintain their control over governments by controlling money and its issuance."—James Madison, former president of the U.S.[351]
- "A great industrial nation is controlled by its system of credit. Our system of credit is concentrated in the hands of a few men. We have come to be one of the worst ruled, one of the most completely controlled and dominated governments in the world– no longer a government of free opinion, no longer a government by conviction and vote of the majority, but a government by the opinion and duress of small groups of dominant men." —Woodrow Wilson, former president of the U.S.[352]
- "The modern banking system manufactures money out of nothing. The process is perhaps the most astounding piece of sleight of hand that was ever invented. Banking was conceived in inequity and born in sin. Bankers own the earth. Take it away from them but leave them the power to create money, and with a flick of a pen, they will create enough money to buy it back again. Take this great power away from them and all great fortunes like mine will disappear, for then this would be a better and happier world to live in. But if you want to continue to be the slaves of bankers and pay the cost of your own slavery, then let bankers continue to create money and control credit." —Sir Josiah Stamp, president of the Rothschild Bank of England and the second-richest man in Britain in the 1920s, speaking at the University of Texas in 1927[353]
- "It is well enough that people of the nation do not understand our banking and money system, for if they did, I believe there would be a revolution before tomorrow morning." —Henry Ford, founder of the Ford Motor Company.[354]
- "The Federal Reserve banks are one of the most corrupt institutions the world has ever seen. There is not a man within the sound of my voice who does not know that this nation is run by

the International bankers." —Congressman Louis T. McFadden (Rep. PA)[355]

- "Most Americans have no real understanding of the operation of the international money lenders. The accounts of the Federal Reserve System have never been audited. It operates outside the control of Congress and manipulates the credit of the United States."—Sen. Barry Goldwater (Rep. AR)[356]

An economy is "the production, distribution, or trade and consumption of goods and services by different agents in a given geographical location." In the broadest sense, it is "a social domain that emphasizes the practices, discourses, and material expressions associated with the production, use and management of resources."[357]

By extension, economic power is the condition to trade what one has produced. "In a free market, all prices, wages, and profits are determined—not by the arbitrary whim of the rich or of the poor, not by anyone's 'greed' or by anyone's need—but by the law of supply and demand." The globalists do not want a free market; rather, they seek an economy run by them.[358]

Consider five areas in which the globalists elite seek to control the world's economy in order to create wealth for themselves, not to improve the lives of the masses. After all, as elite-owned, giant, multinational corporations acquire more economic power, they exercise significant control over our lives. They acquire that power through control of these five areas.

Economic Control #1: Big Banks and International Finance

"The real truth of the matter is, as you and I know that a financial element in the large centers has owned the government ever since the days of Andrew Jackson."
—President Franklin Delano Roosevelt[359]

Wall Street tycoons and international financers lead the charge for globalism by promoting the one-world consumer culture. They push governments to embrace consumer-friendly trade agreements and franchises such as the European Union, the Trans-Pacific Partnership (TPP), and North American Free Trade Agreement (NAFTA).

Who really controls the big banks and international finance? Yes, much of that industry is in the hands of the globalists elite, and it has significant consequences for government.

The largest five banks in the U.S. now control nearly half of the industry's total assets, according to SNL Financial. Those institutions—JPMorgan Chase, Bank of America, Wells Fargo, Citigroup, and U.S. Bancorp—had just under $7 trillion in total assets at the end of 2014. The balance of the country's private assets is divided among 6,504 other institutions, according to the Federal Reserve.[360]

The top U.S. bank is JPMorgan Chase, which ranks sixth in the world, with $2.6 trillion in assets. Who owns JPMorgan's nearly 3.8 billion shares? You may own some of those shares if you have a 401K, a tax-qualified pension account. After all, 77 percent of JPMorgan is owned by institutional investors, and the balance (23 percent) is owned by individuals like James Schinke Crown, the director of JPMorgan Chase & Company. The second-largest investor is JPMorgan's chief executive officer Jamie Dimon, who previously served on the board of directors of the Federal Reserve Bank of New York. He is identified by *Time* magazine as one of the world's most influential people.[361]

It isn't an accident that Crown and Dimon are among the many globalists elite who oversee our financial futures.

The world's largest banks are not American owned, however. China operates four of the five largest banks in the world. The world's top bank is the Beijing-based Industrial & Commercial Bank of China (ICBC), which at last report had assets valued at $3.5 trillion, or more than the entire value of the British economy.[362]

The ICBC is a Chinese government-owned bank. It was established in 1984 and today has a total of 490 million retail customers and 5,320 thousand corporate customers across much of the world.[363]

Just how do big banks like ICBC and JPMorgan, which are run by the globalists elite, manipulate international finance? Some elite bankers use their influence with government to manipulate our Federal Reserve System.

Bankers like those identified above can create problems for our economy if they pressure government to influence the Federal Reserve monetary policy for political gain. The Federal Reserve states that the "goals of monetary policy should be established by the political authorities, but the conduct of monetary policy in pursuit of those goals should be free from political influence." That's not always the case, even though the Federal Reserve's congressionally mandated goals are "price stability, maximum employment, and moderate long-term interest rates...a growth rate consistent with the expansion in its underlying productive capacity."[364]

A serious problem occurs when government and nongovernment entities like banks use short-term political influence to pressure the Federal Reserve to overstimulate the economy to achieve short-term output and employment gains. This can generate boom-bust cycles that lead to a less stable economy, higher inflation, and a less productive economy.

Therefore, when the U.S. Federal Reserve or another nation's central bank caves to political influence for short-term gains, and as a result is not deemed credible, then "businesses and consumers will expect higher inflation and, accordingly, workers will demand higher wages, and businesses will demand more-rapid increases in prices."[365]

Currency manipulation is another elite technique to influence exchange rates, which pads progressive pockets like those of George Soros and the Chinese. We have seen China manipulate its currency exchange rates over the past few years to favor that economy.

Presidential candidate Trump, during the campaign, repeatedly accused China of currency manipulation because it drove the value of the *renminbi* (the Chinese currency) to gain a trade advantage. That move hurt American companies and workers by making Chinese goods cheaper for U.S. consumers and U.S. exports more expensive for Chinese buyers.[366]

The Chinese campaign to weaken its currency relative to the U.S. dollar contributed to the trade gap, which was $347 billion in 2016.

Globalists elite influence our economy through their control of the money supply. They influence interest, credit, and currency exchange rates, which are supposed to be regulated by governments for the good of all citizens.

Economic Control #2: Trade and Business

The progressive elite use multinational corporations to seek control over trade and business, which explains their lust for control of every key strategic resource—oil, water, and food—in order to dominate society.

They use their deep pockets to establish resource dominance, which leads to dependent societies. To accomplish this goal, they must eliminate national boundaries and create super-states such as the European Union. These super-state arrangements, so-called free trade agreements like TPP and NAFTA, allow mega corporations power and control of the masses while maximizing profits.

These trade agreements bring enormous profits for Wall Street and, by association, the globalists elite. But that outcome requires deregulated trade and a transfer of wealth to poorer countries.

The elite who pocket massive financial benefits from these agreements use their corporate influence to persuade the average worker to support "open world markets…mainly because market access is so important to poor countries." Some elite journalists even label those who oppose this transfer of wealth as "selfish" toward people in "poverty more grinding and miserable than anything even the worst-off Americans have experienced in recent years."[367]

Zack Beauchamp of Vox says this transfer of wealth is a moral question: "How much [are we]…willing to hurt the world's poor in order to help ourselves[?]" This is fake morality which, as one writer said, "It is no more convincing than Chevron or Exxon ads that proclaim their corporate purpose is to protect the environment."[368]

The mainstream media, which helps promote such shallow morality, are hypocritical. These paid pontificators and their globalists elite business sponsors put the burden on the low-and middle-income Americans who suffer economically because of globalization. When these average Americans complain about job loss, the left dismisses them as "Trump's people" and blame their discontent on gun control, anti-immigration, and homosexual marriage.

There is no doubt the globalists elite who build big business enterprises make decisions that move governments and disadvantage workers in order to enrich themselves.

Economic Control #3: Health and Medicine

Health and medicine is a big issue for everyone. However, for the globalists elite, health and medical interests tend to be about extending their own lives, reducing costs to increase their corporate profits, and controlling the world's population.

Some globalists elite really do want to reduce the world's population. Globalists elite like CNN's Ted Turner suggest this planet can only sustain a population of less than one billion people out of the current 7.5 billion. Therefore, under the iron fist of a globalist-elite world government, there will be draconian measures to reduce earth's population to a sustainable level. You guessed it: They could employ a host of measures to reduce the population—wars, sterilization, euthanization, abortion, denial of food, and other means. And yes, they want to create a completely new society where only the "best" (read "their") genes are allowed to proliferate.

The United Nations' climate chief Christiana Figueres agrees with Turner's anti-life view. She claims that humanity "really should make every effort" to reduce global population. Why? She asserts that we need to reduce global population to protect the environment. So goes the argument that unless something is done, the U.N. predicts, the global population will surpass nine billion people by 2050.[369]

The U.N. report warns that food and water resources will soon be overstretched by the exploding population. The same report indicates that the world will soon have enough water to meet just 60 percent of our needs. Of course, that's ridiculous, because water is recycled. The problem is distribution, not vanishing H_2O.[370]

What do the globalists elite recommend? One U.N. report says more people need to eat insects for protein, thus reducing the demand for traditional meat. Does that mean fillets of cockroach will soon gain popularity?

U.N. climate chief Figueres calls for radical population reduction, in part because of diminished resources. "We can definitely change those [projected population] numbers and really should make every effort to change those numbers because we are already, today exceeding the planet's planetary carrying capacity, today."[371]

Environmentalist activists have long sounded alarms about the earth's alleged overpopulation. John Holdren, a former White House science czar, argued in the 1970s that governments need to take measures to reduce population or suffer ecological calamity. Later, in the 1980s and 1990s, others sounded similar alarms, such as former Vice President Al Gore and Microsoft founder Bill Gates, who said "fertility management" was the key to fighting global warming.[372]

Gore offered some recommendations at the World Economic Forum in 2014: "Depressing the rate of child mortality, educating girls, empowering women and making fertility management ubiquitously available…is crucial to the future shape of human civilization." Fertility management is a synonym for abortion on demand, something enthusiastically promoted by progressives.[373]

The future elite world envisioned by progressives like Gore will also move to a post-industrial society based on a form of scientific feudalism.

That may require, according to some elite, the means to completely control society, which includes implanting microchips in every human in order to track their every move—and these elite masters will also adopt a cashless medium of exchange, which will be as a means of controlling the surviving "peons." And yes, these elite embrace transhumanism, whereby they prolong life—mostly their own with their superior genes—and the quality of life, thanks to combining technology and biology.

Part of their transhumanist agenda is the control of the world's population through genetic engineering, which serves their desire to control reproduction and the "quality" of the gene pool. Only the "best" will survive in the globalists elite future world.

Many elite believe they are special and, as a result, prolonging their personal existence is critical for the future of the human race. How utterly arrogant but so typical of globalists elite. That view explains their fetish with the whole transhumanist movement, which uses the best of modern technology to mesh with biology to extend life.

Some elite see transhumanism are the path to immortality. They seek a future where machines and humans merge into immortal cyborg-like beings. Is this really true?

Wealthy humans "will become God-like cyborgs within 200 years," claims Yuval Noah Harari, a history professor at the Hebrew University of Jerusalem. Harari said the amalgamation of man and machine will be the "biggest evolution in biology" since life on earth began.[374]

"I think it is likely in the next 200 years or so Homo sapiens will upgrade themselves into some idea of a divine being, either through biological manipulation or genetic engineering or by the creation of cyborgs, part organic part non-organic," said Harari to the *London Telegraph*.[375]

He warned that the "cyborg" transhumanist technology would be restricted to the wealthiest (elite) in society, however. Harari speculated that the widening gap between the elite and the poor in society will widen to the point that the rich may live forever and the poor will die out.

Talk about an elite breakaway civilization. These people are going to upgrade themselves into their own gods.

Finally, the elite are all about making a profit and minimizing costs. That may explain their interest in Obamacare (President Obama's failing Affordable Care Act), which promised to insure more Americans but in fact became an elite program to end "unproductive" lives for lack of care.

Globalists also seek to control healthcare in general because it is a sure money maker. Russell Andrews, a neurosurgeon and author of *Too Big to Succeed*, says "The morphing of American medicine from a function of humanitarian society into a revenue stream for healthcare profits, drug and medical device companies, hospitals, and insurance companies. In essence, we have transformed healthcare in the U.S. into an industry whose goal is to be profitable."[376]

Another physician, Sachin Shah, contrasts in *Forbes* magazine the "struggles patients have paying for their medical bills to the enormous profits of American insurance companies." Shah states that "he five largest health insurance companies—WellPoint, United Health, Aetna Humana, and Cigna—...earned over $3.3 billion in profits [between April and June 2011]." Shah continued: "Profit in the health insurance industry is the single greatest barrier to building an efficient, sustainable system of healthcare in this country."[377]

Insurance companies exist to make a profit, not to make sick people well. Further, the globalists elite who manage these health insurance companies and influence government regulation regarding the health industry are in the business to make money, and some could care less about the average citizen's life. After all, many globalists elite want a smaller population, and healthcare "management" is yet another tool to reach that goal.

Who owns these companies? You guessed it. You own some healthcare stock through your 401K, but the globalists elite own a disproportionate share, and they manage healthcare companies for their own benefit.

Economic Control #4: Science and Technology

> It seems to me that the nature of the ultimate revolution with
> which we are now faced is precisely this: That we are in process
> of developing a whole series of techniques which will enable the
> controlling oligarchy who have always existed and presumably
> will always exist to get people to love their servitude.
> —Aldous Huxley, author of *Brave New World*,
>   in a 1962 Berkeley speech[378]

Technology is a craven force when left in the hands of globalists and progressives to create more efficient consumerist economies. It ravages everything in its wake—government, family, faith, freedom, and life. The modern technological society as guided by globalists welcomes whatever facilitates the consumerist economy, such as immigration and multiculturalism, because those forces facilitate greater efficiency and, by association, capital growth. After all, the flow of immigrants in industrialized countries tends to lower wages while replacing the native population, and at the same time creates new cohort of consumers. Meanwhile, the elite get richer.

Technology also allows us better trade and produce globally. Thanks to technology, the West is globalizing faster than much of the world because it exercises more openness and can buy the best science that drives cutting-edge technologies.

The elite, through their foundations and directed government grants and philanthropy, fuels science research, and most of that effort is accountable to the source of the funding—elite-controlled government and the deep-pocketed corporate elite. That makes the scientists lackeys for the elite.

Most of that funded scientific development comes about to make a profit for the likes of pharmaceutical firms, weapons developers, and other for-profit businesses. For example, the Pentagon's Defense Advanced Research Projects Agency (DARPA) fuels basic research that may provide a new weapon or technology, but ultimately it enriches giant arms merchants run mostly by corporate elite.

DARPA helped develop many of the modern communication devices, giant money-making machines. Some of those same devices make monitoring what we buy and sell easy to track. After all, Big Brother knows most everything about us as a result. Besides, many of these devices are also now harnessed to manipulate our thinking by enticing us to buy certain cars, foods, and clothing.

Science and technology belong to the globalists elite and keep them equipped with tools that fill their purses and better help to control the masses. Thus we do live in a Brave New World!

Economic Control #5: Energy

> In searching for a new enemy to unite us, we came up with the idea that pollution, the threat of global warming, water shortages, famine and the like would fit the bill. In their total-ity and in their interactions these phenomena do constitute a common threat with demands the solidarity of all peoples. But in designating them as the enemy, we fall into the trap about which we have already warned namely mistaking systems for causes. All these dangers are caused by human intervention and it is only through changed attitudes and behaviour that they can be overcome. The real enemy, then, is humanity itself.
> —Club of Rome, The First Global Revolution, 1991[379]

The globalists elite have harnessed "global warming" as an ally to wrestle more control over the world's economy. They intend to promote global warming, which has become the modern bogeyman, giving the globalists an opening to promote a worldwide system of taxation and control.

Decades ago, the globalists tried a different scare tactic. At the time, they invoked the scare message that the world was running on empty.

On April 18, 1977, progressive President Jimmy Carter and CFR member announced to the American people that "onight I want to have an unpleasant talk with you about a problem unprecedented in our history. With the exception of preventing war, this is the greatest challenge our country will face during our lifetimes."[380]

Then Carter said we faced an unprecedented problem due to the lack of energy. One can almost hear fellow progressive icons Brzezinski and Rockefeller whispering into Carter's Trilateralist ears as he weaved his dire prediction. "We simply must balance our demand for energy with our rapidly shrinking resources," said the thirty-ninth president. "The oil and natural gas we rely on for 75 percent of our energy are running out."[381]

That's a pretty sobering announcement coming from the occupant of the Oval Office. Few at the time questioned Carter's forecast even though he was very wrong. Was he simply duped by his progressive elite advisers in order to justify pouring more resources into alternative energy projects? Of course, time would totally disprove Carter's dire message. There are plenty of oil and natural gas reserves in North America, Russia, Saudi Arabia, and other areas of the world—trillions of untapped fuel reserves for many decades to come.

Once Carter's prediction fell flat, Americans began to hear the other shoe drop from the alarmist progressives: global warming, thanks to former Vice President Al Gore's siren call. He warned we were on the verge of burning ourselves to a crisp. Gore's alarmist call soon faded to be replaced by yet another horror: the coming climate -hange apocalypse.

Why all the energy alarm? Those claims came from progressives with a mission: control the world's energy resources.

The good news is that after extracting seventy billion barrels of oil from the earth, geophysicists keep finding new sources of fuel. Even when oil becomes scarce in the far-distant future, there are plenty of other sources of energy: coal, atomic nuclei, and the sun. Man is progressing in harnessing theses forces to his advantage all the time.

Few readers have heard about hydrogenating coal to form liquid fuels, a major future energy source. In fact, South Africa, which has no oil wells, fuels its automobiles by converting three thousand tons of coal into oil each day. The earth has plenty of untapped coal for a long future. The U.S. government estimates that our recoverable coal reserves will last about 256 years.[382]

Once the globalists found out they could no longer force people to abandon carbon fuel by scaring them into believing the resource would soon be gone, they turned to global warming and then climate change. Once again, the progressives intend to scare us into abandoning carbon-based fuels for alternative green energy, but the science isn't settled.

Obviously, there are many myths promoted by the climate change alarmists, such as global temperatures are rising at a rapid, unprecedented rate. The fact is, the earth has seen surface temperature rise and fall for decades at a time. The HadCRUT3 surface temperature index, a product of the Climate Research Unit of the University of East Anglia, shows six distinctive multi-decade cycles of first global cooling followed by warming.[383]

Another myth indicates the "earth has experienced a steady, very gradual temperature decrease for 1,000 years, then recently began a sudden increase." Climate changes are evident throughout geologic time, such as the Medieval Warm Period (A.D. 1000 to 1200) was followed by a period known as the "Little Ice Age."[384]

The major bogeyman for climate-change alarmists is carbon dioxide, which is blamed for adding to the Greenhouse Effect. Yes, carbon dioxide levels have changed over time, and man is partially responsible. However, there is no proof that carbon dioxide is the main driver of global warming. What is known is that, as temperatures rise and fall naturally thanks to solar radiation and other influences, the earth's warming surface expels more carbon dioxide, a life-sustaining outcome.

The globalists' energy grab is about power, and they use climate-change alarms as a ruse to divert attention from their true agenda.

CONCLUSION: POWER CENTER
OF ECONOMICS

Many factors influence the world's economy, not just the five outlined above. However, should the globalists elite exercise significant leverage over just these five factors, there is little doubt they will have their way with the world's economy.

Being the master of the world's economy is pretty significant, but true domination requires control of two other power centers: political and cultural.

WORLD'S POLITICAL POWER CENTERS

The Rockefellers and their allies have, for at least fifty years, been carefully following a plan to use their economic power to gain political control of first America, and then the rest of the world. Do I mean conspiracy? Yes, I do. I am convinced there is such a plot, international in scope, generations old in planning, and incredibly evil in intent.

—Congressman Larry P. McDonald, November 1975, from the introduction to a book titled *The Rockefeller File*[385]

The globalists elite must exercise control over the world's political power centers in order to attain their goal of one world government. That means they must acquire the ability to control the behavior of people through a variety of mechanisms.

Political power is the "ability to influence, condition, shape, and control the content and direction of public policy." Those who possess and exercise political power are found both inside and outside of government—political authority and political influence.[386]

Globalist progressives who are inside of government like Roosevelt,

Wilson, Kennedy, and Johnson exercise political authority to advance their ideas. The formal legal authority associated with their public office gives them the opportunity to adopt and implement authoritative decisions that have the force of law and are therefore binding on all citizens. Thus political authority is the legal right to govern society and the consequence in a democratic system of the voters' right to select their leaders.[387]

The other tool available to globalists is political influence, which is the ability of private individuals (like progressive financier George Soros) and groups (like Soros' Open Society Institute) to impact government decisions. Although such individuals and groups do not possess formal legal authority to make official government decisions, they do shape and often control government behavior through political influence to the extent that it is taken into account by government officials.

What constitutes political influence? It is the ability of non-government individuals or groups to persuade officials to vote or decide a certain way on legislation or on the implementation of a policy. That persuasion can come in various forms such as campaign contributions, access to politically influential families who can tap into the "old boys" network, demonstrations and protests, political patronage, party loyalty, telephone calls, letter writing, and personal visits with officials.

We have seen throughout the twentieth century efforts by progressives to migrate power first from individuals and states to the federal government and then to world bodies. This is done by creating new "rights" by taking away aspects of the private sector and local government decisions.

In this section, the reader will examine how globalist progressives employ both political authority as government insiders and political influence as outsiders to favor their agenda.

We begin by examining the migration of power from the citizens to the federal government, and then examine the consolidation of power from nation-states to international bodies.

CONCENTRATION OF POWER WITH THE FEDERAL GOVERNMENT

Although the majority of Americans prefer state over federal government power (55 percent v. 37 percent), according to a 2016 Gallup poll, over the course of the twentieth century, progressives have succeeded in concentrating more power at the federal government level, an outcome never intended by our founders.[388]

The Heritage Foundation rightly points out that "over the past 100 years, our government has been transformed from a limited, constitutional, federal republic to a centralized administrative state that for the most part exists outside the structure of the Constitution and wields nearly unlimited power. This administrative state has been constructed as a result of a massive expansion of the national government's power."[389]

Of course, that transfer of power is music to the ears of progressives who favor big government. Our founders wanted to entrust only limited powers to the federal government, but over the life of our country, the federal governments grew to regulate the citizens rather than protect their rights. That outcome was predicted by Alexis de Tocqueville, who warned in his early nineteenth-century work, *Democracy in America*, that under such a government, citizens would become "nothing more than a herd of timid and industrious animals, of which the government is the shepherd."[390]

The transfer of power to the federal government happened in spite of the 10th Amendment to the Constitution, which states, "The powers not delegated to the United States by the Constitution, nor prohibited by it to the States, are reserved to the States respectively, or to the people." After all, our founders expected most power and authority to be left to the states and the people, but progressives have successfully transformed this nation into a nanny-state overseeing virtually every aspect of the citizens' lives. Unelected bureaucrats now have vast powers to run every aspect of our lives, thanks to progressives.

Take inventory over the past one hundred years of the federal government's changes, programs, and mandates, which are mostly thanks to the progressive Democrat Party. This transfer of power is almost an audible sound, if one listens carefully, of the power being sucked out of local communities by progressives and placed in the hands of big government and its legions of federal bureaucrats.

The following is a short list of progressive big government initiatives dating back over more than one hundred years. As you read through these initiatives, ask yourself: Who profited from these initiatives?

- **THE FEDERAL RESERVE BANK** became an entity thanks to Congress and progressive President Woodrow Wilson, a Democrat. A severe panic in 1907 resulted in bank runs, which led Congress in 1913 to write the Federal Reserve Act. The emergent Federal Reserve System was intended to address the banking panics, but soon took on much broader responsibilities thanks to progressives bent on growing big government. Today it supervises and regulates banks and other financial institutions to "ensure the safety and soundness of the nation's banking and financial system and to protect the credit rights of consumers."[391] Some founders feared that a central bank was a dangerous consolidation of power that would benefit investors, banks, and businesses above the wider population. President Andrew Jackson was more suspicious, calling a central bank "a den of vipers and thieves."[392]

- **LEAGUE OF NATIONS** was proposed by President Woodrow Wilson as well. Fortunately, the League was rejected by the Congress in part because membership in that organization meant a loss of sovereignty and created greater international obligations.

- **FEDERAL INCOME TAX** became the law of the land through the 16th Amendment to the Constitution that was proposed by President William Howard Taft, a Republican, in a 1909 address to Congress. The ever-increasing federal income tax fuels the progressives' dream of a big spending, all-encompassing government.

Most Americans agree our tax code is too complicated and the burden of paying for the government is not equitably shared across the population.

- **THE NEW DEAL** was proposed by President Franklin Roosevelt, a Democrat. It consisted of a host of social programs and government interference in the private sector that arguably extended the Great Depression for at least a decade.

- **UNITED NATIONS** was proposed by President Franklin Roosevelt, a Democrat. Roosevelt's U.N. became an intrusive international organization designed by members of the CFR and guided by Roosevelt's globalist vision. Today, as we will see shortly, it is a power-grabbing international forum for every radical agenda and home to the globalists elite.

- **SOCIAL SECURITY ACT** was proposed by President Franklin Roosevelt, a Democrat. That act was another enormous big government program that included several provisions for the general welfare to include a social insurance program to pay retired workers a continuing income after retirement. The major complaint today is that it is failing in part because there isn't enough income from the taxpayers to sustain the costs in part because people are living longer. The problem is the Baby Boomer bulge and the decreased number of wage earners paying for the Boomer "entitlements."

- **THE GREAT SOCIETY** was proposed by President Lyndon Johnson, a Democrat, allegedly to eliminate poverty and racial injustice. It too was a big government program pushed by progressives. It's no more than another socialist redistribution system that removes much of the incentive to work for millions of Americans.

- **MEDICARE** was signed into law in 1965 by President Lyndon Johnson, a progressive Democrat. It is the federal health insurance program for people who are age 65 or older, and those young people with disabilities or with end-stage renal disease.

One byproduct of this program is to relieve people the responsibility for saving for their old-age health care, a progressive agenda item that makes citizens dependent on big government.

- **MEDICAID** was signed into law in 1965 by President Lyndon Johnson. It is a joint federal-state program that provides health coverage and nursing home coverage for certain groups of less-privileged people. Once again, this is a program that transfers political authority from the states to the federal government.

- **FIRST AUTO BAILOUTS** was done thanks to President George W. Bush, a Republican in 2008 to the tune of $17.4 billion. Bush made the loan contingent upon the companies hitting "Restructuring Targets." This was a wealth transfer program and indicative of big government playing god with our economy.

- **COMMUNITY REINVESTMENT ACT** was created during President Jimmy Carter's administration, a progressive Democrat. The CRA states that "regulated financial institutions have continuing and affirmative obligations to help meet the credit needs of the local communities in which they are chartered."[393] This is an example of the collusion of big government and big banks, a marriage that our founders warned about.

- **NORTH AMERICAN FREE TRADE AGREEMENT** was created and strongly supported for progressive President William Clinton, a Democrat. It is an agreement by Canada, Mexico, and the United States, creating a trilateral trade bloc in North America. It is great for big corporations' bottom line, but has drained jobs from the American workforce.

- **PATRIOT ACT** was passed during Republican President George W. Bush's administration. It came in response to the terrorist attacks on September 11, 2001, and grants big government the power to research and obstruct any person or group believed to support or advertise any domestic or foreign terrorist activity. Many rightly argue the Act robs Americans of some of their civil liberties and continues even today to infringe on our 4th Amendment rights against search and seizure.

- **TROUBLED ASSET RELIEF PROGRAM (TARP) BAIL-OUT** was a program signed into law by President Bush to purchase toxic assets and equity from financial institutions to strengthen the financial sector. Two years after Bush signed TARP, then President Barack Obama, a Democrat, signed into law a TARP-like act, the Dodd-Frank Wall Street Reform and Consumer Protection Act, at a cost of $431 billion. Dodd-Frank was a winner for two big banks, Bank of America and Wells Fargo, and the losers were the American taxpayers. No, TARP did not turn a profit as some rumored. Mark Gongloff with the *Huffington Post* reported that half of the funds repaid to the U.S. government were repaid with funds that came from loans from other government programs.[394]

- **$1 TRILLION "STIMULUS"** was enacted by President Obama in 2009 to create jobs, but because of debt service, the overall cost rose to $1.2 trillion. The spending was in three broad categories: tax benefits to individuals and businesses ($290.7 billion); entitlements, including Medicare, Medicaid, food stamps, and unemployment benefits ($264.4 billion); and contracts, grants, and loans in such areas as education, transportation, infrastructure, energy, science, and health ($261.2 billion).[395] We are still looking for those jobs.

- **CAP AND TRADE** is an environmental policy tool pushed by Presidents Ronald Reagan, George H. W. Bush, and George W. Bush to reduce emissions of a pollutant by placing a limit (or cap) on the total amount of emissions that can be released by sources covered. It's like a game of musical chairs; "polluters must scramble to match allowances to emissions."[396] Cap and trade has its critics. They argue it increases the price of energy, does not reduce emissions, and harms the poor it vowed to protect, harms energy security, marginally impacts the environment, and drives out some industries out of business.[397]

- **SECOND AUTO BAILOUT** was pushed by President Obama in 2009 to the tune of $85 billion in restructuring GM. In 2012, the *Detroit News* said the government expected at the time to lose $23.6 billion on the bailout.[398]

- **AFFORDABLE CARE ACT, aka Obamacare,** was signed into law by President Obama in 2010. It promised to provide affordable health-insurance coverage via a Health Insurance Marketplace, but it is proving to be unprofitable, thus leading toward a single-payer, socialized medical system. Not surprisingly, the big winners are the managed-care companies, according to the *New York Times.* The Standard & Poor's 500-stock index—United-Health, Aetna, Anthem, Cigna, Humana and Centene—have risen far more than the overall stock index. In fact, as a whole, those stocks have gained nearly 300 percent, according to Bespoke Investment Group.[399] Now, because the profits are leaving under Obamacare, so are the insurance companies—which means the burden will eventually fall on the struggling taxpayer.

What's your conclusion from reading summaries of these eighteen government programs? Likely, if you are like me, the beneficiary is always the big corporation and big government. The citizen gets stuck with the bill, and as a result, we have less say about our exploding-in-size government.

CONCENTRATION OF POWER WITH INTERNATIONAL BODIES

The progressives are concentrating power at the federal level in many nation-states. That is a necessary step before that power is next transferred to international bodies. Of course, in some situations, we have already seen evidence of that transfer.

Progressive leader Hillary Clinton demonstrates through her past government work and her 2016 presidential campaign how political power once concentrated at the nation-state level can be shifted to international forums.

Hillary Clinton loves the United Nations and would turn over American sovereignty on many issues to that international body. For example, while serving in the U.S. Senate, Clinton said, "a strong United Nations is in America's interest." Then again, as secretary of state under President Obama, Clinton gushed that the U.N. "remains the single most important global institution," and she added, "we are constantly reminded of its value." Of course, she remains rather vague about the positive attributes, perhaps because she understands the potential backlash.[400]

Clinton sought to use the U.N. as a platform to promote her "progressive internationalism." She pushed the international body to infringe on nation-state sovereignty in such areas as parents' authority over their children, gun control, and who should be admitted into a country.[401]

She loved the U.N. even while serving as the first lady. Her progressive colors shined brightly when attending an award ceremony for the late CBS news anchor Walter Cronkite. The broadcaster said at the event hosted by the World Federalist Association, "We must strengthen the United Nations as a first step toward a world government patterned after our own government with a legislature, executive and judiciary, and police to enforce."[402]

Clinton verbally applauded Cronkite's call for a world government. She said of Cronkite that there is "no better captain that I can imagine" to "sail across the un-navigated seas of the twenty-first century." Then she added, "For decades you told us 'the way it is,' but tonight we honor you for fighting for the way it could be."[403]

In 1973, Hillary Rodham worked for the Children's Defense Fund as a staff lawyer researching why millions of children were not in school. She found by knocking on doors and talking to families across America that many schools were denying access to children with disabilities, children who couldn't afford to pay for books, non-English speakers, and others. Her work and the Children's Defense Fund report contributed to the eventual passage of a federal law guaranteeing access to public schools for children with disabilities.[404]

Clinton's work for the Children's Defense Fund is admirable, but her work many years later as a child advocate undermines families. Specifically, she advanced "progressive internationalism" by putting down stay-at-home mothers and lambasted parents in her advocacy for the U.N. Convention on the Rights of the Child. That treaty empowers children to bring their parents to court "to seek, receive and impart information and ideas of all kinds, regardless of frontiers, either orally, in writing or in print, in the form of art, or through any other media of the child's choice."[405]

Ms. Clinton has never been a supporter of gun rights, which is why few were surprised by an October 4, 2015, leaked e-mail written by Clinton campaign press secretary Brian Fallon that exposed the candidate's anti-gun plans. The e-mail stated:

> Circling back around on guns as a follow up to the Friday morning discussion: the Today Show has indicated they definitely plan to ask about guns, and so to have the discussion be more of a news event than her previous times discussing guns, we are going to background reporters tonight on a few of the specific proposals she would support as President— universal background checks of course, but also closing the gun show loophole by executive order and imposing manufacturer liability.[406]

Hillary Clinton would seek to confiscate most firearms if she ever regains political authority. She once labeled Australia's firearms confiscation operation a "good example," which she said was "worth looking at" for America. A reporter for *Business Insider* wrote that Australia required "all firearm-license applicants to show 'genuine reason' for owning a gun, which couldn't include self-defense."[407]

Brian Fallon's leaked e-mail is consistent with Clinton's use of the

U.N. Arms Trade Treaty. That treaty would maintain a firearms "control list" registry for all signatories. Predictably, Clinton said during her presidential bid that "guns, in and of themselves, will not make Americans safer," and "arming more people is not [an] appropriate response to terrorism." In fact, Clinton as president would have tried to go well beyond "closing the gun show loophole by executive order."[408]

Progressive Clinton also used international forums to advance her antireligious views as well. She attacked "deep-seated cultural codes, religious beliefs and structural biases" at the 2015 Women in the World Summit. She even pushed the U.N. to treat homosexuality as a matter of universal human rights, another slap-down of many religions that consider homosexual behavior wrong.[409]

Mrs. Clinton used a speech at the U.N. in Geneva to advance her support for homosexuals and to attack people of faith. In that speech, Clinton said the "most challenging issue arises when people cite religious or cultural values as a reason to violate or not to protect the human rights of LGBT [lesbian, gay, bisexual and transgender] citizens." Then she compared those religion-based objections to "the justification offered for violent practices towards women like honor killings, widow burning, or female genital mutilation."[410]

Progressive Clinton even used her political authority as secretary of state to call for the U.N. to push for the admission of more Syrian refugees. She called for the U.N. to host an "emergency global gathering where the U.N. literally tries to get commitments" to admit more refugees. Then she promised, "I obviously want the United States to do our part," and she said "this is an international problem that demands an international response."[411]

What would have happened regarding the refugee issue had Clinton been elected president? Her speeches make that answer clear: She would expand the U.N.'s role in pushing countries to admit more refugees and migrants, irrespective of the risks and costs. In fact, during her 2016 presidential quest, she called for admitting at least sixty-five thousand Syrian refugees annually in the U.S.—a 500 percent increase over Obama's level.[412]

Clinton's use of political authority and influence over the years illustrates the progressives' intention to drain nation-states of their sovereignty over virtually all issues of importance. She obviously sees transnational entities like the U.N. and the European Union as being morally superior to the nation-state and will do whatever necessary to marginalize opposition to the transfer of sovereign authority.

Before advancing to the next power center, it is worth reviewing how globalists have already successfully diverted political power from nation-states to unelected international government and nongovernment organizations.

There are at least sixty-nine thousand international nongovernmental organizations (INGOs) and intergovernmental organizations (IGOs).[413] Each exercises some degree of either political authority or political influence within nation-state governments.

The IGO is an entity created by treaty, which includes at least two nations, working on common interests. Those IGOs formed by treaty are subject to international law and have the ability to enter into enforceable agreements.[414]

IGOs are the progressives' tools to create mechanisms to work more successfully together on a broad range of issues. Further, globalization is a boon for IGOs, because they are expanding their role in international political systems and global governance. Some IGOs in fact have the ability to make rules and exercise power within their member countries, and as a result have a global impact.[415]

Consider the political authority exercised by a few of the most prominent IGOs.

United Nations is the favorite IGO of progressives, as evidenced by accounts like Ms. Clinton's statements above. Its announced purpose is to maintain international peace and security, develop relations among nations, and solve a host of international issues. Members agree to settle any disputes peacefully, not to use force against other members, and to refrain from helping countries that oppose the U.N. It is funded by members' dues, which is based on wealth—explaining why the U.S. pays 22 percent of the U.N.'s regular budget.[416]

The U.N. has six functional bodies: the General Assembly, Security Council, Economic and Social Council, Trusteeship Council, Secretariat, and an International Court of Justice. Each body has specific purposes and jurisdictions, such as the Security Council and the International Court of Justices, which helps develop and enforce international law. Further, the Security Council is the only entity with the power to declare international uses of legitimate military force.

What political power is exercised by the U.N.? The U.N. is accused of moral relativism because today it is more amenable to the requirements of dictatorships than of free democracies, according to former Israeli ambassador to the U.N. Dore Gold, author of *Tower of Babble: How the United Nations Has Fueled Global Chaos*. The U.N. is also widely accused of being an instrument of globalism, which is evidenced by Hillary Clinton's views expressed above. Further, it is a strong advocate for population control, a progressive agenda item.[417]

North Atlantic Treaty Organization (NATO) was founded to safeguard the freedom and security of its current twenty-eight members. Politically, it promotes democratic values and encourages consultation and cooperation to prevent conflict. Militarily, it is committed to resolving disputes when Article 5 of the Washington Treaty is invoked by one of the member states.[418]

What political power is exercised by NATO? Membership in NATO is a concession of U.S. sovereignty because taking part in a mutual defense pact means having to defend other countries that may run contrary to our own interests. There is also the expense, as President Trump explained during his campaign for the presidency, which falls disproportionately on the U.S. Those funds could be better spent at home rather than mutual defense on the other side of the Atlantic Ocean.

European Union (EU) was initially created to be the economic and political union among six European countries to increase economic cooperation. However, it evolved into a twenty-eight-member organization spanning policy areas from climate to healthcare. Its actions are based on treaties entered by the member countries, such as the abolition of border controls between EU members known as the Schengen Agreement, and it promotes human rights.[419]

What political power is exercised by the EU? The integration of the member states weakens the nation-state by encroaching on national sovereignty. For example, by April 2017, sixteen EU member states had signed off on the controversial scheme to grant the European Public Prosecutor's Office (EPPO) the powers to investigate and prosecute tax fraud and corruption. So far, "major EU states the Netherlands, Sweden, Poland, Hungary and Malta announced they would opt out amid fears of the creation of an EU super state."[420]

Organization of the Petroleum Exporting Countries (OPEC) exists to "coordinate and unify the petroleum policies of its member countries and ensure the stabilization of oil markets in order to secure an efficient, economic and regular supply of petroleum to consumers, a steady income to producers and a fair return on capital for those investing in the petroleum industry."[421]

What political power is exercised by OPEC? It acts like a cartel by getting members to restrain production so that prices rise, thus gaining higher income for less production. Unfortunately, OPEC isn't sanctioned for such behavior, because it's an IGO with members joining together to achieve their price goal at the expense of the consumers. However, America's fracking industry impacts OPEC's pricing leverage because it restrains the cartel's pricing freedom, a good outcome for the global consumer.[422]

World Trade Organization (WTO) "is the only global international organization dealing with the rules of trade between nations. At its heart are the WTO agreements, negotiated and signed by the bulk of the world's trading nations and ratified in their parliaments. The goal is to help producers of goods and services, exporters, and importers conduct their business."[423]

What political power is exercised by the WTO? The WTO is undemocratic and not transparent. Its rules are written by and for corporations with inside access to the negotiations. Also, it is not creating a world of "free trade," its alleged mission. Rather, rich countries and mega corporations dominate international trade for their own reasons. Its rules put corporate profits ahead of human and labor rights.[424]

Organization of American States (OAS) "is the world's oldest regional organization, dating back to the First International Conference of American States, held in Washington, D.C., from October 1889 to April 1890. That meeting approved the establishment of the International Union of American Republics, and the stage was set for the weaving of a web of provisions and institutions that came to be known as the inter-American system, the oldest international institutional system."[425]

What political power is exercised by the OAS? The OAS is accused by some Latin governments like Cuba of being overly influenced by U.S. foreign policy. Cuban President Raul Castro called the OAS "an imperialist instrument."[426] Congressional Republicans tried to defund OAS because it supported undemocratic regimes in Latin America, yet it continues to soak the U.S. taxpayer for more than $50 million annually.[427]

Africa Union (AU) is an organization of African countries that promotes democracy, unity, economy, and development—an organization modeled after the European Union. It strives to promote and protect human and peoples' rights in accordance with the African Charter on Human and Peoples' Rights and other relevant human rights instruments, as well as establish the necessary conditions which enable the continent to play its rightful role in the global economy and in international negotiations.[428]

What political power is exercised by the AU? The AU is slow to respond to security threats, prioritizes power over justice, and doesn't appropriately represent all African people. It is also criticized as a platform for tyrants and as an ineffective bureaucracy focused more on per diems than on political challenges.[429] China wields significant influence within the AU, however. Beijing paid for a new, twenty-story AU headquarters in Addis Ababa at the cost of $200 million, which was built by a Chinese company with Chinese labor. Many people rightly conclude that China was buying influence with the new building in order to extend its economic presence on the continent, which includes dumping its goods in Africa.[430]

It is evident from the above examples that nation-states have surrendered considerable political authority to IGOs. That loss of nation-state sovereignty is exacerbated by the political influence granted to those organizations.

An international nongovernmental organization (INGO) is not created by an international treaty like an IGO. Rather, it tends to focus on a specific set of issues, such as hunger or disease. INGOs are funded by philanthropies, but also by government grants. For example, the U.S. Agency for International Development (USAID) is a U.S. government agency that awards taxpayer-funded grants to nongovernmental organizations to address specific problems. In fiscal year 2016, USAID awarded $22.7 billion in grants.[431]

Typically, INGOs rise from the ashes of human disaster, such as the reaction of a single nineteenth-century man who saw an urgent moral imperative. That man, Henri Dunant, wrote a book and lobbied governments that led to the creation of an INGO, the International Committee of the Red Cross. He campaigned to adopt the first Geneva Convention in 1864 that introduced international humanitarian law.[432]

INGOs are more often than not tethered to IGOs than nation-states. For example, INGOs successfully used their political influence to strengthen the wording in the U.N.'s Charter regarding the role on human rights, economic and social questions, and equality for women. Today, many thousands of NGOs lobby the U.N. by circulating statements to government delegates and host meetings as "side events" to the official proceedings.

INGOs exercise significant influence across the globe, either working with IGOs or with nation-states. Consider the work of some of the largest INGOs and their influence.

Bangladesh Rural Advancement Committee (BRAC) is the largest nongovernmental development organization on the planet. BRAC is a microcredit and microfinance pioneer that diversified into a wide suite of activities, ranging from agriculture to education to climate change risk reduction to child health. It is an entire international development sector in one organization, with an annual income of $684 million. *The Economist* reports that the government of Bangladesh "has been unusually friendly to NGOs, perhaps because, to begin with, it realized it needed all the help it could get." BRAC answered that call by distributing emergency aid after the war of independence, and now it claims to have helped three-quarters of all Bangladeshis.[433]

Danish Refugee Council (DRC) formed after World War II and the European refugee crises following the Soviet Union's invasion of Hungary in 1956. DRC uses its nearly 299-million-euro annual budget to meet a variety of needs. Specifically, it is dedicated to humanitarian land mine removal, housing and small-scale infrastructure, income generation through grants and microfinance, food security, and agricultural rehabilitation. It is noteworthy that the DRC influences the execution of government policy by helping to fill the Danish Refugee Appeals Board, an official government activity overseen by the Danish Immigration Service.[434]

CARE International began after World War II, and at that time was known as the Cooperative for American Remittances to Europe, which incorporated twenty-two American charities of civic, religious, cooperative, and labor backgrounds. At that time, CARE distributed 2.8 million U.S. Army surplus food packages to needy Europeans. Today, CARE is one of the largest poverty-fighting organizations in the world, providing relief to the people hit by disasters and emergencies.[435] The CARE International website announces its intention to "influence the national and international policies that affect the lives of the poorest and most vulnerable communities around the world." CARE intends to play a "pivotal role" in global advocacy of many issues such as women, peace and security; women and food security; sexual, reproduction and maternal health and gender and climate change. "The CARE International Secretariat carries out policy and advocacy work through its offices in Geneva, New York and Brussels, where we seek to influence governments, United Nations institutions, the European Union and other multilateral organizations to actively promote change. In conjunction with CARE members and Country Offices, the CARE International Secretariat coordinates advocacy efforts across the globe."[436]

Globalists have successfully drained sovereignty from nation-states through the use of IGOs and INGOs. Yes, many of these organizations perform wonderful, needed work around the world helping to meet the needs of millions of people. However, many also advance the globalist agenda by transferring political power from nation-states to international organizations that in time will be networked into a on- world political system, aka one world government.

Well known globalists use both IGOs and INGOs to advance their agenda. For example, one study claims globalist billionaire George Soros funds at least in part 187 INGOs attempting to subvert the course of especially American democracy. Those groups reflect the well-established progressive agenda: abortion, open borders, socialist health care, climate change, and many more.[437]

WORLD'S CULTURAL POWER CENTERS

The third leg of the progressives' power center stool is culture. Globalists are using a number of cultural institutions to help transform nation-states like the U.S. into multicultural societies, a critical step to their ultimate goal of establishing a one-world government.

Anthropologist E. B. Tylor defines culture as the "complex whole which includes knowledge, belief, art, morals, law, custom and any other capabilities and habits acquired by man as a member of society."[438]

How are globalists capturing the cultural power centers? By monopolizing key cultural institutions in order to get them to spout the progressive agenda or at least remain silent, and therefore provide an opportunity to remold the minds of the masses.

Progressives can monopolize cultural institutions through either political authority—elected officials who direct policy decisions—or private enterprises that promote a politically correct view of history and society.

This volume identifies numerous examples of global progressives employing political authority to advance their agenda. We certainly saw examples of progressives employing political authority (Wilson, Roosevelt, Johnson, Carter, and Obama) pushing their radical agenda.

The use of political authority to impose cultural transformation is illustrated by the lifting of the U.S. military's ban on service by open homosexuals. In 1992, progressive presidential candidate Bill Clinton promised that if elected, he would lift the military's two-centuries-old homosexual ban. He tried to do just that shortly after his January 1993 inauguration, but he ran into a buzz saw of opposition from the Pentagon brass and on Capitol Hill.

Jump forward to the 2008 election of progressive Barack Obama, the most pro-homosexual leader ever elected to the White House. He used every bit of his political authority to push the homosexual agenda across the government, and in particular at the Pentagon. Eventually, with the support of a Democrat-controlled Congress and a host of cowardly flag officers at the Pentagon, Obama succeeded in lifting the ban. But that wasn't enough. It took years of browbeating by elected officials and threats through mandatory re-education by the military chain of command to make service members stuff their well-founded opposition to open homosexual service. But, as expected, that wasn't enough for progressive Obama. No, Obama pushed the transgender agenda at the Pentagon in his final year in office and came very close to getting those truly sick people officially embraced by the brass, thanks to the imposition of political authority and a cadre of culture changing political appointees and spineless senior uniformed officers.

Employing political authority to force cultural change through policy initiatives requires top elected officials. That's likely to be less effective in the long-term than a more subtle tool described by Angelo Codevilla, a senior fellow of the Claremont Institute and professor emeritus of international relations at Boston University.

Miss Codevilla writes that progressives seek to take control of culture through a concept first attributed to Antonio Gramsci (1891–1937), a communist theoretician. Gramsci created the concept known as "cultural hegemony" which, according to Codevilla, "envisage[s] a totalitarianism that eliminates the very possibility of cultural resistance to progressivism." In part, that's what the senior military leaders did to the armed forces once Obama's political authority changed the rules.[439]

Gramsci's "cultural hegemony" transforms the enemy rather than killing him, the preferred approach used by Marxists. Specifically, the progressive focuses on cultural matters by "persuading minds not through reasoning on what is true or false, good and bad…but rather by creating a new historical reality." In other words, the progressives rewrite history to fit their agenda and then re-educate the population.[440]

Gramsci turned to Niccolo Machiavelli, the fifteenth-century historian and philosopher, to understand how to change a culture to a new set of beliefs. Machiavelli wrote, according to Codevilla, in *The Prince* (1513), that "nothing is more difficult than to establish 'new modes and orders,' that this requires 'persuading' peoples of certain things, that it is necessary 'when they no longer believe to make them believe by force.'"[441]

Machiavelli said that once the people are inculcated with a new set of beliefs, then the rulers can count on being "powerful, secure, honored and happy." Of course, Machiavelli suggests in *Discourses on Livy Book II*, according to Codevilla, that the new set of beliefs is a religion of sorts, a view about progressivism outlined earlier in this volume. Then Machiavelli explained, "When it happens that the founders of the new religion speak a different language, the destruction of the old religion is easily effected."[442]

Codevilla indicates that modern progressives are employing the Gramscian vision of hegemony—a new religion—over culture by waging cultural warfare within institutions. They began their cultural warfare logically by rewriting history. She illustrated the point by outlining a national progressive version of American history: "America was born tainted by western civilization's original sins—racism, sexism, greed, genocide against natives and the environment, all wrapped in religious obscurantism, and on the basis of hypocritical promises of freedom and equality."[443]

So how do progressives rewrite history and then transmit that revisionist perspective to the masses? They wage cultural war from government pedestals (as outlined by Obama's pro-homosexual agenda above), through their dominance of news and entertainment media, within our educational establishment, and through globalist controlled major corporations.

Of course, progressives are an intolerant cabal; just think about Hillary Clinton's "basket of deplorables" label for Trump followers. Progressives speak their "religious" language to the masses demanding universal obedience to their elite leaders and agenda, enforced by political correctness.

We have seen this evidenced in spades, especially over the past couple of decades in regards to the progressive social agenda such as the redefinition of marriage—now defined as a relationship between two men or two women as well as the traditional one man, one woman—and the politically correct branding of any dissent to such an understanding as culpable psychopathology called "homophobia," punishable by a number of official sanctions such as fines. More recently, progressives started pushing a transsexual agenda suggesting that, as Codevilla wrote, "not until 2015–16 did it occur to anyone that requiring persons with male personal plumbing to use public bathrooms reserved for men was a sign of the same pathology."[444]

Consider how progressives are using "cultural hegemony"—through the mechanism of political correctness—to transform society through two key institutions (education and media), thus adding the third leg of the power center stool to the progressives' camp.

Progressive cultural hegemony through education

Coexistence on this tightly knit earth should be viewed as an existence not only without wars…but also without [the government] telling us how to live, what to say, what to think, what to know, and what not to know.
—Aleksandra Solzhenitsyn, from a speech given September 11, 1973[445]

Solzhenitsyn's statement is antithetical to the progressive who believes he knows best for humanity and long ago started to make inroads into the institution of education to drive home his radical agenda. Today, our government-run educational establishment propagandizes our children from kindergarten through the best universities on the progressive's politically correct way to live, speak, think, and understand, and what to do with their lives.

Progressive intrusion into education has been unimpressive on the surface and totally counterproductive for those concerned about truth. Although per-pupil federal expenditures on education tripled over the past half century (now at $156,000 per student) with dozens of federal education programs, reading proficiency remains unchanged since the early 1970s, and mathematics achievement is no better. Further, graduation rates for disadvantaged children remain stagnate as well.[446]

Government-run educational institutions deserve their bad reputation. They are no better than our dysfunctional, big-government agencies in Washington. So, what in fact does big-government education do?

Big-government education "legally enforce[s] diluting of parental authority over the raising of children, with [read "progressive"] intellectual and moral lessons, goals and methods regulated by the government," according to Daren Jonescu in his book, *The Case Against Public Education.* As if that doesn't sound bad enough, government-run schools are "under the supervision of various levels of government agents trained in accordance with government [progressivism ala John Dewey] standards to represent and administer [progressive] government policy regarding the proper rank-ordering of society, the attitudes and skills deemed by the government to be most socially useful, and pre-emptive extinguishing or subduing of beliefs, attitudes, and behavior judged to be undesirable to the government for any reasons."[447]

That sounds pretty draconian, and besides, the system weakens the family and familial associations in favor of "cultivating alternative attachments to government officers, and to the artificial, government-designed social order of the school," according to Joenscu.[448] In other words, the government educational establishment generally succeeds at remolding society's culture to fit its progressive agenda.

No doubt government education institutions are very powerful agents of cultural change. They employ Gramsci's concept of "cultural hegemony" by re-educating our children to the progressive agenda, as outlined above. For example, government schools often indoctrinate our children that white people are inherently evil simply because of the color of their skin. Of course, most schools are more nuanced, suggesting that society's problem is so-called "white privilege" or "systemic racism" to persuade children to believe in "white guilt."

Feminism is a cultural issue pushed by progressive public schools, another weapon in their arsenal to attack mostly white men, who are also labeled the biggest oppressors in history and women are victims of patriarchy. Further, those same progressive revisionists mock and attack traditional-thinking mothers who remain home to raise their children.

Many feminists join ranks with the radical homosexual movement to work against the traditional family unit and intolerantly attack those who hold a faith-based view of homosexual behavior. They have no patience for those who disagree regarding accepting homosexuality as the moral equivalent to heterosexuality.

These problems are especially evident at so-called institutions of higher education (read "colleges and universities") that seethe with progressive politically correct intolerance.

Emory University students were upset when someone chalked "Trump 2016" on sidewalks. Evidently, those snowflakes felt "fear" and "pain," and they demanded the university's administration "decry the support for this fascist, racist candidate [Trump]." Another Emory student complained to the school paper: "I'm supposed to feel comfortable and safe (here). But this man [Trump] is being supported by students on our campus and our administration shows that they, by their silence, support it [him] as well.... I don't deserve to feel afraid at my school."[449]

James Wagner, Emory's president, promised to identify and discipline the offending sidewalk chalk-writing author(s). The school paper reported that Wagner promised "the University will review footage 'up by the hospital [from] security cameras' to identify those who made the chalkings." Wagner also told the protesters "that if they're students, they will go through the conduct violation process, while if they are from outside of the University, trespassing charges will be pressed."[450]

Similarly fragile, politically correct university students and spineless administrators are at the University of Pennsylvania as well. There, more snowflakes demanded, according to NBC News, that the university's English department remove a portrait of William Shakespeare (the single most important figure in the formation of the modern English language) and replace it with a photograph of Audre Lorde, a "self-described black lesbian, mother, warrior, poet." That change would affirm, according to dissenting snowflakes, the university's "commitment to a more inclusive mission for the English department."[451]

Ignorance and political correctness are close cousins among today's progressives, a phenomenon infecting even high schools. Public schools in Accomack County, Virginia, removed classics from libraries and classrooms after a parent complained the volumes contained racial slurs.

Yes, Mark Twain's *The Adventures of Huckleberry Finn* and Harper Lee's *To Kill a Mockingbird* were removed even though they in fact expose racism.[452]

Unfortunately, progressive snowflakery isn't confined to America. Evidently, students at London University demanded that figures such as Plato, Immanuel Kant, and Rene Descartes be removed from philosophy curriculum because they represent "the structural and epistemological legacy of colonialism."[453]

Sir Anthony Seldon, the vice-chancellor for Buckingham University, reacted to the snowflakes demand by stating there's a "real danger political correctness is getting out of control."[454]

Evidently, historical facts hurt modern sensibilities, but such political correctness advances the progressive agenda to homogenize and weaken the next generation. They will evidently become non-thinking boobs vulnerable to manipulation by the progressive elite.

Another institution co-opted and crippled by progressives is the news and entertainment media.

Progressive cultural hegemony through the media

> The conscious and intelligent manipulation of the organized habits and opinions of the masses is an important element in democratic society. Those who manipulate this unseen mechanism of society constitute an invisible government which is the true ruling power of our country.
> —Edward Bernays, from his book, *Propaganda*[455]

Certainly Edward Bernays, a twentieth-century Austrian-American pioneer in the field of public relations and propaganda, understood the influence of mass media outlets to promote the progressive agenda. Not surprisingly, Donald Trump also understood the media's progressive agenda during the 2016 presidential campaign and made that an issue.

President Trump made the so-called mainstream media a story during the 2016 presidential campaign by exposing them for what they really are: liars, cheaters, crooks, and agents of the progressive elite. Trump exposed them for consistently failing to objectively report on the campaign demonstrating a clear bias against him.

Reporting bias is an extremely powerful weapon under the thumb of the progressive-controlled media. Many of these outlets, exposed earlier in this volume, are a propaganda arm for the left and as a result create a cultural bias that promotes the progressive agenda. That bias was especially evident on virtually every major topic in the 2016 campaign and especially regarding the topic of Trump's views on immigration such as the building of a wall on our southern border, deporting illegals, and expecting English as the national language. Those who disagreed with the progressive anti-Trump media bias were openly labeled bigots and xenophobic. Remember what Hillary Clinton said about Trump supporters?

Ms. Clinton, the Democratic presidential nominee at the time, described Trump's supporters as "a basket of deplorables." She continued, "Right? Racist, sexist, homophobic, xenophobic, Islamaphobic, you name it."[456]

The power of the media is widely understood, which makes it a powerful cultural tool. But media alone, thanks to modern technology, has created the possibility of granting the progressives' third leg of their power center goal, creating a global culture.

There are two media-related mechanisms for reaching that goal: technology and the message.

The technology piece is pretty evident today. The Internet, satellites, cable television, social media (Facebook, Instagram, Twitter, and more) collectively sweep away most cultural boundaries. They open up new audiences for global news and entertainment companies to shape perceptions and by association homogenize culture. The result is "televisual globalization is not only the uninformization of culture…but also the total obliteration of culture," according to Bianca-Marina Mitu, who wrote for the journal *Economics, Management, and Financial Markets*.[457]

The other media mechanism is a combination of programming content and the creation of celebrities who promote the progressive agenda.

The mass media's programming influence is indisputable and frankly frightening. It is controlled by too few outlets and, due to editorial control it has created a socially engineered construct, or, as some would state, a psychological prison of a different reality Like the co-opted educational system, the media more often than not distorts reality and does so on a massive scale, further homogenizing culture to the progressives' applause.

Entertainment media (Hollywood) outlets create programming that aims to change perceptions about groups of people and concepts. Certainly, the global view about the acceptability of homosexuality is a case in point. Public attitudes about the acceptability of that lifestyle changed by design because media outlets presented a consistently positive image through outlets so that today there is a growing positive view of the lifestyle, even though the defining behavior associated with homosexuals remains the same.

Another aspect of the media's manipulation is how some people idolize entertainment media celebrities; in some cases, it's an obsession. Too often, celebrities become bigger than life in spite of real lives that are truly train wrecks.

Naturally, the politicians recognize the value of celebrity endorsements, especially for liberal Democrats who swoon for television and movie personality endorsements. Some celebrities have become especially politically active by using their status to influence politics and push the progressive agenda.

Politically based television shows like *The View* and *The Daily Show with Jon Stewart* are venues used by politicians to tap into celebrity endorsements. Of course, as astute observers realize, some of the content discussed on such shows are either fact-free or more often than not totally based on the celebrity's uninformed opinions.

Fact or opinion, most politically active celebrities are out in force pushing the progressive, globalist agenda. For example, actor George

Lopez used his celebrity status to incorrectly advance the idea during the 2016 campaign that Mr. Trump would deport Mexicans born in this country, a view not supported by the U.S. Constitution, which forbids deportation of anyone who is a U.S. citizen—nor is it a position Trump espoused.[458]

Actress Whoopi Goldberg consistently uses her appearances on *The View* to push a progressive Democratic Party agenda. One of her favorite distortions is that pro-life President Trump will reverse Roe vs. Wade, stopping a woman's ability to get an abortion. Of course, that so-called right to choose is an interpretation of the U.S. Constitution approved by the U.S. Supreme Court in 1973 that allows women to have an abortion. Trump can't strike down Roe vs. Wade, but he can appoint new Supreme Court justices, which might in the future reverse that sad, immoral decision.

There are other fact-free celebrity scare tactics, such as the assertion that Trump will separate blacks and whites, bringing back slavery. The media and politicians like former President Obama fan the race-relations issue, pushing itback to earlier years when race-based discrimination was truly a significant topic.

The progressive Democrats have successfully played the race card to control black Americans. History shows the Democrats reaching back to the American Civil War were the instigators and protectors of slavery, yet they have managed to obscure the facts and promote themselves as the defenders of the poor blacks who need a government handout. It is control, pure and simple.

CONCLUSION

This chapter makes the case that globalists are succeeding at capturing three critical power centers: economic, political, and cultural. Once they reach that goal, the inevitable next step is the imposition of one-world government.

CHAPTER ELEVEN

Globalism v. Religion

Spiritual Warfare and Prophetic End Times

Everyone chooses a side in the ongoing war between globalism and religion. Most people choose sides by default because they have no clue—much less care—that there is such a war. Meanwhile, globalists are so self-absorbed and arrogant that they discount most of us as expendable peons and, like good Marxists, these totalitarian progressives see our religions as an obstacle in their drive to transform the global society to their liking. Of course, the globalists elite don't understand that they are being spiritually manipulated as part of a grand scheme by the evil forces of the unseen realm that will ultimately usher in the prophetic end times.

In this chapter, we will explore the globalists' view of religion and the challenges people of most faiths pose for them. We will then explore a biblical view of globalism, the evidence of spiritual warfare motivating the warring parties, and how that conflict is setting the stage for the prophetic end times.

GLOBALISTS' VIEW OF RELIGION
AND THEIR CHALLENGES

Imagine there's no countries. It isn't hard to do. Nothing to kill
or die for. And no religion, too.
—John Lennon song, "Imagine," 1971

John Lennon, the former Beatle, commented on his song, "Imagine,"
stating, "'Imagine that there was no more religion, no more country, no
more politics,' is virtually the communist manifesto, even though I'm
not particularly a communist and I do not belong to any movement."[459]
He didn't openly embrace communism, but his words put a smile on
the faces of Marxists who, like most globalists, totally reject religion.
Unfortunately for them, religion and especially evangelical Christianity
will prove to be the globalists' worst nightmare.

The globalists aim to either marginalize or replace religion with their
own version of religious secularism. These secularists promise a utopian
world with all men paying tribute to the globalists elite, whom they hope
will rule their future one-world government. The unified globalist future
world has no borders, as Wallace Henley, associate pastor at Second Baptist
Church in Houston, Texas, explains: "Because within borders a particular
civilization can choose to uphold those principles that we [as Christians]
believe are at the heart of what makes a civilization a civilization."[460]

The globalists rightly understand that nation-states without borders, something President Obama and former Secretary of State Hillary
Clinton sought, advance the globalist agenda toward their one-world
government goal. That means for the globalist that "the only alternative
to [a nation without borders]…is a global governance scenario, which is
terrifying," Henley cautioned.[461]

William "Jerry" Boykin, a retired U.S. Army lieutenant general and
current executive vice president for the Washington, D.C.-based Family
Research Council, believes the globalist movement is not just progressive
in its philosophy, but is really Marxist at its core. Boykin also believes

globalist leaders like billionaire George Soros fund Marxist-like activities of groups such as Black Lives Matter whose mission is to destroy America. Part of their effort is focused directly on religion and especially Christianity, which rejects the globalist agenda.[462]

The course of least resistance for the globalist cabal is to co-opt religion by relativizing it, or in other words, by watering it down to make religion just one of many influencers in our multicultural society. General Boykin says the globalists are already at work co-opting, diluting religion by trying to persuade religious leaders to accept freedom of worship rather than freedom of religion. There is a major distinction between the two. If religious leaders accept freedom of worship over freedom of religion, the faith community will have no moral authority and therefore won't be able to influence anything in the public discourse. But there is a problem with this strategy[463].

Most religious leaders want nothing to do with globalism because the movement's progressive philosophy for society leads to secularization, which is antithetical to most faiths. That tension explains the ongoing battle between secular globalists and religious people across the world.

Scholar Bruce Lawrence, a humanities professor of religion at Duke University, explains that globalist-religious tension. Lawrence states that tension is evident thanks to a sharp rise in religious activism he labels "fundamentalism" manifested by revolt "against the secular ideology that often accompanies modern society."[464]

Mark Juergensmeyer, a professor of sociology at the University of California, echoes Lawrence's view in his book *Global Rebellion*. Globalization and religious people are natural enemies no matter the religion and geographical setting, according to Juergensmeyer. This adversarial relationship presents a significant challenge, especially for the globalists who seek to transform global society. In fact, their struggle represents a different interpretation of a commonly understood concept, antimodernism or fundamentalism—"a religious revolt against the secular ideology that often accompanies modern society" associated with the differences between religious cultures.[465]

Most readers have likely heard about Harvard Professor Samuel Huntington's famous "clash of civilization" thesis, which puts flesh on the globalist-religion struggle. Typically, this thesis is famously used to juxtapose Islam and Christianity and/or Western culture. However, when put in the context of globalism versus religion, the thesis becomes a "clash" between secularization and almost all religions. Let me illustrate.

The pre-Islamic revolutionary Iranian leader Ayatollah Ruhollah Khomeini warned his followers about secularization's attack on religion. He referred to this attack as the "West-Toxification" or "WestOmani." That was Khomeini's way of describing the unacceptable influence of Western secularism on Islamic society. The ayatollah said the enforcement of "WestOmania" against Islamic people started in the eighth century and continued up to the time of the 1979 Islamic Revolution. Khomeini also charged "WestOmania" for converting the last of the twentieth century's Iranian shahs, Mohammad Reza Pahlavi, with the help of the Central Intelligence Agency, into a secular Western figure that Islamists rejected.[466]

Pause for a second to consider a sidebar issue. It is noteworthy and not a mistake that the shah of Iran was rescued just prior to the 1979 Iranian Revolution by David Rockefeller, the elite globalist, who convinced his fellow CFR member and then-President Carter to grant exile to the Iranian shah under the guise of medical treatment. In reality, the rescue was to save him from the coming religious revolution, which appears to erupt because of "WestOmania."

Khomeini's rejection of "WestOmania" is an all-too-common complaint among religious leaders worldwide. After all, with very few exceptions, religious leaders attribute their society's moral decline to secularist (read "Western") influences and many, in fact, believe secularism is sinister if not outright demonic.[467]

Labeling secularism as sinister and/or demonic may explain why some religionists embrace radicalism—as Lawrence suggested above—to defend their faith. A study that considered a database of 462 suicide terrorists demonstrates secular government's lack of knowledge of religion and its powerful influence on the faithful.[468]

The Chicago Project on Suicide Terrorism Study found a very different motivation for suicide bombers than what is commonly heard from secular governments. Secularists tend to profile suicide bombers as "mainly poor, uneducated, immature religious zealots or social losers." The study found a radically different profile. Most suicide bombers, according to the Chicago study, harbored "the sense that their territory or culture has been invaded by an alien [secular] power that cannot be overthrown."[469]

The bomber's "alien power" reference is secularism, which is radically contrary to the governance of a state under the watchful eye of a religion, whether Christianity as in the West or Islam in the Middle East. Religion-based states exposed to secularist "aliens" more often than not generate radical responses from fundamentalists such as suicide bombers. To a certain extent, this view explains the emergence of suicide bomber attacks in places where Western forces are fighting Islamists like in Iraq and Afghanistan.

Obviously, the globalist's ignorance about the influence of religion is a major problem and stands between him and his control of the global society. It is especially noteworthy that the globalist's cabal of academic and government elite dismisses religion as an important societal influencer, a view traceable to the Greek historian and general Thucydides (460–400 BC).

Thucydides is known as the father of the school of political realism, which generally ignores/rejects the role of religion in public affairs and especially in the international relations arena. He viewed religion solely as a private affair of the citizens, not as most modern sociologists understand religion to be at the core of every culture. After all, religion defines the nature of good and evil as well as provides insight into life after death, an age-old quest for all mankind.

Secular globalization offers no such insight to mankind, nor does it provide hope. Rather, globalists seek to replace religion with an anything-goes, secular value system. How might this be accomplished and to what end?

The globalists want to defang religion, a view posited by Thomas McFaul in *The Futurist*. McFaul proposed the outcome of the ongoing globalist-versus-religion war might be what he labels "Becoming One Family," translated: All faith (religious) groups abandon orthodox views to hold hands and sing Kumbaya. After all, homogenizing "global culture" will require significant tempering of orthodox religious views, an unlikely outcome but one pressed by globalists.

Religion also plays a significant psychological role that secularists shouldn't ignore. Keep in mind that "religion," which comes from the Latin *religare*, means "to bind together again that which was once bound but has since been torn apart or broken." Religion thus provides a sense of psychological well-being, which must be replaced with something that supports the globalists' aim. That is a tall if not impossible order.

Of course, globalists would like to ignore religion, but that would be a fatal mistake as well. Scholar Timothy Shah, associate director of the Religious Freedom Project at the Berkeley Center for Religion, Peace, and World Affairs, asserts: "Religion has become one of the most influential factors in world affairs in the last generation but remains one of the least examined factors in the professional study and practice of world affairs."[470]

Why are globalists so blind to religion's influence? That blindness might be attributable to their rigid universal adherence to the "secularization thesis," which holds to the view "that as the world modernizes, religion will, in Marx's famous phrase about the state, 'wither away'—in contemporary social science, including international relations." Sorry globalists. Religion is not fading and, in fact, as Shah said, it is a significant source of international problems and will fight your modernization efforts.

Most globalists naively and rigidly subscribe to the "secularization thesis" in spite of contrary evidence. After all, Rodney Stark, a professor of sociology and of comparative religion at the University of Washington, grants globalists a false promise "that modernization is the causal engine dragging the gods into retirement." No, Professor Stark, the "gods" of religion are not abandoning the fight for the hearts of man.[471]

Globalists like Stark are likely for the time being going to continue to blindly push their "secularization thesis," which embraces three misinformed aims intended to marginalize religion's influence on society and therefore provide secular globalism an opening. First, there is the false claim that there is an increasing distinction between the religious and secular realms. Second, religious belief becomes most appropriately consigned to the private sphere; and finally, the privatization of religion is indicative of liberal democracy.

So far, there is no evidence of those three aims diminishing religion's global influence. In fact, Harvard Professor Samuel Huntington believes the products of globalization such as economic modernization are in fact weakening the nation-tate, a globalist agenda item. But, according to Huntington, the void left by the weakened nation-state is being filled by world religions "often in the form of movements that are labeled fundamentalist." That's a significant setback for the secular globalists, who must capture global culture in order to reach their one-world government goal.[472]

A more distressing aspect of the rise of religion's influence for the globalists is the growing threat of violence in the name of faith. Globalists pushing their secularist agenda in a world of growing religious fundamentalism will likely confront violence. In fact, pressing the secularist agenda typically ends badly. Theologian William Cavanaugh argues that the "so-called wars of religion appear as wars fought by state-building elites [globalists] for the purpose of consolidating their power over the church and other rivals."[473]

It appears that the "secularization thesis" is not holding up against religion. Further, the world is not becoming less religious, which is a serious problem for globalists. In other words, the world is becoming more, rather than less, religious. The most striking evidence for this view is that those claiming to be "nonreligious" or "atheists" are growing at the slowest rate of all, well below the rate of population growth.[474]

News that the world is becoming more religious is also bad for the globalists' secular agenda, because "since 1823 the general trend has been toward more wars involving different religious actors on either side." That view is supported by a study that examined a long list of wars over the past two centuries that identified the casus belli of the conflicts.[475]

Globalists are challenged by a very tenacious opponent, religion. They must defeat, neutralize religion's influence by secularizing society in order to ever expect to control the global society. However, there is evidence that religion is growing in its influence, and it is also becoming part of the reason for more and widespread violence.

BIBLICAL VIEW OF GLOBALISM

Globalism is a secular humanistic religion that is antithetical to a Christian worldview. Globalists push a global value system that is radically different from a Christian value system, a view expressed by Pastor Henley, a former high-level official in the Nixon White House.

Pastor Henley said there is an anti-Christ spirit at work in the secular world that opposes the kingdom of Christ. "The Kingdom of the Lord Jesus Christ is the highest form of civilization," Henley explained. "The anti-civilization represented by anti-Christ is the opposite of that. So if the kingdom of Christ is righteousness, the anti-civilization is evil and injustice. If the kingdom of Christ is peace, the kingdom of anti-Christ is conflict. If the kingdom of Christ is joy in the Holy Spirit, anti-civilization is misery."[476]

The apostle Paul records in Romans 1 much of the globalists' social agenda that evidences anti-God, evil thoughts and the depravity of the secular world. Consider the following verses from Romans 1:18–25 (KJV) that evidence man's consuming drive to pull away from God and create his own global order.

For the wrath of God is revealed from heaven against all ungodliness and unrighteousness of men, who hold the truth in unrighteousness; Because that which may be known of God is manifest in them; for God hath shewed it unto them. For the invisible things of him from the creation of the world are clearly seen, being understood by the things that are made, even his eternal power and Godhead; so that they are without excuse: Because that, when they knew God, they glorified him not as God, neither were thankful; but became vain in their imaginations, and their foolish heart was darkened. Professing themselves to be wise, they became fools, And changed the glory of the uncorruptible God into an image made like to corruptible man, and to birds, and four-footed beasts, and creeping things. Wherefore God also gave them up to uncleanness through the lusts of their own hearts, to dishonor their own bodies between themselves: Who changed the truth of God into a lie, and worshipped and served the creature more than the Creator, who is blessed forever. Amen.

These verses describe the globalists to a "T"—ungodly, unrighteous, vain, self-serving, and dark, fools, unclean, lustful, dishonoring, liars, serving the creature. These words describe the globalists identified in prior chapters: Rockefeller, Clinton, Soros, and the rest of their elitist cabal.

Globalists seek a boundary-free world, but God said it is best that man have nations with boundaries. Acts 17:26–27 (NIV) states:

From one man he made all the nations, that they should inhabit the whole earth; and he marked out their appointed times in history and the boundaries of their lands. [27] God did this so that they would seek him and perhaps reach out for him and find him, though he is not far from any one of us.

Those of us who worship the true God of the Bible are a serious hindrance to secular globalists, who despise religionists and especially evangelical Christians. They hate us and the One we represent. "We are called [by globalists] narrow, hateful, bigoted, and anti-progressive moralists," according to Jan Larue, a senior legal analyst for the American Civil Rights Union. She continued, "We are a reminder to secular globalists that God is sovereign, not man."[477]

Empire building through military conquest is one form of globalism seen in God's Word as well. The Old Testament explains that the Assyrians were bent on world conquest and eventually did control vast swaths of the Middle East. In fact, God used these brutal warriors to punish and exile the ten northern tribes of Israel, as evidenced in 2 Kings 17.

The best known Biblical example of globalization is the attempt to construct the Tower of Babel (Genesis 9:1). Once again, as outlined earlier, Noah's great-grandson, King Nimrod (translated "the rebel") was perhaps the first globalist. God responded to Nimrod's globalist ambitions to build a tower by confusing their languages and forcing the people to scatter (Genesis 11:8–9).

Daniel 2 evidences other globalization attempts that were revealed to King Nebuchadnezzar in a dream. Daniel interpreted the king's dream, which featured a huge statute of a man. Its head was "made of pure gold, its chest and arms of silver, its belly and thighs of bronze, its legs of iron, its feet partly of iron and partly of baked clay" (Daniel 2:32–33, NIV). The Scripture goes on to explain that a rock cut "not by human hands" (Daniel 2:34, NIV) hit the foot of the statue, and the whole edifice "became like chaff on a threshing floor," while the rock "became a huge mountain and filled the world earth" (Daniel 2:35, NIV).

Daniel's interpretation, thanks to a revelation from God, was that each major feature of the destroyed statue represented a future kingdom that would fall: Babylonian, Persian, Greek and the Roman empires. The fifth and final empire to fall has yet to rise, and that kingdom is likely the product of the modern globalization movement.

That fifth and final globalist empire will be a true one-world government, ruled by the Antichrist, the beast, and the lawless one (Revelation 13:4). The Antichrist will have "authority over every tribe, people, language and nation," the globalists' aim. He will control all financial transactions (Revelation 13:17) and demand religious observance (Revelation 13:8), whereby he is the object of his secularist worship.

It is clear in the Bible that man's many past efforts to globalize resulted in ungodly empires, and that will be true of the current elitist efforts to globalize, as we shall see in the next section.

Of course, there is a globalization plan Christians will celebrate: the return of Jesus Christ (Revelation 19–20). He will rule the nations with righteousness and truth (Isaiah 11:3–5). Amen!

SPIRITUAL WARFARE: GLOBALISTS VERSUS CHRISTIANS

Any movement away from God's prescription for living on this planet is by definition demonic, which is manifested in the spiritual realm that drives and governs the physical, sin-fallen world.

The present globalist-versus-Christian war is taking place in both the seen and unseen (spiritual) realms, which are traceable to the beginning of mankind, according to theologian Michael Heiser, author of *The Unseen Realm.* The original Edenic design outlined in Genesis failed due to man's sin and was replaced by a new family from Abraham (Deuteronomy 32:8–9). That resulted in the disinherited nations being put under the authority of lesser gods, divine sons of God who became corrupted, thus resulting in the long spiritual war that continues today between Yahweh (the God of the Bible) and the fallen gods, demons.[478]

Heiser speculates that these fallen gods (demons) wage war today as disembodied spirits of Nephilim mostly guided by the chief liar, Satan. If we had spiritual eyes, Heiser wrote, we would see our world as mostly darkness peppered with lights of Yahweh's (God's) presence in the form of believers scattered across the globe, and we would see clearly that globalism and its followers are truly demonic.[479]

This view of the spiritual battleground is shared by Pastor Jim Garlow, of the Skyline Church in San Diego, who said, "It [globalism] is spiritual and demonic at its core. Few—very few—understand this. Do your homework on this one. Think 'principalities and powers.'" Even people of other faiths see the demonic aspect of the current war.[480]

The apostle Paul, who warned us in Romans 1 earlier in this chapter, also warns us about the current spiritual warfare in Ephesians 6:10–17 (NIV):

> Finally, be strong in the Lord and in his mighty power. Put on the full armor of God, so that you can take your stand against the devil's schemes. For our struggle is not against flesh and blood, but against the rulers, against the authorities, against the powers of this dark world and against the spiritual forces of evil in the heavenly realms. Therefore put on the full armor of God, so that when the day of evil comes, you may be able to stand your ground, and after you have done everything, to stand. Stand firm then, with the belt of truth buckled around your waist, with the breastplate of righteousness in place, and with your feet fitted with the readiness that comes from the gospel of peace. In addition to all this, take up the shield of faith, with which you can extinguish all the flaming arrows of the evil one. Take the helmet of salvation and the sword of the Spirit, which is the word of God.

There is no doubt about the call to arms in this spiritual battle. Paul calls us to suit up—armor, belt, helmet, shield, and sword—to struggle against "spiritual forces of evil in the heavenly realms." We are to stand firm "in His mighty power."

Even non-Christians understand the spiritual stakes. Professor

Jeremy Rabkin, a Jew and law professor at George Mason University, alleged that globalism is threatening: "It's almost demonic."[481] Attorney Jan Larue said much the same: "There is most definitely a spiritual and demonic component to globalization," it is "the twenty-first-century version of the tower of Babel—politically correct Babel. Satan has always sought worship and dominion."[482]

General Boykin comes to the same conclusion: "This globalization will not have a good ending. I believe globalization is demonic because what it does is rob us of our constitutional freedoms our founders provided us. Those freedoms will not be provided under a global government."[483]

Pastor Henley calls out "philosophical globalism" because it pushes a shared secular (anti-Christian) value system and global governance. "This is what really got my attention. In the 1990s the United Nations began a push for global shared values," he said. He continued, stating that under such a regime, "nations would be forced into it, into a very secular humanistic set of ethics." Then he cautioned that globalism goes much deeper than a set of humanistic ethics and values:[484]

"As I moved deeper in my study of it [globalization], into the spiritual dynamics of nations, I became very interested in this and so I realized in studying Genesis that the fundamental temptation in the Garden of Eden was the temptation of power and for humans to take power over themselves," Henley said. "This is what Saint John calls the anti-Christ spirit, which he said was at work in the world even in his day."

There is such a concept, according to Henley, known as spiritual globalism, which co-opts the world's major religions harnessing them to the globalist agenda of promoting man rather than God. This agenda is about power. Henley asked, "Who is going to have power over the whole of the world?" to which he added, "And the only way you can have that kind of power is to make sure it is a unit that can be seized instead of a world where there are value systems [like Christian values] that hold out and resist."[485]

That is why globalists seek to destroy civilization as we know it, as

Henley explained. The anti-Christ spirit seeks to oppose the kingdom of God and impose itself in the place of Christ on the throne of the whole world.

This evil power struggle is not just evident to those of faith but also to some in the secular world. Zero Hedge, a popular business blog, examined the issue and concluded that "globalists are in fact evil." The blog writers continued, "The globalists have basically constructed a festering belief system around everything that is contrary to our moral compass." Then the authors elaborated on the globalists' association with occultism, luciferianism, and moral relativism.[486]

Zero Hedge claims that occultism isn't necessarily "evil," the term only means "secret knowledge." President John F. Kennedy warned of secret societies (think CFR and Trilateral Commission) and secret proceedings that withheld "valuable knowledge from the masses as a means to influence behavior and control the direction of society." We saw that behavior in our examination of secret societies in a prior chapter.

The problem with occultism, according to Zero Hedge, is that "occult knowledge, secret knowledge, is driven by the selfish desire of one group [globalist elite] to maintain a sense of dominance over another. Is it evil to withhold knowledge that could save lives for the sake of self-elevation? I would say absolutely."

Zero Hedge considers the nexus between globalism and luciferianism. "Do globalists really believe in a devil with a pitchfork and hooves and horns? I really don't know," admit the authors. But they continued, "What I do know is that many of them believe in the ideas behind the mythology of the figure" such as Saul Alinsky, Clinton's idol, who dedicated his book, *Rules for Radicals,* to Lucifer.

"The Lucifer mythology is one of rebellion, a rebellion against the Christian God," writes Zero Hedge. Luciferians are rebelling against the restrictions put in place by God and instead they favor self-esteem as they seek "their own 'godhood.'" A world controlled by those with such beliefs "will suffer in the scorched path of [globalist] elites seeking to revolt against inherent moral and natural boundaries as they role play in an ignorant daydream of satanic hero worship, and this is without a doubt evil."

Finally, Zero Hedge paints globalists as moral relativists, a concept addressed earlier in this volume as well. "Moral relativism is the act of rationalizing a destructive or evil process by claiming that a positive end result or intention washes away responsibility," according to the authors. The rub, according to Zero Hedge, is "globalists could not care less about the consequences of their actions to others [sound familiar?], but they do feel the need to justify those actions in a way that people will embrace." So what do globalists do? They spout propaganda based on the concept of moral relativism and "the lie that good is only about perception while evil is a 'gray area,' or illusion."

Zero Hedge's solution calls for confronting "the organized evil of the globalist cabal," which is pretty sobering. They are highly critical of those who excuse globalists as "misunderstood" or "not important." Rather, they call for "the eradication of the globalists."

Globalism has demonic aspects and some of its elites are vessels for waging spiritual war in the physical realm while those forces of evil wage a war in the unseen realm, which only those with spiritual insights can even imagine.

Might this spiritual war usher in the prophetic end times?

Author and speaker for raptureready.com, Terry James, told me:

We are well into the "end times" and globalization is at the heart of all the rebellion today. In fact, Satan is furious because God has slowed the process that was going at full throttle, that is, until the 2016 presidential election. That process isn't stopped, but it has been throttled back a bit. We see the insanity of those who are what God calls "rebellious earth dwellers." They are driven to lunacy because they don't want their debased way of living evidenced as outlined in Romans 1—"all ungodliness and unrighteousness of men"—interfered with by those who would "impose their morality" on them.[487]

Discerning Christians see the indicators of the end times cascading all about us, but only God knows whether in fact globalization is the fifth and final empire of Daniel 2 and the spiritual warfare so evident today is leading to the prophetic end times.

Jan Larue volunteered: "It [globalism] may be the catalyst [ushering in the end times]." She quoted 1 John 5:19–20 as evidence:

> Dear children, this is the last hour; and as you have heard that the anti-Christ is coming, even now many anti-christs have come. This is how we know it is the last hour. They went out from us, but they did not really belong to us. For if they had belonged to us, they would have remained with us; but their going showed that none of them belonged to us.[488]

General Boykin also believes the contemporary globalist movement is pushing toward a one-world government led by the Antichrist. The general believes either the United Nations or a like-minded global seat of international government could actually become a reality under at least two believable scenarios.[489]

The United Nations or a similar entity could become the global seat of government if there is a global economic meltdown or a nuclear exchange. Both would be devastating, and under either circumstance, people would eagerly surrender their sovereignty for the next meal, surmised the general. Either scenario could be the one prophesied in Revelation 4–6, the final confrontation between Yahweh and His believers and the powers of darkness, which results in the emergence of a one-world government led by the Antichrist, the beast, and the lawless one (2 Thessalonians 2:8).

There is yet another possibility that initially may seem strange, but on reflection makes sense. But first we must understand more truth about the globalist cabal, especially those co-opted for religious purposes.

Carl Teichrib, a Canadian Christian researcher, travels the world visiting globalist venues to better understand the "enemy." For example,

Teichrib has visited many globalist events to learn about their one-world government views, their desire for a global "king" who rules the world through one global currency, a unified world religion, and their elusive one-world government.[490]

Mr. Teichrib described to me the bizarre scene at the 2015 Parliament of the World's Religions that took place at the Salt Palace, Salt Lake City, Utah. It was a gathering of some ten thousand religious leaders representing fifty faiths and spiritual movements who converged around the official theme, "Reclaiming the Heart of Our Humanity: Working Together for a World of Compassion, Peace, Justice, and Sustainability."[491]

The five-day assembly, October 15–19, opened with a song that echoed across the plenary hall and set the tone for the globalist assembly of religious leaders: "Remember who you are; Goddess, Mother, Shakti of this Earth," sang Hindu author Vandana Shiva. The audience responded: "Goddess, Mother, Shakti of this Earth."[492]

Globalist speakers included Karenna Gore, the daughter of climate alarmist former Vice President Al Gore, and Brian McLaren, a leading figure in the emerging church movement. McLaren said religions must organize for the "common good" to create a "global, passionate, dynamic movement of contemplative activists to heal the world and protect all living things." Pope Francis even provided a video that called for global action to "solve the climate crisis."[493]

The assembly included numerous examples of efforts to unify faith and spiritual communities around the "common good." For example, the Federation of Zoroastrian Associations of North America presented a workshop to create a "Religious Arm of the United Nations" to provide a global moral and spiritual guide.[494]

Teichrib observed that even though the religious globalists at the parliament shared a central aim—global, unified, spiritual movement— they came to the event with very diverse agendas and in the end failed to reach agreement on much of anything. They just could not get along—a common problem, according to Teichrib, which he observes at every one of these globalist conferences.

Why can't they get along, and why does that matter? Well, globalist leaders—religious, corporate, academic, nongovernment groups, government—typically have giant egos, and as a result of their pride and arrogance, they seldom reach consensus on important issues. That failure makes it highly unlikely they will ever produce a single, governing global entity. That may sound like good news, but it contradicts God's prophetic Word, which clearly states there is ultimately to be a global order under one dictator, the man of sin, and the future Antichrist.

Since there can never be harmony on a worldwide scale that will bring order like that indicated in Revelation 13:16–18, how will the Antichrist's regime ever come to fulfillment? Terry James said when he was "thinking on such things, I was struck with the realization—upon reading an article by Wilfred Hahn, a global economist/strategist and former head of a large global investment company—that globalism is, itself, a *non sequitur*, a nonstarter."[495]

Hahn, an expert on global economic matters whose articles appear on Rapture Ready, wrote the following, quoting Moisés Naím, the well-known former editor-in-chief of *Foreign Policy* magazine and former executive director of the World Bank:

> When was the last time you heard that a large number of countries agreed to a major international accord on a pressing issue? Not in more than a decade.... These failures represent not only the perpetual lack of international consensus, but also a flawed obsession with multilateralism as the panacea for all the world's ills. It has become far too dangerous to continue to rely on large-scale multilateral negotiations that stopped yielding results almost two decades ago. So what is to be done? To start, let's forget about trying to get the planet's nearly two hundred countries to agree. We need to abandon that fool's errand in favor of a new idea: minilateralism. By minilateralism, I mean a smarter, more targeted approach: We should bring to the table the smallest

possible number of countries needed to have the largest possible impact on solving a particular problem.[496]

"This recommended minilateralist approach seems to precisely foreshadow the global configuration that will vault Antichrist to his dictatorship and sustain his power," James said. He continued:

It will be constructed by the principalities the apostle Paul exposes as recorded in Ephesians 6:12. We see this global arrangement for the climax of history just prior to Christ's return in the following scriptural passage: "And the ten horns which thou saw are ten kings, which have received no kingdom as yet; but receive power as kings one hour with the beast. These have one mind, and shall give their power and strength unto the beast" (Revelation 17:12–13).

Since the prideful human power wielders will never easily come to consensus on governing on a worldwide basis, the most powerful dictator ever to be upon planet earth will use his demonic force of will to wrest control from the holdouts.

Daniel wrote:

After that, in my vision at night I looked, and there before me was a fourth beast—terrifying and frightening and very powerful. It had large iron teeth; it crushed and devoured its victims and trampled underfoot whatever was left. It was different from all the former beasts, and it had ten horns. While I was thinking about the horns, there before me was another horn, a little one, which came up among them; and three of the first horns were uprooted before it. This horn had eyes like the eyes of a human being and a mouth that spoke boastfully. (Daniel 7:7–8, NIV)

James concludes:

Yes, this is a frightening scenario and it will happen. But for the believer there is great news as we see our world moving closer to the biblical end times. There is a time our King and Redeemer, Jesus Christ, will reign over the nations in righteousness and truth (Isaiah 11:3–5).[497]

That globalized Christ-kingdom is described in Isaiah 12:3–4 (NIV): "With joy you will draw water from the wells of salvation. In that day you will say: Give praise to the LORD, proclaim his name; make known among the nations what he has done, and proclaim that his name is exalted."

CONCLUSION

This chapter demonstrates that religion is a major obstacle to the globalist agenda to secularize the world's society, but could also be a major tool to achieve complete control, as Teichrib found at the religious parliament. Further, the chapter provides a biblical view of globalization and outlines evidence of the ongoing spiritual dimension of the globalist-versus-Christian war, and concludes with a possible scenario that leads the world to the biblical end times.

CAN GLOBALISTS ELITE BE STOPPED?

INTRODUCTION

The final section answers the question, "Can globalists elite be stopped?"

We begin with chapter 12, which examines recent attempts to stop the globalists elite, the lessons learned from those anti-globalist efforts, and how resistance to globalism feeds dangerous authoritarianism.

Chapter 13 demonstrates that the globalist movement is genuinely a communist cabal that rides the globalist bandwagon that promises to create a hell on earth for future earthlings. However, there is a brief opportunity to reverse the current direction.

Finally, chapter 14 outlines the Christian's responsibility in the ongoing war between the globalists elite and the Christian church, especially as events lead to the biblical end times. Our guide through this chapter is the old leader and builder, Nehemiah.

Can we make a difference or has God preordained mankind's final outcome? Yes, God has preordained the final outcome, and we can make a difference in spite of the rigid and seemingly overwhelming push by the globalist and their ally in the unseen realm.

Never forget, fellow Christian, that we are called to be about the Lord's work until He comes again. This means we sound the alarm! So, yes, we can make a difference, as our work is hopefully going to bring more into the Christian fold—even while planet earth deteriorates into chaos as we approach the end times.

CHAPTER TWELVE

Countering the Globalist Movement and Lessons

Earlier in this volume, I suggested that globalism became a major worldwide factor after the fall of the Iron Curtain in 1991. That event accelerated the free movement of capital, people, and goods across most borders. Now, decades later, many people are reacting to what globalization has wrought and whether it is good and might lead to something far worse.

Less than a decade after the end of the Cold War, anti-globalists reacted violently in places like Seattle, Washington, during the World Trade Organization meeting, which reflected some of the ills wrought by globalism. More recently (June 2016), voters in Britain made a significant statement with their decision to exit the European Union known as "Brexit," and months later, Donald Trump's surprise election was more of a shock. These reactions although significant were just the latest in a series of efforts to turn back the globalization tide.

I witnessed arguably the first nationwide anti-globalization reaction almost twenty years ago, and that effort likely set the stage for the anti-globalization populist movements now exploding across much of Europe as well as here in America.

In February 2000, I was in Vienna, Austria, to observe the globalist EU train its big guns in that tiny country and its alleged boister-
ous demagogue, Joerg Haider, the leader of the upstart Freedom Party
(Freiheitliche Partei Osterreichs). Despite having ignored the human-
rights records of many communists and former communists at the time
serving in European governments, including those of France, Italy, and
Poland, the EU bureaucrats expressed outrage at Haider.

At that time, American columnist George Will correctly described
Haider as "frequently adolescent and reptilian in a populist sort of
way."[498] Haider's anti-immigrant rhetoric and his reference to Nazi concentration camps as "punishment camps" convinced some in the then-
Clinton administration that he was Europe's next dictator.[499]

Yet the EU's indignation at the time appeared to be highly selec-
tive. *The Black Book of Communism*, then recently (1997) published in
France, documented European leftists' complicity in an international
party record that cost eighty-five million people their lives, and untold
millions more their freedom. But the EU said nothing about the red
terror or its toll.

I believed at the time that Austria's nationalistic revolution was worth
studying in depth, because Europe was facing, among other maladies,
a population implosion. European socialist governments had encouraged abortion, homosexuality, and the breakdown of marriage. As a
result, few European states were even at replacement levels for population. Consequently, the ancient states of Europe were seeing millions of
immigrants attracted to higher-paying jobs and Europe's very generous
unemployment and welfare systems.

Austria's "right" attacked those immigrants instead of focusing on
universal themes of faith, family, and freedom. Evidently, it was easier to
deplore another mosque being built in Europe's old cities than to summon the will to fill the continent's magnificent cathedrals with worshipers.

My visit to Austria was to study the political climate and cut through
the media's spin to find the truth. That fact-finding tour included
numerous interviews with ordinary Austrians as well as the nation's lead-

ing political and government leaders, to include Freedom Party leader Haider and the vice prime minister, a member of the Freedom Party.

Just prior to my arrival, Austria formed its controversial new government from a coalition of the People's Party and the Freedom Party. Immediately, the EU, as well as several non-EU countries, notably Israel, sanctioned Austria for including Haider's Freedom Party in the new government. In fact, the U.S. government recalled its ambassador for "consultations"—an act normally done only prior to war. Then Secretary of State Madeleine Albright made harsh comments about Austria's new government. The U.S. Congress considered whether to condemn Haider and his party officially as "extremist, racist, and xenophobic," even though little actual fact-finding had occurred. There were demonstrations in Vienna and elsewhere across the globe opposing Austria's new government.

Christiane Boutin, a pro-life French parliamentarian at the time, was astonished that the EU so readily rejected the will of the Austrian people. "I worry about this totalitarian attitude of the EU," said Boutin. "At the level of principle, this is very grave."[500]

The collective disdain for Austria's new government at the time had no parallel until 2016. At that time, the EU ignored the crises in Bosnia and Kosovo, and had never condemned countries, such as Poland and Italy, with communists serving in government positions. Nor did the EU ostracize the late French president François Mitterrand, a former member of the Vichy government, which collaborated with the Nazis during their occupation of France.[501]

"I find what he [Haider] has said repugnant," said Secretary Albright. She accused Haider of unacceptably promoting "xenophobic, anti-immigration and anti-human rights policies."[502] Albright was pretty free with her comments against Austrian populists like Haider, especially given the EU's moves to threaten nation-state sovereignty. But the EU pushed and continues to push far beyond its original charter.

Austria was at the time arguably the first European nation to react against the globalist agenda pushed by the EU, a perspective that still dominates that organization. It is noteworthy even today that the entrance to the European Parliament building in Brussels displays the national flags of all the world's countries. The explanation given for flying the flags of even non-European countries is that the globalist organization's vision is that one day all countries will be part of a single world federation—a one-world government.

It certainly appears that Brussels has globalist ambitions, and even back in the year 2000, at least a sizable minority of Austrians believed that to be so, which explains why they pushed back against the EU's Babel-like concept of one universal voice. The Austrian election should have given the EU pause, but obviously not enough.

Many of the same problems that brought the Freedom Party to prominence in 2000 were once again evident in 2016 and 2017, when the British went to the polls to decide whether to remain with the globalist EU. Then again, the same issues erupted during the U.S. presidential campaign, and more recently, populist sentiment skyrocketed in the May 2017 French presidential contest and many other nations are on a similar course.

What triggered the anti-globalist revolts?

An anti-globalist movement is gathering steam, especially in the West. We will examine that movement, the triggers creating the backlash, and the lessons learned from a number of the recent activists' campaigns.

Beginning in 2016, the world watched as Western politics was shaken by a series of anti-globalist responses of historic significance: Britain's successful Brexit campaign, Donald Trump's election, and the significant surge of anti-globalists in countries like France, Austria, the Netherlands, and elsewhere across Western Europe. This uproar of opposition shows a new divide between the globalist progressive establishment and the anti-globalist nationalists/populists movement.

Earlier in this volume, I outlined numerous, very specific consequences of globalization. Those consequences are gaining attention and push-back by an ever-larger segment of especially Western populations. What is behind this growing revolution?

Western populations are especially disturbed by the pace of global change, which is putting great stress on them, their communities, and governments. Further, government efforts to mitigate that stress are evidently less than satisfactory, which explains in part the groundswell of protest verging on outright violence, and a growing chorus of calls for action across much of Europe.

That growing chorus of calls for action was especially evident in January 2017, when European political leaders opposed to globalization met in Koblenz, Germany, to cement their alliance and plan their Europe-wide campaign ahead. That gathering was organized by the pro-sovereignty "Europe of Nations and Freedom" alliance, which featured senior leaders from most major European countries, who rallied to explicitly reject the EU's performance and its failing globalist agenda, and to chart their collective future campaign.[503]

Consider the specific issues by country that triggered the groundswell of anti-globalist reaction.

UNITED KINGDOM

The British made a strong anti-globalist statement with their June 2016 referendum to leave the EU—Brexit. This rejection happened for a host of reasons, but in general, the average British citizen was fed up with his life, and he blamed the EU's push for globalization. The issues piled atop that frustration are palpable.

The following globalization-related frustrations were enumerated thanks to the British columnist Peter Hitchens.[504]

The average British citizen faces significant financial woes. His money is worth less, and besides, it is harder to earn today than in the past. Further, his job doesn't seem all that secure, and meanwhile, his country is overflowing with migrants (legal and illegal) who soak up all the available housing, which sends lodging costs through the roof.

Commuting to work is more expensive and frustrating for the average Brit, explained Hitchens. Not only is the typical commute taking longer, it is also becoming very expensive. British roads are more congested, public transport is costly, and those few public spaces are packed with people speaking strange languages more than ever before.

British schools aren't especially good and are very crowded. Parents who want to send their children to private schools can't afford them, and they understand that school choice impacts their children's future competitiveness for the best jobs.

The British government is tethered to significant national debt, and yet Parliament refuses to cut its appetite for more of the same. Meanwhile, social services grow with the debt and the average worker's income tends to run out before the end of the month adding to escalating private debt.

These frustrated citizens of the EU (former citizens of the British Crown) don't have a bright future because their collective savings are down and they have good reason to fear their pensions will be plundered by private corporations now on life support due to global competition. Even the jobs they now have are subject to being snatched away by migrants willing to accept less money.

Membership in the globalist EU means that British jobs are easily available to East European "citizens" attracted to higher English wages. These EU migrants are especially competitive for British jobs, because East European education and vocational training tends to be superior to that in much of England.

There is also a cultural phenomenon at play regarding jobs. British merchants have a problem finding young Brits willing to take less challenging jobs such as childcare, waiting tables at restaurants, and harvesting crops. Those jobs are filled by migrants, thanks to the EU's openborders policy.

The British blame the EU and their government, and some rightly blame themselves for this sad predicament. That collective disenchantment with their increasingly drab existence pushed a simple majority of Brits to strike a blow for national sovereignty by voting to leave the EU and take a shot across the bow of the EU's distasteful globalization agenda.

FRANCE

The French people gave a thumbs-down to the anti-globalist candidate in their May 2017 presidential election. Although sentiment ran high to kick out the EU globalists, at least for now, France's Marine Le Pen's populous Front National Party returns to the sidelines to wait for another chance to capture a majority of the votes.

Le Pen was soundly defeated by Emmanuel Macron, a pro-EU centrist, but the populist Le Pen earned an impressive 35 percent of the vote, a significant share of the French voters and a clear warning sign that her message has significant national support. Her anti-immigration, anti-EU, pro-national sovereignty Front National agenda earned a central place as a leading opposition force in France.

"In 2017, I am sure, the people of continental Europe will wake up. It's no longer a question of if, but when," Le Pen explained her optimism for the future just prior to the May election. Indeed, her voice was heard, and her party and its allies across the continent are gaining a voice. Time will tell whether President Macron delivers on his reform promises, but that's doubtful, because for the French, the situation is rather dire; optimism is hard to find.

French citizen concerns expressed just prior to the election demonstrate why they are so opposed to globalization and generally a pro-EU agenda that President Macron supports.

The EU's open borders and economic policies are having a significant negative effect. Dominique Perriaux, 63, a self-identified moderate French voter, said, "We're heading towards a catastrophe. Unemployment is high. The taxes are just crazy. Our country isn't safe." She said the rising living costs and attacks by Islamists persuaded her to vote for Le Pen.[505]

Lost French jobs is a big issue for many Frenchmen. In 2017, French unemployment was nearly 13 percent, and among the youth it was 23 percent nationwide.

Andre Robert is one of many unemployed blue-collar Frenchmen suffering from job loss. "Fifty years ago, France produced everything for France," Robert said. "Now everything comes from Italy, Spain, [and] China. We struggle to find work, while immigrants profit from the system." Jean Messiah, the then-project coordinator for Le Pen's campaign, addressed the effect of globalization: "The Eurozone isn't viable. It's better to jump on a life raft [Le Pen] than to stay on the Titanic [the EU]!"

The French are especially concerned about the cultural price of globalization. Louis Aliot, then vice president of the National Front, attacked the media, the tyranny of the EU, and the loss of Christian traditions: "We must defend our culture, our heritage, our identity!" French citizen Eveline Fouche echoes that concern: "We're losing our values, our roots."

"I feel like I'm not even in France," Ms. Fouche said. "I don't hear French in the market. I don't see French products in the stores. All I hear is Arabic music. These people don't do anything all day, and they don't respect our country."

The widespread French concern about the future of their country is evidenced elsewhere on the continent, where the issues are much the same.

THE NETHERLANDS

The March 16, 2017, Dutch election was a litmus test for the anti-globalization populist movement. Although the centre-right candidate won over populist Geert Wilders of the Party for Freedom (PVV), the wave of nationalism is far from fading away. Mr. Wilders' party won the second most seats in parliament with 20 of 150.[506]

The flamboyant Wilders, often dubbed the "Dutch Trump," founded the PVV as a marriage between economic liberalism and criticism of Islam and immigration. He made his name by producing a provocative film, *Fitna*, which features the aftermath of terrorist attacks with verses from the Koran.

Wilders advocated a "prohibition of halal slaughter, restrictions on Islamic headscarves, and a program of repatriating criminals of foreign and dual citizenships." The Netherlands have a significant Muslim population, estimated at 5 percent of the total.[507]

Wilders promised, if elected, to host a Brexit-like referendum on the Netherlands' membership in the EU and called for the "de-Islamification" of the Netherlands. That will have to wait until the Dutch grow wearier of globalization and install either Wilders or another populist.

GERMANY

German chancellor Angela Merkel is firmly in the globalist camp and most often blamed by Europeans for the tsunami of immigrants that flooded much of Western Europe in 2015–2016. Her endorsement of an immigrant welcoming EU encouraged the emergence of the anti-EU/globalist populist Alternative for Germany (AfD) party.

Support for the Eurosceptic AfD spiked after Trump's election in 2016, but sputtered through mid-2017. But the group's anti-globalist agenda, which includes calls for the reintroduction of German border controls, strict sanctions on Muslims, and a referendum on EU membership is very much alive, a rallying cry of sorts for a growing cross-section of Germans.

That skepticism is fed by other outrageous government intrusions such as what happened in Hamburg. In early 2017, Hamburg authorities confiscated six privately owned residential units in a gestapo-like fashion and then contracted to have the units repaired and the renovation bills were then sent to the owners. Why? City officials want to accommodate the more than four hundred new migrants arriving daily, and the city has insufficient shelter.[508]

In 2015, the Hamburg Parliament (Hamburgische Bürgerschaft) passed a law that allows the city to seize vacant commercial real estate and use it to house migrants. Andre Trepoll of the center-right Christian

Democratic Union said such seizures are "a massive attack on the property rights of the citizens of Hamburg." Further, Trepoll said the act amounts to a "political dam-break with far-reaching implications."

Some German citizens correctly argue that government efforts to seize private property is communist and autocratic, while others ask what is next: "Will authorities now limit the maximum amount of living space per person, and force those with large apartments to share them with strangers?"

Understandably, such outrages as the property-seizure story fuel opposition to Merkel and her pro-EU, globalist push. That was especially evident at the January 2017 Koblenz conference mentioned above.

Marcus Pretzel with the AfD, who participated in the conference, verbally attacked the *Frankfurter Allgemeine* newspaper, a leading German news source. The crowd responded with wild applause and chanted *luggenpresse* or "lying press." That was the German catchphrase used in Nazi propaganda to smash dissent to Adolf Hitler's Third Reich.[509]

Frauke Petry, an AfD candidate at the Koblenz rally, shouted to the gathering, "Merkel must go." Petry explained "We don't want this diversity [a reference to Merkel's decision to allow hundreds of thousands of refugees into Germany]." He continued, "Mass migration is sold to us as 'diversity.' Well, we don't want this 'diversity' that Brussels [the EU] dictates to us."[510]

Petry rallied support with a clarion call: "Together with patriots of Europe, the nation state will come back. But we have to be courageous to rethink Europe and Europe's freedom."[511]

ITALY

In December 2016, a referendum in Italy gave a shot in the arm to populist parties. That outcome led to the resignation of the prime minister and raised the stature of the populist Five Star Movement, led by Italian comedian Beppe Grillo.[512]

Italian political observers believe that, should Grillo become the prime minister, he will call a referendum to scrap the euro (the EU's currency), then reintroduce the Italian lira and possibly exit the European Union.

AUSTRIA

Earlier in this chapter, I introduced the emergence of the Austrian Freedom Party as the first in the wave of anti-globalist assaults on the EU. In December 2016, Austrians narrowly elected a left-wing independent candidate over the Freedom Party's candidate, Norbert Hofer. However, much as the 2000 election guided by Haider, the 2016 election demonstrates there is significant popular support for pushing back on the EU's open-borders, pro-globalization policies.

The anti-globalist agenda is spreading across the entire continent with no indication that it is fading, and many nations are poised to revolt in the coming years. The only question is whether delay means defeat.

What are the lessons from the anti-globalist revolts?

The anti-globalist revolts outlined above produced numerous lessons. Those lessons should be studied and applied as the globalist-populist/nationalist battles continue.

Cultural conservatives and especially Christians are among the most offended by globalists. Progressives feign their tolerance, but absolutely hate devout Christians who disagree with their radical globalist agenda.

Consider eight lessons from the anti-globalist revolt across Western Europe and the U.S.

Lesson #1: The first lesson learned by anti-globalist Americans is that progressives like Obama and Clinton have absolutely no tolerance for the freedom of evangelical Christian expression. Dissenting views earn attacks from the likes of then presidential candidate Obama, who said in April 2008 about his opposition: "They get bitter, they cling to guns or religion or antipathy to people who aren't like them or anti-immigrant sentiment or anti-trade sentiment as a way to explain their frustrations.[513]

Consider what a fellow evangelical wrote about the palpable progressive intolerance of Christians:

> Doubt me? Try standing up for Jesus, unborn babies, strong borders or gun rights on social media. Defend marriage as being between one man and one woman. Support Israel and see what happens. You'll face an assault on your intellect, your reputation, your genetics, and even your right to exist.[514]

Lesson #2: The second lesson is that globalists/progressives play by uncivilized rules. The same author who wrote the description for the lesson above explained the set of rules globalists (leftists) use.

> The truth is, two different sets of rules play out now—one for each side. Although the right has been deeply despaired with the elections of Obama, and with his "Make America Weak" policies, they never rioted in the streets, burned businesses, beat up bystanders, threatened to kill electors, shot cops, formed filthy communes in public places, encouraged assassinations, promoted anarchy, bankrolled mobs, shut down free speech, nor asked for safe rooms, teddy bears, pet therapy, and Play-Doh. The right is imperfect, but the conduct of the left is outrageously wrong.[515]

Lesson #3: Countries like the U.S. that abandon manufacturing capabilities will find in time that they spend less and less money on innovation and infrastructure and thus become less competitive, all thanks to globalization. This lesson is based on a study that found a long-term downturn in productivity, which significantly impacts the affected countries. The logical results are suppressed income, consumption, and general welfare. CNN reports that in 1960, one in four American workers had a manufacturing job, but today only one in ten is employed in that sector.[516] President Trump will find returning manufacturing jobs to the American economy and very challenging endeavor.

Lesson #4: Mass immigration can potentially destroy a country. The British experienced mass immigration in the 1950s and 1960s and the result was "slums, dilapidated urban areas, an overburdened welfare state, and wage competition among poorly qualified workers." More recently, the EU-facilitated mass migration of 2015–2016, which enabled poverty-driven migration that totally discredited the EU in the eyes of the Brexit voters. Now, as illustrated earlier, a significant part of the EU population fears that mass migration will negatively impact their domestic culture, the character of their countries, and competition over a limited amount of resources for redistribution through their welfare services. Further, a significant portion of the new migrants will fail to assimilate, and a certain element is directly behind the worst spate of terrorism in Europe in many decades.

Lesson #5: There is a trade-off that nationalists/populists must understand about globalization: It creates winners and losers, and the later (the many losers) must not be forgotten. An emerging market means that exporting firms are more productive and pay higher wages than those who serve only a domestic market. That is why most of America's exports go to countries with which it has a free-trade deal. This dynamic understandably attracts popular attention, because, as Austrian economist Joseph Schumpeter argues, capitalism inevitably involves a process of "creative destruction." While competition stimulates firms to innovate, it also can destroy entire industries and regions, or at least marginalize them as "more innovative competitors take the lead in a given sector." This results in unemployment and destitution for some communities.[517]

Lesson #6: Protectionism hurts consumers and workers. A study of forty countries found the richest consumers would lose 28 percent of their purchasing power if free trade ended, and the poorest consumers would lose 63 percent.[518] However, protectionism sustains jobs for inefficient domestic producers, which has short-term political pay-offs but the underlying lack of competitiveness must be addressed.

Lesson #7: Globalists seek to destroy virtually everything we conservatives hold dear. One writer explained the globalist push for one-world government and the carnage it will leave in the wake:

> They [the globalists] advance the sketchy premises of climate change in order to enforce a universal set of rules. They promote dissolution of borders to blur sovereign territories. They over-regulate economies to weaken nations. They violate basic laws to incite chaos and promote controls on society, and they defend illegal immigration to overwhelm political and legal systems and to introduce confusion.[519]

Lesson #8: Populism/nationalism run-amok can lead to dangerous authoritarianism. The U.S. and European representative republics must be careful, because at the core of populous political forces is the potential for authoritarians to emerge. Once any leader starts to reject constraints to his/her political decision making, we will begin to see the emergence of fascism, an ugly phenomenon. As Andrzej Lepper, the late leader of Poland's populist authoritarian party Samoobrona (Self-Defense), put it, "If the law works against people and generally accepted notions of legality then it isn't law. The only thing to do is to break it for the sake of the majority."[520]

This final lesson—populism leading to authoritarianism—is absolutely essential to dissect, because there are potentially serious consequences for all involved.

How do populist/nationalist moral views become authoritarian and dangerous?

Social psychologist Jonathan Haidt explains a major divide between globalist and populists. His approach may help put into context the final anti-globalist lesson outlined above and the triggers behind the potential for populists/nationalists to revert to authoritarianism.[521]

It appears the globalists don't understand the right's discontent over globalization, so they say, and they wonder out loud why Trump, Wilders, Le Pin, Brexit, and much of the growing anti-globalist populist movement is gaining momentum. Haidt suggests the globalists ask: "Doesn't the right see this ends badly for our collective nation-states? Do they really not care?"

The problem, as many on the right will explain, is that this isn't just about economics any more than globalization is just about money, jobs, and trade.

Yes, globalization has raised prosperity across the world with some exceptions, such as among the Western middle class as well as among the less educated and those with low-skilled jobs.

What has especially alarmed many is the rise of authoritarianism behind the populist movements' response to the ugliness of globalization. We saw some of that earlier in this chapter. The rhetoric is heated and civility is becoming rare.

To understand the radical differences in views, we must examine the dividing line, which French populist Marine Le Pen says is "a battle between globalists and patriots." Is it really that simple?

Haidt explains that globalization has changed the values and behavior of the urban elite—the center of globalist views in the West—which antagonizes the nationalists, causing them to behave in a more authoritarian fashion. Let's explore this issue using the controversial issue of immigration.

Haidt argues that immigration is a good vehicle to illustrate this issue, because it is at the heart of the nationalist agenda with the globalists. Specifically, Haidt argues from a "moral psychology" perspective, which he believes offers some help to potentially reduce the conflict through mutual understanding.

Haidt uses the World Values Survey to illustrate values changes across sixty countries to suggest two propositions.

First, as nations industrialize, they move away from "traditional values" in which religion, ritual, and deference to authorities are important, and to "secular rational" values that are more open to change, progress, and social engineering.

His second proposition is that, as countries become more prosperous, more people move into the service sector and away from "survival values" emphasizing the economic and physical security found in one's family, tribe, or other groupings and to "self-expression" or "emancipative values" that emphasize individual rights and protections.

These changes, according to Haidt, are addressed by Christian Welzel's book, *Freedom Rising:*

> ...fading existential pressures [i.e., threats and challenges to survival] open people's minds, making them prioritize freedom over security, autonomy over authority, diversity over uniformity, and creativity over discipline. By the same token, persistent existential pressures keep people's minds closed, in which case they emphasize the opposite priorities...the existentially relieved state of mind is the source of tolerance and solidarity beyond one's in-group; the existentially stressed state of mind is the source of discrimination and hostility against out-groups.

Haidt concludes, based on Welzel's proposition, that democratic capitalist societies, which enjoy a high living standard and existential security are more open and tolerant. Combine that view with all the goodies associated with Western affluence, and this openness leads to a cosmopolitan attitude or a view that especially Western urbanites are citizens of the world as opposed to citizens of Los Angeles, Seattle, or Kansas City. Remember what then presidential candidate Obama said in Berlin in 2008? "People of Berlin, people of the world, this is our moment. This is our time," Obama said to the German audience. Then he offered himself "not as a candidate for president, but as a citizen, a proud citizen of the United States and a fellow citizen of the world."[522]

Obama, like so many other progressive elite, embraces universalism as opposed to parochialism. Haidt quotes George Monbiot, a British leftist, to further illustrate the point.

> Internationalism…tells us that someone living in Kinshasa is of no less worth than someone living in Kensington…. Patriotism, if it means anything, tells us we should favour the interests of British people [before the Congolese]. How do you reconcile this choice with liberalism? How…do you distinguish it from racism?

Monbiot's racism accusation fits his multicultural globalist philosophy, but for the nationalists, that view is naïve.

Haidt next juxtaposes the nationalist who views patriotism as a virtue. Like many Americans, the nationalist believes his country and culture are worth preserving, and such a view is not indicative of racism. Haidt explains, "As many defenders of patriotism have pointed out, you love your spouse because she or he is yours, not because you think your spouse is superior to all others."

You feel a bond with your spouse, and similarly, a patriot is bonded to his country and has a sense of duty to love, serve, and protect his own people. That's not racism, but a measure of trust that creates many benefits for society, such as lower crime and better prosperity.

Haidt then asks: "So how have nationalists and globalists responded to the European immigration crisis?" He explains that the globalists are thrilled with Angela Merkel's open-door policy whereby more than a million mostly Islamic people flooded into Europe in 2015–2016. Not surprisingly, the nationalists were terrified by her act, but few did anything to stop the migrant tsunami.

The globalists elite cheered the flood of migrants, demanding that every EU member state accept large numbers of refugees. Not surprisingly, those demands came mostly from the EU elite in Brussels who were deaf to Europe's dissenting nationalists, who argued the continent already had enough Islamic immigrants who mostly refused to assimilate. Those immigrants who refuse to assimilate endanger European societies, and the problem got much worse with the new flood of Muslim immigrants who made themselves unwelcomed by their riots, terrorism, attacks on trains and buses and the slaughter of the likes of the Charlie Hebdo staff in Paris in January 2015.

The fight between globalists and nationalists was already at a high pitch when in the summer of 2015 globalists proclaimed, "Let us open the floodgates, it's the compassionate thing to do, and if you oppose us you are a racist."[523]

The globalists' arrogant finger-pointing accusation of "racism" against nationalist objections to mass immigration sparked anger and fed the growth of populist sentiment. Of course, admits Haidt, some nationalists may be racists, but that's not the full story.

There are serious "moral" issues associated with the nationalist concerns that globalists too easily dismiss. Haidt explains the "moral" by stating: "People don't hate others just because they have darker skin or differently shaped noses; they hate people whom they perceive as having values that are incompatible with their own, or who (they believe) engage in behaviors they find abhorrent, or whom they perceive to be a threat to something they hold dear." Rather, Haidt says to understand the anti-immigration populism as "racism" or "authoritarianism" is a totally incomplete explanation.[524]

Karen Stenner, author of *The Authoritarian Dynamic*, finds that "authoritarianism is not a stable personality trait." Rather, as Haidt interprets Stenner, authoritarianism is "a psychological predisposition to become intolerant when the person perceives a certain kind of threat. When people are faced with such a threat they are attracted to a strongman and may favor the use of force."[525]

What kind of threat might trigger such a reaction? Stenner calls it a "normative threat," or a threat to the moral order. Stenner is quoted:

The experience or perception of disobedience to group authorities or authorities unworthy of respect, nonconformity to
group norms or norms proving questionable, lack of consensus in group values and beliefs and, in general, diversity and
freedom 'run amok' should activate the predisposition and
increase the manifestation of these characteristic attitudes and
behaviors.[526]

Understandably, the nationalist wants to protect his home and family, his community and culture when they are threatened by outsiders.
They become authoritarians, according to Stenner, when important values such as obedience are compromised.

Stenner found in her research that nationalists must be triggered
before crossing the authoritarian line. Specifically, she found that when
nationalists learned about Americans becoming more morally diverse,
the authoritarian trigger was pulled and they became more intolerant.
For example, Haidt cites Stenner, "maintaining order in the nation" was
a high priority for nationalists, while "protecting freedom of speech" was
not. Issues such as homosexuality, abortion, and divorce earned special
criticism from nationalists.[527]

Haidt indicates that one of Stenner's most helpful contributions is
that authoritarians are "psychologically distinct from 'status quo conservatives' who are the more prototypical conservatives—cautious about
radical change." The two—conservatives and authoritarians—are not
natural allies because the average conservative tends to avoid big risks.[528]

Haidt believes status-quo conservatives can align themselves with
authoritarians when progressives subvert the country's traditions and
identity. That is when dramatic political action such as Brexit becomes
necessary. Haidt explained the view: "Brexit [for many British voters]
can seem less radical than the prospect of absorption into the 'ever closer
union' of the EU."[529]

Now go back to Haidt's thesis as to why immigration caused such a polarizing reaction in Europe as well as in America. He explained, "Muslim Middle Eastern immigrants are seen by nationalists as posing a far greater threat of terrorism than are immigrants from any other region or religion." The issue isn't just the security aspect, but, as Stenner would argue, it tramples on other important values. "Islam asks adherents to live in ways that can make assimilation into secular egalitarian western societies more difficult compared to other groups."[530]

Immigrant Muslims frequently fail to assimilate into Western culture, a topic I examine in detail in my 2015 book, *Never Submit: Will the Extermination of Christians Get Worse Before It Gets Better?* In that volume, I explain their cultural bias is to demand accommodation by the host nation to their traditions, whether they be veiling and covering of women, gender segregation, or much more.[531] Americas, like communities in Europe, experience first-hand this phenomenon, which results in ghetto-like Islamic communities popping up across the landscape.

Haidt concludes that for the average conservative concerned about rapid change in his society, he often agrees with the conclusion that "high levels of Muslim immigration into your Western nation are likely to threaten your core moral concerns." But of course, if a conservative expresses those core moral concerns, the globalist automatically labels him a "racist." That marginalization by globalists pushes many conservatives into the authoritarian's arms.[532]

Haidt argues that Stenner's authoritarian dynamic is like a "Rosetta stone," a means for interpreting the rise of right-wing populism. Then Stenner contrasts her authoritarian theory with the globalist view of an "unstoppable tide of history moving away from traditions and 'toward greater respect for individual freedom and difference,' and an expectation people will continue evolving 'into more perfect liberal democratic citizens.'"[533]

Stenner's interpretation of the nationalists' transition to authoritarianism may be correct, but her view of mankind's evolution is very much a globalist perspective. Specifically, she evidently supports Hegel's philosophy outlined earlier in this volume that mankind is evolving into a "perfect" humanity, but that process requires a government to tame man's raw impulses (perhaps the nationalists' tendency to authoritarianism), the basis for progressive policies.

Communism rejected the socialist view that the state apparatus would gradually wither away as citizens learned to cooperate for the greater good and man was perfected. The Communists used a strict authoritarian approach to seizing and ruthlessly retaining all forms of power. The result was a two-class society: the majority poor workers and the minority controllers. And here in a nutshell is the Communist attitude, mindset, and objectives today embedded in the liberal progressives and globalists.

I can agree with Stenner's prediction that "intolerance is not a thing of the past, it is very much a thing of the future." However, I also believe her dreamy globalist view of the future is far off track.

CONCLUSION

Globalization sparked an explosive reaction among citizens especially in the West and that spark will continue to spread to other regions. Hopefully, the lessons from past anti-globalization campaigns will help new efforts to turn back the progressives' global campaign.

I recognize up to this point the reaction to globalism is more situational and issue-specific. Most Westerners are not accustomed to using the term "globalist" and "globalism." However, they are beginning to react in an appropriate manner to the symptoms of globalization, but they have yet to incorporate their belief into the broader perspective that they are in fact consciously opposed to the consequences of globalists/globalism. That is one of the objectives of this volume: educate the public that there is a higher issue in play. I've led the reader through a strategic consideration of the threat thus far, while more often than not, the reader is understanding and operating at a tactical level. I'm hoping this volume will raise general awareness to the higher level.

The next chapter will advance a proposition that has broad geopolitical implications to help the reader understand the globalist movement from a different perspective as well as offer approaches to defeat its advance.

CHAPTER THIRTEEN

Fueling Globalism and Pushing Back

Earlier in this volume, I addressed the spiritual issues behind global-ism and explored whether evil forces are ushering us into the end times. Theologian Michael Heiser, author of *The Unseen Realm,* is skep-tical about that theory, but admits he doesn't know, which brings up an alternative view as to what's really going on with globalism and what we must do to stop the radical parts of that agenda.

I begin by posing a rhetorical question: Do the globalists elite really seek a one-world government under their control and, if true, what might that future globalist-controlled world be like?

The answer to this question is simple: Yes, many globalists elite cer-tainly claim to seek a one-world government, and that sort of thinking is demonic if not psychotic! Further, globalism for many adherents is really a ruse for something far more sinister, and in the end, should they be successful at taking over the world, then life under these evil people will be truly horrible. Allow me to explain.

My interview with General Boykin confirmed the view there is a spiritual dimension to the current conflict with so-called globalists. Yes, "it is demonic and anti-Christ," but "globalists" are more than egotistical rich people who are encouraged by demonic forces. Rather, they are also wolves in sheep's clothing, according to the general.[534]

Dr. Heiser shares that view, as evidenced by his observation that "intelligent evil has a role to play" today, but the theologian hesitates to put all the blame for man's contemporary problems on disembodied spirits. Rather, Heiser asserts, "We (mankind) are capable of messing up our own lives" and by inference he meant we don't need demons to help us "mess up."[535]

Although we shouldn't ignore the influence of "intelligent evil," Heiser warns, we ought to try to understand who or what are today's wolves in sheep's clothing. For me, that metaphor became clear after I considered all the material covered in this volume—the obvious consequences of globalism, the globalists' radical agenda, the globalist fathers' corrupted worldview, and their elite contemporary offspring, their secret societies and how they are capturing the world's power centers, the escalating spiritual warfare, and in the last chapter, how the anti-globalist revolts are shaking up much of the West.

I asked myself whether all the evidence about the globalists' agenda and actions really points to some grand human scheme—a conspiracy—to control the world. After all, we already know the unseen realm is busy tripping up mankind through sin. Of course, we make enough mistakes (read "sin") that dishonor God without the encouragement of the demonic world. However, we should ask ourselves whether there is a real conspiracy other than the obvious globalists elite doing their secret work aimed at world dominance.

I believe it is likely, and yes, it sounds conspiratorial, but stay with me because it isn't what you may think.

General Boykin told me the modern globalist cabal is really modern Marxists—thus the metaphor, wolves in sheep's clothing. He explained: "The globalist movement is based on Marxism…their leadership and funding is at the heart, Marxism," and their supporters are "useful idiots thinking they are doing something good for mankind but they are only helping the Marxist movement."[536]

Boykin explained that every Marxist movement has the wealthy, like the globalists elite. He also called attention to those who came out of Marxism, who then explained that "an objective look at communist (Marxist) regimes always includes a wealthy elite controlling everything—production, distribution, prices." The result is a cabal of globalists elite making a lot of money while the majority depends on their governments for handouts.

There is one major distinction between our understanding of modern globalists and Marxists, however. Boykin explained that present-day globalists wedded to a Marxist ideology really do want to destroy capitalism as opposed to a certain cohort of other globalists who are focused primarily on exploiting capitalism for self-enrichment. That distinction explains why those globalists driven by Marxist ambitions invest in anarchy through groups like Black Lives Matter (read "George Soros"), hoping, according to the general, to "take over the United States." He said, "I'm not being conspiratorial. I think that's what we are seeing."

Boykin drew my attention to the 1958 book, *The Naked Communist,* in which one of the things cited in that volume as necessary to take over America is to move the country from a revealed to a social religion. He believes the globalist Marxists are doing just that—pushing for a strong movement to get the religious community to accept freedom of worship versus freedom of religion. Boykin explained this is a smart line of attack because so few Americans are truly informed about our Constitution and the Bill of Rights; that is, they really don't know their rights. Further, the only religion not falling prey to this strategy is the Islamic faith, which itself is very authoritarian.

The globalist (Marxist) movement's effort to co-opt the world's religious communities appears to be working, if we are to believe the account in chapter 11 about the 2015 Parliament of the World's Religions.

Jim Simpson, an author and former White House budget official, is an investigative journalist who helps organize communities to fight the left's immigration push in this country. Mr. Simpson agrees with General

Boykin about "globalists," but he refers to them as "communists" rather than Boykin's use of the label "Marxists."

Simpson tracked the emergence of the politically correct "globalist" label in lieu of "communist," which is widely associated with the unpopular fallout associated with the controversial U.S. Senator Joseph McCarthy's congressional hearings in the 1950s held after the senator claimed to have a list of 205 State Department employees who were members of the American Communist Party. Those hearings were inconclusive, but the senator's name—"McCarthyism"—became synonymous with the practice of making accusations of subversion or treason, especially involving suspected communists without proper regard for evidence.

Since that time, the communists in America have enjoyed a relatively free hand to organize and create powerful leftist organizations like the American Civil Liberties Union and the Southern Poverty Law Center, which, according to Simpson, are really communist fronts. They seek to subvert our society by undermining our law and sovereignty, push for open borders, and promote cultural implosion through sexual deviance.

Simpson also explained that the neutral label "globalism" emerged as a much more acceptable descriptor for the blood-soaked term "communism." No matter the label, Simpson argues, the result is the same. Communist-controlled regimes and their proxies haven't changed recently, and they have no intention of merging with other nations, much less Western republics, as part of some future global government or watering down their intentions. Rather, according to Simpson, the communists' (globalists') real objective remains to tear down the West by forcing it to "surrender its will to the will of a central organization," such as the United Nations, which was created in part and is now "controlled" by those sympathetic with the communists.

Anyone who has studied the history of communism understands its leaders are dedicated to destroying Western society, the first phase of their grand strategy of global conquest, Simpson said. He explained that contemporary communists are not people necessarily tethered to Karl Marx's teachings, however. Rather, "they are people who understand the utility of using communist propaganda." He said they "put themselves in power and [then] seize absolute power and wealth."

Their instrument of choice for taking over the West is the United Nations, according to Simpson. He points out that American Alger Hiss, who was convicted in 1950 of perjury for denying that he had been a Soviet spy, played a key role in creating the United Nations with a communist bias.

Once the Soviet Union collapsed in 1991, historians gained access to Moscow's archives and settled the question about Hiss. The Central Intelligence Agency reports, "Although no specific file on Hiss has been released from the KGB or GRU archives, enough material has been found in other files—in Moscow, Eastern Europe, and Washington—to enable historians to write several new works that leave almost no room for doubt about Hiss's guilt. These developments also have significant implications for the intelligence professional today."[537]

Hiss was positioned to influence the creation of the United Nations. Prior to World War II, he served President Franklin Roosevelt in a variety of positions, and finally "settled at the State Department in 1936 as an aide to assistant secretary of state Francis B. Sayre, who was President Woodrow Wilson's son-in-law."[538] Don't forget that President Wilson was the nation's leading progressive in the early part of the twentieth century and the primary American proponent for the League of Nations, the precursor to the United Nations. Possibly this isn't guilt by association, but it is a curious circumstance.

While at the State Department, Hiss was heavily involved in the planning for the foundations of the United Nations, and, in the spring of 1945, he served as secretary-general of the United Nations' organizing conference in San Francisco, according to the Central Intelligence Agency.[539]

Was Hiss' association with the Soviets and his contribution to the United Nations just a coincidence? Not according to Simpson, and evidently the CIA agrees, based on its report on Hiss. Simpson believes Hiss' role in writing the United Nations' charter from his presidential-appointed roost at the State Department resulted in a document and organization that was an "extension of [Russia's] foreign policy" and by design communist-favoring, and therefore "compulsively anti-American."

Simpson goes on to explain that communists have never given up their quest to control the world, especially the West, even after the fall of the Soviet Union. In fact, the communist imperative to control the world was strengthened after the Soviet's fall, but, according to Simpson, that strategy morphed into a brilliant although opaque marketing plan.

The neo-communist marketing plan uses as a subterfuge a promise pushed by its modern proxy, globalization, to save the oppressed world, which it claims is threatened by globalist agenda issues: climate change, overpopulation, violence, unjust economic disparities, and much more. Meanwhile, Simpson argues, communism's true aim is to transform the world into a tightly controlled, monarchy-like government overseen by a small cabal of elite globalists—a one-world government. He indicates that the Castro brothers' tight grip in Cuba illustrates the communists' end game for the world, a regime that exercises absolute control.

How might such a global outcome be possible? Simpson argues that's simple. All globalists elite need is a seared conscience with the willingness to use mass murder to remove all opposition, such as the purges conducted by Mao in China and Stalin in Russia. We shouldn't be too quick to say "never again," either.

Earlier in this text, I cited CNN owner Ted Turner as advocating for a radical reduction in the world's population because our planet, according to Turner, can't sustain such a large population. Turner doesn't explain just how the world will cut 80 percent of the population, however. But given a relatively recent history of genocide in many places—Congo, Rwanda, Cambodia, Russia, China, and involving Mideast Christians—it's not too hard to imagine similar tragedies happening again, but next time on a much more massive scale.

The only barriers between today's world and a morally corrupt future brutal, genocidal communist, worldwide regime are a few legitimate governments like the United States. That's why, as Boykin and

Simpson agree, the globalists elite (many who are closet hardline communists) are pulling out all stops to destroy America, to remove one of the last barriers to world dominance.

We may already be heading down that road. Remember from earlier chapters the siren song of the globalists who push cheap labor, unfettered immigration, unconstrained global markets, and higher profits? They promise great rewards—a slick marketing plan. Yes, they did deliver short-term results, but, as we have seen with China, in the long term, the globalist tools turned that Asian country into a global military competitor that has also saturated America with her agents (called guest workers) that drain us of our industrial and intellectual secrets, and made the communist giant the world's largest economy. Now Beijing has come upon a new strategy to infiltrate the United States.

A May 2017 *New York Times* article, "China's Chase of the 'Golden Visa' Abroad, By the Numbers," exposes a very grandiose new globalization effort. Well-heeled Chinese citizens are "spending literally billions on new passports and visas to move their families away from their homeland." Ostensibly, Beijing's objective is to help "China's middle and upper classes find better schools, cleaner air and more secure life for their children." Old China hands know nothing is done without Beijing's approval and to suit its strategic purposes.[540]

Those visas for Chinese citizens to move abroad are very pricey. Specifically, as the *Times* cites, a Chinese citizen can buy citizenship in Antigua and Barbuda for a $50,000 government fee and a local investment of at least $250,000. It's more expensive here in the U.S. For a minimum business investment of $500,000 via the EB-5 program, with a "green card," the Chinaman enjoys permanent resident status.[541]

Evidently, according to the *Times*, a lot of wealthy Chinese are buying their way into the United States. Annually, at least $7.7 billion of Chinese funds are invested in the U.S. as part of the EB-5 program. So why does China want so many of its wealthy citizens abroad?

China is globally hegemonic. It has a long history of expanding its reach into the West beginning two millennia ago with the Silk Road, and more recently with its expansive economic enterprises across much of Africa, South America, and Southeast Asia, and it is making very significant inroads in the West. Many of these people remain beholden to Beijing's communist leverage due to families left behind, which creates a growing sympathetic population abroad.

Russia is re-emerging to do much the same.

At this point, let me be perfectly clear. Communists, whether of Chinese, Russian, or other origins disguised as globalists are full of empty promises that help them subvert the gullible West into putting enough of them into powerful positions. The end result is that they will facilitate a peaceful transition to global power. Then, as Simpson warns, we will be overpowered and subject to a horrible future. That's the globalists' intention, and they are making genuine progress.

Simpson believes that the Soviet Union never really collapsed, which seriously begs his credibility given all the contrary evidence. He also contends that the Soviets created a ruse before the "transition" (end of the Cold war in 1991) whereby they would pretend to fall apart and then sit back, allowing the rise of democracy among former client-states in Eastern Europe and capitalist markets within Russia.

I don't buy Simpson's views about a Soviet ruse to feign collapse in order to manipulate the West. However, it is true that the West did let down its guard after the collapse of the Soviet Union, which led to naïve Western views that Russia all of a sudden became a geopolitical teddy bear, a nonthreat, and welcomed closer ties with the West. Of course, that was a very temporary outcome, but soon, for a host of reasons, Moscow quickly abandoned *perestroika* to re-embrace its old confrontational ways, thanks to the former KGB operative at the helm of that country, President Vladimir Putin.

Just as the West turned a blind eye to Moscow, it also took a defense acquisition holiday. Soon, the old-line Soviets crawled back to the helm in Moscow to modernize its military, increase intelligence operations (spying) especially in the West, and reestablish itself internationally in places like Iran and Syria, while in the meantime, the West naïvely opened itself to significant Russian immigration as it has for Chinese immigrants. Today, the Russian diaspora in the West is poised to provide critical information to those running the Kremlin, to our collective demise.

What should we understand from the above? Well, many globalists elite are closet communists who seek world dominance, and they are seeding much of the globe, especially the West, with their agents thanks to our naïvety. Globalists and their legion of followers are rising in power, much as the old hardliners who controlled the Soviet Kremlin are nudging their way back into prominence.

What should we expect from the globalists (communists) in the future?

Logically, the globalists will do what's possible to advance their often-articulated goal of world domination. In fact, Professor Heiser believes we are already "on the fast track toward a global society." He said there are "all sorts of indictors" of progress.[542]

Heiser claims the globalists elite are great marketers, as are their ideological fathers (the communists and progressives). They will continue to use their marketing skills in the future to sell a deceptive view of the globalist world with lots of benefits, but at the same time, they will squelch all dissent. After all, Heiser argues, once the globalists have their global system in place, they will have to deal with dissent like a disease, much as Mao used passive measures (like re-education) and active measures (such as rounding up dissenters to slaughter them by the millions).

General Boykin believes that, under globalists, our future "will not have a good ending." It is demonic and will "rob us of our constitutional freedoms," he said. No one should be so delusional as "to believe globalists will provide the same level of individual freedom and choice we enjoy in America today."[543]

Dr. Heiser sees much the same outcome should globalists rule the future world. "The elite will do whatever needs to be done to maintain the system," he said. "They won't tolerate dissent" and our freedom of speech will be gone. All information will be manipulated into Orwellian propaganda and our history will be rewritten to alter the thinking of future generations. This is very much reminiscent of life under communism past and, to a certain degree, similar to present life in oppressive places like North Korea.

Many readers may not be aware of what life was like under communism and therefore won't appreciate the threat globalists inspired by communism pose for a future one-world government. I got a brief glimpse of that possible future in 1982 when visiting the former Soviet Union, and that was enough to make me incredibly thankful for my American freedoms.

My memories of that visit are stark images of a sea of sad-faced people, massive concrete structures, bad food, an inefficient transportation system, and the feeling of being constantly watched.

Our Russian minder (tour guide) was certainly a government agent who told me we were "so brave" to bring our infant daughter on the trip. I didn't know what she meant at the time, but understood there were more than well-wishes behind her comment. Was that a threat?

We took an overnight train ride as part of our tour from Moscow to then Leningrad (now St. Petersburg). For much of that overnight journey, we were "entertained" by an inquisitive Russian man who spoke good English and stood in the car's hall outside our sleeping compartment passing around a flask of vodka. He was especially inquisitive about our jobs. At the time, I was an Army captain stationed in Europe, but on the advice of my command, I wrote on my visa application that I was an engineer, a true statement given my education at West Point. I guess the man was a KGB agent trying to pry intelligence from our tour group, which was made up of military families stationed in West Germany at the time.

It was a stressful trip, but once the Aeroflot jet touched down in Frankfurt, West Germany, the stress was gone and most of the passengers erupted in cheers. Evidently, I wasn't the only person on the tour to be glad to return to freedom and leave behind the oppressive Soviet Union.

My brief visit behind the Iron Curtain didn't provide nearly enough insight to properly describe life for the average Russian under communism, much less to suggest what a future world might be like under communistic-leaning globalists. So I turned to another who looked in detail at life under the former Soviet regime.

British columnist Peter Hitchens lived in Moscow in 1990, just a year after the collapse of the Soviet Union. He captured some keen insights about life under the failed regime from Moscow residents, and those insights are especially instructive for those considering a future life under an ideological, communist-inspired, one-world globalist government.

Hitchens lived in "the very center of the capital city of a (former) great empire (Moscow)." Officially, the former Soviet Union had a liberal constitution, law courts, newspapers, and alleged deliberative assemblies. But, as Hitchens discovered within "sight, sound, and stink of these things," many Russians were murdered by government agents for the most trivial statements against the regime, and this brutality came from a cabal of people who promised a utopia. Hitchens explained it is hard for the foreigner to "understand the cynicism and darkness of the lives of normal people in such countries, or of the liberation they felt when the last traces of the communist party were scrubbed away."[544]

Life for the average citizen was harsh beyond belief, which, according to Hitchens, literally made the Russian people appear much older than their actual years. Even Russian births (which were outnumbered by abortions during the regime's long rule) were harsh experiences at terrifying maternity hospitals where nurses snatched newborns from moms, wrapped them tightly, and brought them around only for brief feedings. Hitchens wrote, "Fathers were not allowed to visit for many days, and mothers would hang strings from the [hospital] windows, bearing notes pleading for bars of chocolate or other comforts and giving news of the baby's progress."

Family life was precarious and frequently marred by easy divorce. Hitchens said, "I do not think I ever met a Soviet couple with two children who were full brothers and sisters. Invariably, it was a merger of two broken marriages into one new one." Why so many broken families? The Soviet system was designed to ensure that middle-class families needed two full-time salaries to survive, and children were "abandoned in early infancy to state nurseries and became the state's charges."

Hitchens saw a documentary film, *Tak Zhit Nel'zya* (translated "We Can't Go on Living Like This") that provided a good picture of the squalor, cynicism, and despair so common in Soviet life. The film was produced by Stanislav Govorukhin, a friend of Alexander Solzhenitsyn. Hitchens characterized the film, which was never shown in the West, as a "frank and sometimes jeering parade of failure and unhappiness unrolled on the screen." He explained that as he sat in the theater watching the film, "I became aware that everyone else in the theater was weeping. For the first time, they were seeing an honest account of how harsh their lives were, contrary to the unceasing propaganda proclaiming the U.S.S.R. an unmatched, enviable success. Now they were free of the lies, and free to mourn."

Is that a snapshot of the future world under communist-inspired globalists? Think about what you've read in this volume. Globalists make big rosy promises (a future utopia) through their slick marketing campaigns. Are they to be trusted to deliver on those rosy promises? Most certainly not!

What must we do to stop these globalists?

Sun Tzu was a Chinese general and philosopher more than two millennia ago who wrote about the importance of strategy and wisdom. His words remain extremely applicable to the modern world and the modern fight with the globalists. He wrote, "If you know the enemy and know yourself, you need not fear the result of a hundred battles."[545]

What does this mean for the globalist threat to our future? It means we must understand both our strengths and weaknesses as well as those of our competitors, the globalists.

Throughout this volume, we've examined compelling evidence that points to a clear globalist agenda intending to undermine our liberties, economic prosperity, and freedom. Further, we learned the globalists elite have massive power to move the world community in their direction, and besides, they appear to be in league with the unseen realm as well.

This means we have some very tough times ahead, and perhaps this scenario will lead to the end times. Simpson believes a civil war between the globalists elite and the populists is quite possible—that, is unless the populists revert to authoritarians as suggested in the prior chapter, and then conspire for self-serving reasons with the globalist totalitarians. Fortunately, there is still time to avoid the worst outcome, Heiser believes. "We still have a lot of people who understand what's at stake and will resist," he points out.[546]

What's the solution to the globalist onslaught? I'll provide a detailed Christian call to action in the next chapter. However, on the broader secular front, we need to elect constitutionally savvy and courageous leaders to all levels of government. Those leaders must roll back the globalists on all fronts.

We received a temporary reprieve from the globalists' advance with the election of Donald Trump. He appears to be taking some important action to reverse the radicalism created by the progressive Obama, and more broadly, he is putting in place some people who respect our Constitution. Hopefully he'll fulfill his promise "to drain the swamp" in Washington. Time will tell whether Trump's initiatives are enough to repair the damage already done by globalists and to reverse their global progress.

CONCLUSION

This chapter asserts that many globalists are really closet communists in their ideology, which threatens a horrendous future if they reach their goal of world domination. That outcome is not a foregone conclusion, especially if freedom-loving people everywhere wake up to the serious nature of the threat and push back.

CHAPTER FOURTEEN

Nehemiah's Call to Action

This section began with an overview of efforts to push back against the globalists here in the U.S. vis-à-vis the Trump campaign as well as in a number of European countries. We learned many lessons from those efforts to include the risk that emergent nationalists/populists resisting the globalist cabal might morph into authoritarians, which could usher in significant violence to include civil war.

The next chapter unveiled the globalist movement as an ideological communist inspired confederacy that promises the world a utopia. But the evidence from history suggests if given the reigns over the world, globalist governance will create a hell on earth much as millions endured communist atrocities in the past. This outcome may in fact trigger the prophetic end times. The chapter concludes with a secular prescription to turn back the globalist assault, albeit for only a brief window of opportunity.

Finally, this concluding chapter exposes the globalist threat for Bible-believing Christians by outlining how the enemy tries to co-opt Christendom. I round out this chapter with an Old Testament illustration to demonstrate how Christians must counter the globalists' multipronged assault if we are to have any hope for a peaceful future.

GLOBALISTS TARGET CHRISTENDOM

It is paramount that Christians understand they (Christendom) are targeted for elimination by globalists who "tend to be actively antagonistic against religion in general, seeing it as divisive and the course of violence and anti-social behaviours…and [specifically against] Christians [who are] (outdated, irrelevant, centres of child abuse)," so states Doctor Philip Doecke, a professor at the Royal Melbourne Institute of Technology University, Melbourne, Australia. Others agree with the professor, including Carl Teichrib, a Christian researcher who frequently participates in globalist conferences.[547]

Mr. Teichrib states that most globalists believe "man is master of himself"…and "master of his own destiny." Teichrib said globalists intend to "marginalize Christianity" by forcing Christians to "put aside their distinctions" by sacrificing "truth on the altar of peace."[548]

Theologian Fay Voshell believes globalists won't stop at just marginalizing Christianity, however. No, they want to replace Christianity with the globalists' religion, secular humanism. She writes in the *American Thinker* that globalists intend to replace "the beatific vision of Christianity with its secularist faith in humanity by which men grant their allegiance to a global city of men ruled by elite priests who act as gods for the masses."[549]

The globalists' world has no tolerance for Christianity, Voshell argues:

> The secularist vision requires complete destruction of the old [read "Christianity"]; including nations, institutions, faith and even historical memory itself; hence, for instance, the constant attacks on the Christian Church and on the reality and concept of nation and the human being. Devotion to faith, family, nation is not only suspect, but considered positively injurious.[550]

Globalism intends to strip "humanity of its former and unique status as beings created in *imago Dei* [Latin for "image of God"] and the substitution of the idea of humanity as genderless units," writes Vosell.

There is a growing consensus among many Christian observers of globalism that the globalists elite seek to substitute Christian faith with their humanist gospel of salvation. Rousas J. Rushdoony, a twentieth-century Calvinist philosopher and father of Christian Reconstructionism, observed that globalists seek to replace Christianity with humanist institutions like the United Nations that offer salvation without a savior, "the brotherhood of man without union with God."[551]

Let Christians have no doubt about the threat. Globalists have religion in general and Christianity in particular in their crosshairs. And ironically, they are free to use false religions such as Islam to rain terror on Christianity and Christian nations.

NEW-AGE CHRISTIANS NEED TO FOLLOW AN OLD TESTAMENT BUILDER'S EXAMPLE

Christians ought to embrace the example of an Old Testament hero in their physical and metaphysical war with globalists. Specifically, Nehemiah was a godly man who evidenced the type of leadership needed in the twenty-first century with globalists.

The story of Nehemiah is found in the Old Testament book by the same name. In fact, the biblical books of Ezra and Nehemiah are lumped together in the Hebrew Bible because the two men were ancient contemporaries, as was Esther, a young Jewish maiden whom God raised to the throne of Persia as queen. Esther's husband, King Artaxerxes I, the son of Xerxes, commonly called Longimanus, reigned over the Persian Empire from 465 to 424 B.C. He was the heathen king who allowed Nehemiah to return to Jerusalem to rebuild the holy city's walls.

Consider the steps God used in Nehemiah's life to restore Jerusalem's walls. Those steps outline a process available to God's people today to reverse the threat posed by anti-Christian globalists and their agents of the unseen realm—that is, unless globalism proves to be the instrument that ushers in the prophetic end times.

Rebuilding begins with conviction.

City walls for the ancient Israeli meant strength and protection, the only means of defense against marauding enemy armies. Jerusalem's walls and that city were very special to the Jews, who considered it God's dwelling place and the center of life for the world, but they had been destroyed by Nebuchadnezzar's armies in 586 B.C.

We see in Ezra 4:11–23 a failed attempt to rebuild the walls, because some Samaritans and other pagans complained to King Artaxerxes, who stopped the project. Subsequently, in late 444 B.C., Nehemiah was with Artaxerxes in his winter capital in Susa when "he had a life-changing conversation with his brother, Hanani and some other men who had just come from Jerusalem."[552] Nehemiah inquired about the city, and they responded: "The remnant there in the province who survived the captivity are in great distress and reproach, and the wall of Jerusalem is broken down and its gates are burned with fire" (Nehemiah 1:3, NASB).

Once Nehemiah learned that Jerusalem's walls were still in ruins, he turned to God with tears and prayer: "When I heard these words I sat down and wept, and mourned for days; and he continued fasting and praying before the god of heaven" (Nehemiah 1:4, NASB).

Nehemiah's response to the news of Jerusalem illustrates how modern Christians should react to the current wreckage of the present world. Our world is corrupt, immoral, and declining into the globalists' humanist hell. Like Nehemiah, Christians must respond with tears, prayer, and fasting before God over our contemporary "ruins."

First, confess.

Nehemiah prayed hopefully:

Remember the instruction you gave your servant Moses, saying, "If you are unfaithful, I will scatter you among the nations, but if you return to me and obey my commands, then even if your exiled people are at the farthest horizon, I will gather them from there and bring them to the place I have chosen as a dwelling for my Name." (Nehemiah 1:8–9, NIV)

At the time, most Israelites [or Jews] were exiled in far-off Persia (present-day Iran) because they had forsaken God. That's why Nehemiah had to first confess to God and acknowledge His justice. Nehemiah's commitment follows that confession: "O LORD, let thy ear be attentive to the prayer of thy servant, and to the prayer of thy servants who delight to fear thy name; and give success to thy servant today," (Nehemiah 1:11a, RSV).[553]

Nehemiah made a commitment on the heels of confession to rebuild Jerusalem's walls, and with that determination, a plan began to emerge in his mind.

Nehemiah asked that the Lord "grant him [Nehemiah] mercy in the sight of this man" (Nehemiah 1:11b, RSV). "This man" was King Artaxerxes, who had the authority to grant Nehemiah's request to return to Jerusalem and rebuild the walls.

Like Nehemiah, Christians today must confess to God and acknowledge His justice has allowed the present-day persecution of His church. We have turned our back on Him and, like Nehemiah, God put us in a contemporary "exile" dominated by anti-Christian globalists who force-feed us their secular humanism.

It is past time to awaken to this oppressive threat and turn back to God, especially as the time may be short.

Second, prayerfully assemble a plan.

Nehemiah began planning the restoration of Jerusalem by petitioning God in prayer to prepare the heart of the king for Nehemiah's anticipated request. At the time, Nehemiah was the king's cupbearer, a trusted servant. Only the king had the authority to grant permission for Nehemiah to travel back to Jerusalem to rebuild the walls.

Nehemiah saw the problem clearly: God's city lacked protective walls, and they had to be restored. He gave considerable thought and prayer to rebuilding the walls before he went about pursuing that goal— asking the king to grant his request.

Similarly, Christians living in this anti-Christian humanist world must pray for the opportunity to rectify the globalist wrongs, but at the same time, we must begin to make a plan and trust God to open the doors as he did for Nehemiah.

Third, be prepared to move forward.

Nehemiah committed himself to the building project, but first he needed God to arrange the circumstances over which he had no control. Nehemiah prayed about going to speak with the king.

Nehemiah was granted an audience with the king, who saw the sadness of Nehemiah's face and asked what he wanted. Meanwhile, God had been softening the king's heart through his Jewish wife, Queen Esther. Nehemiah wrote in Nehemiah 2:1–5, NIV:

> In the month of Nisan in the twentieth year of King Artaxerxes, when wine was brought for him, I took the wine and gave it to the king. I had not been sad in his presence before, so the king asked me, "Why does your face look so sad when you are not ill? This can be nothing but sadness of heart." I was very much afraid, but I said to the king, "May the king live forever! Why should my face not look sad when the city where my ancestors are buried lies in ruins, and its gates have been destroyed by fire?" The king said to me, "What is it you want?"
>
> Then I prayed to the God of heaven, and I answered the king, "If it pleases the king and if your servant has found favor in

his sight, let him send me to the city in Judah where my ancestors are buried so that I can rebuild it."

The king was responsive to Nehemiah's plea for permission to return to Jerusalem in order to rebuild the wall.

How many of us know what God wants but fail to ask for guidance? Today, Christians have clear scriptural prescriptions for how to live in a corrupt world, yet we cower before the enemy (1 Thessalonians 4:7). We need to be like Nehemiah and be bold, tell "the king" what we want, and then be ready to act once "He" opens the door!

Remember who you are in Christ: "For we are his workmanship, created in Christ Jesus for good works, which God prepared beforehand, that we should walk in them" (Ephesians 2:10, NIV).

Fourth, find the courage to move out.

Nehemiah had the king's blessing to return to Jerusalem and begin rebuilding. But Jerusalem was a great distance from Persia, and not everyone agreed with the Persian king's endorsement of Nehemiah's request.

It took great courage for Nehemiah to travel home and confront Israel's old enemies in the land.

When Sabella the Horonite and Tobiah the Ammonite official heard about this [Nehemiah's return], they were very much disturbed that someone had come to promote the welfare of the Israelites (Nehemiah 2:10, NIV).

Nehemiah threw himself into the task of rebuilding the walls and completed the project in just fifty-two days, in part because he courageously refused to be distracted even by confirmed enemies Sanballat and Tobiah.

These enemies hounded Nehemiah throughout the course of his work. But to his credit, Nehemiah ignored them, asking:

So I sent messengers to them, saying, "I am doing a great work and I cannot come down. Why should the work stop while I leave it and come down to you?" (Nehemiah 6:3, NASB)

Nehemiah's rebuff to his critics is instructive for the contemporary Christian facing a world of secular opposition. We see a very significant task at hand—countering the ruinous work of globalists.

We should throw ourselves into the effort to defeat those opposed to God's will much as did Nehemiah in spite of the criticism and overt opposition. Our mission is to reverse the globalists' successes at building a modern Babel-like one-world government, which is contrary to God's intentions.

Unfortunately, the courage to take a righteous stand is in short supply among modern Christians. Too often we bow to our humanist culture, which intimidates rather than encourages biblical faith. After all, we are criticized at every turn for our so-called hate speech against homosexual behavior, making war on women for opposing abortion, and so-called self-righteous intolerance for claiming to have the truth in Christ alone. We too often do the easy thing when opposed and by giving up to "conform to the world," as the apostle Paul warned in Romans 12:2.

We must stand for the truth! Pastor Ray Stedman, the author and longtime evangelical Christian pastor of Peninsula Bible Church in Palo Alto, California, once told a story about truth that is very relevant today.

One day a man went to visit an old musician. He knocked on the musician's door and said, "What's the good word for today?" The old musician didn't say a word. He turned around and went back across the room to where a tuning fork was hanging. He took a hammer and struck the tuning fork so that the note resounded through the room.[554]

Then the musician said, "That, my friend, is 'A'. It was 'A' yesterday. It was 'A' five thousand years ago and it will be 'A' five thousand years from now." Then he added, "The tenor across the hall sings off-key. The soprano upstairs is flat on her high notes. And the piano in the next room is out of tune." He struck the tuning fork again and said, "That is 'A' and that, my friend, is the good word for today."[555]

Stedman explained, "That is truth. Truth is always the same. It never changes." Christians must muster the courage to stand for the truth of God in a wicked world![556]

Fifth, avoid compromise.

Even though Nehemiah refused to abandon his work due to criticism, he still faced other setbacks during the course of his rebuilding.

> But when Sanballat, Tobiah, the Arabs, the Ammonites and the people of Ashdod heard that the repairs to Jerusalem's walls had gone ahead and that the gaps were being closed, they were very angry. They all plotted together to come and fight against Jerusalem and stir up trouble against it. (Nehemiah 4:7–8, NIV)

Israel's enemies mocked Nehemiah's work, tried to incite rebellion among the Israelites, and discouraged the Israeli population. In spite of those setbacks, Nehemiah succeeded because he refused to be distracted.

Christians must be resilient like Nehemiah in the face of setbacks. We must fight against the globalist humanistic assaults on our faith. Yet too many modern Christians take their eyes off their calling and are co-opted by the siren call of the world to marginalize their faith or outright abandon their faith in favor of secular humanism. Both results are potentially devastating.

Dr. Peter Jones, a Presbyterian minister and executive director of truthxchange, calls this push to compromise our faith "oneism" as opposed to "twoism." Christians allow their faith to be marginalized when they embrace a "oneism" view, which is "multiculturalism whereby there are no value judgments, no distinction between religions, alternative sexuality is embraced, and guilt is a curable psychological illness. This sort of Christianity dishonors Jesus Christ."[557]

Christians are called to "twoism," explained Jones. There are only two options for thinking about this world, according to Romans 1:25. You either worship creation (oneism, which is really paganism), or you worship the creator. Globalists push paganism, which is worshipping creation—for them, everything is ultimately and divinely the same.

We saw evidence of worshipping paganism pushed by globalists at the 2015 Parliament of the World's Religions. Carl Teichrib reported on a talk by Gwendolyn Reece, a priestess of Athena and founder of the Sacred Space Foundation, who spoke about "the pagan concept of citizenship, community, and cosmopolis." Her idea of world community, or world city, "accepts the interconnection of all reality." Teichrib concluded the pagans at the parliament sought "to re-create a sense of the scared with the Earth, with each other, and with 'non-human beings' in the evolution of divinity."[558]

Christians are also too often co-opted to act like pagans when they abandon the spiritual resistance to join the secular effort against globalists. Peter Leithart, theologian and president of Theopolis Institute for Biblical, Liturgical & Cultural Studies in Birmingham, Alabama, warns Christians to refuse the choice of nationalism or globalism; rather, we are to follow Christ's pathway.

Leithart writes:

> We are members of a communion that, now more than ever before, is geographically universal. The church is ecumenical, a worldwide "Abrahamic empire." We are members of a real global community, which is not a Davos elite or a subversive Anonymous but a community that includes all sorts and conditions of men and (today especially) women. Our deepest brotherhood isn't with other citizens of our nation but with those who are united with us by the Spirit in the Son. Baptismal

water is thicker than blood; the Word unites us more basically than commitment to any Constitution, no matter how wise its political institutions. We cannot be nationalists.

On the other hand: The church is a body with many members, each individual member contributing in a unique way to the edification of the whole. The church is a nation of priests that encompasses all nations, tribes, tongues. Nations retain their national identities—their languages, histories, and customs—when they are disciples by the gospel; their national identities are *fulfilled* in service to Christ the King. We cannot be globalists.[559]

It is tempting to align with secular forces against globalists, but Christians must refuse that choice. Christians must always be kingdom-first people.

Finally, be plugged into the power source.

Nehemiah knew he wouldn't succeed without God's help. He began his work on his knees:

> Lord, let your ear be attentive to the prayer of this your servant and to the prayer of your servants who delight in revering your name. Give your servant success today by granting him favor in the presence of this man. (Nehemiah 1:11, NIV)

Modern Christians should take that lesson to heart because the same power available to Nehemiah is available today. The psalmist reminds us of God's Word: "And call on me in the day of trouble; I will deliver you, and you will honor me" (Psalm 50:15, NIV).

Calling on God means, as Dr. Doecke reminds us, is to "continue to focus on Jesus Christ, the One true unifying Saviour, the principles of love and care He taught, in response to total surrender and submission to His will for each of us."

CONCLUSION

Nehemiah's story teaches us that there can be no compromise with evil. Jesus evidenced the same uncompromising view of evil when He came into the temple in Jerusalem and found it filled with the moneychangers. What did He do? He made a whip of cords and drove them out of God's house.

Jesus was righteously angry because man had defiled God's house. Obedient Christians today must do likewise as Nehemiah and Jesus did to move against evil in the world, because we must always be kingdom -first people.

The Deeper State

The globalist movement is the most dangerous threat to Christians, America, and freedom-loving peoples across the globe. It is a stealth enemy with great power pushing our world at a rapid pace toward the prophetic end times.

No doubt there are many other threats at our collective doorstep. Islamic terrorism is a major global threat to our collective way of life. North Korea, Iran, Russia, and China are overtly hostile to America, Israel, and much of the rest of the world as well. We see the growing likelihood of wars, some which could easily involve nuclear weapons, space-based weapon platforms, transhumanist cyclops-like warriors and cyber weapons capable of crippling our critical infrastructure. We also see truly evil men with great power doing terrible things on a daily basis. Even the secular world comments on the general decline in morality and threats across the planet, and they, too, fear societal collapse. But these things are still not the most dangerous threat. They are only what we can see; what we don't see with our naked eyes is the key, and *The Deeper State* gives the reader a glimpse inside that emerging frightening world—the tandem operation of the seen and invisible work of the globalists elite.

While other crises occupy the daily media, globalism moves quietly but quickly in the background. If we can understand that our contemporary crises are largely controlled by the invisible world of Satan and his demons, then we can admit that the true character of this world is, as the Bible declares, truly evil. Globalists, whether they are willing or unwilling dupes, are the servants of the evil one driving events on the prophetic path toward the return of Christ. Interim stops along that path are prophesied wars involving Christians in general—especially Israel and other nations, and almost certainly America. The final stop on the globalists' grand strategy to conquer the earth involves all the nations of the world united under a global leader indwelt by Satan, who will attempt to kill all the Jews and fight against Christ when he visibly appears and invades the earth.

The true character of globalism's ideology as revealed here is therefore evil. As Christians, we are called to fight that evil, and time is short.

Yet, even today, most of the Christian church sits on the sidelines watching radical change all around us and ignores God's sobering call to action. The evidence is undeniable that change is accelerating toward the prophesied end times.

Globalization is changing everything about our world; much of that change is evil-inspired. Today, the nations of the world have become interconnected and interdependent—we're rapidly becoming a giant global village. Technological advances in today's globalized village mean we are more likely than not to share in common most goods (food, clothing, and medicine), money, diseases, security nightmares, and data with diminishing barriers.

This outcome is especially evident in the United States. Americans buy in local stores products that came from manufacturers in many distant countries. We watch our Japanese-made televisions at home or the latest global crises streaming live on our Chinese-made I-Phone-7. We drive our car—or soon will depend on a computer-controlled, self-driven vehicle—made by a foreign-owned enterprise operating here in America, assembled by "green-card" immigrant workers using parts imported from dozens of countries. We routinely call a 1-800 service center in India or Bangladesh for help with our computer or to adjust an airline reservation. We buy goods via the Internet from faceless websites using plastic cards, and those orders are fulfilled at places we can't even pronounce. In this modern globalized village, nation-state borders mean nothing, and each new day, distances and time are collapsed by our growing global interdependence.

The muscle behind this frightening revolution is globalization energized by mega-multinational corporations that are getting richer daily rather than by representative-run sovereign nation-states. Global financial markets secretly know our every purchase, and they manipulate our purchases via mass manipulative media. Increased global migration blends traditional cultures beyond recognition into a global multicultural homogenized society.

The economics of modern trade is truly mind-boggling and transformational. Globalized trade exploded from $320 billion at the end of the Second World War to more than $16 trillion in 2016, according to the World Trade Organization.[560] Such levels of international exchange mean a trade problem such as a factory breakdown or a natural disaster in some distant land will now impact a local store here in America, and vice versa.

The consequences of this surge in interconnectivity and interdependence are truly significant. The upside of globalization is rich, industrialized countries like America, and elite globalists invest in poorer countries to reduce labor costs, which allows for the mixing of people and cultures while making products cheaper for everyone. Further, it enables the sharing of ideas and improves the standard of living and quality of life for many even in those less-developed countries.

The downside of globalization includes job losses in industrialized countries and the "Americanization" of other cultures, as well as the neutering of traditional religions' influence for the masses and its replacement by secular humanism. Meanwhile, globalization enriches wealthy nations, their elite managers, and their multinational corporations by

exploiting workers in developing nations—but those elite who are getting wealthy most often refuse to pour any of their profits back into those
same communities. Thus, the gap between the rich and poor continues to
skyrocket, and discontent feeds unrest, which is becoming more violent.

The Deeper State took a deep dive into the camp of the globalists
elite who profit from the above economic environment while following
their progressive agenda to take over virtually every aspect of human
life. These self-promoting elite meet in their secret societies to formulate
policies and plans for our future world that lands them in the position
to manipulate the world's power centers for too-often destructive ends.

The volume concludes with a biblical template for defeating globalism's tragic agenda. The ancient biblical figure Nehemiah provides
an example for modern Christians to emulate through his God-fearing
efforts to courageously rebuild the walls that once protected the city of
God: Jerusalem.

Applying Nehemiah's prescription to the contemporary Christians'
fight against globalism will at best delay what every Bible student understands is God's plan for the end of time.

Specifically, God warned us about the rise and fall of nations throughout history (Daniel 2). He also warned, as we saw earlier, about the
emerging, fast-paced, globalized, interconnected world and the advances
in technology—those times are now. "But you, Daniel, roll up and seal
the words of the scroll until the time of the end. Many will go here and
there to increase knowledge" (Daniel 12:4, NIV).

At the same time, the apostle Paul warns us: "But know this, that in
the last days perilous times will come (2 Timothy 3:1, NKJV)." Interest-
ingly, the phrase "perilous times" can equally be translated as "raging
insanity." Paul continues with a long list of the conditions that will define
the end times, and one only has to watch a few minutes of the daily news
to see that raging insanity is a rapidly growing global phenomenon.

Then the Bible (Revelation 18) tells us that in the future there will
be a globalized union of nations that dominate the world through economics, military might, and even a universal false church. That's the

prophetic end times—the height of the globalist world—just prior to the triumphant return of Jesus Christ, who will bring the kingdom of God to the earth. Only at that time will we truly become one with God.

In the meantime, we are called to put the kingdom of God first, a tall order given the growing influence of the globalist cabal and the price we must be prepared to pay.

The Globalists Elite

When you go to a Broadway play, the usher provides you with a program at the door. That program identifies information about the play: a synopsis of the script, acknowledgments, credits, and the cast. This appendix provides a similar service by identifying key globalists elite, some not identified earlier in this volume, and many who try to manipulate and or control the world's power centers.

The appendix ends with a biblical reminder as to the appropriate use of wealth and influence, the challenge especially for the globalists elite.

KEY GLOBALISTS ELITE

Chapter 8 of this book examined in detail four contemporary globalists elite: the late David Rockefeller, Henry Kissinger, Hillary Clinton, and George Soros. They represent four distinct groups of modern globalists elite: corporate, academic, government, and nonprofit.

The Global Elite website (http://theglobalelite.org/globalists/) identifies elite who are considered key players of the one-world-order cabal: **1:** Lord Jacob de Rothschild; **2:** His son, Nathaniel; **3:** Baron David de Rothschild; **4:** Sir Evelyn de Rothschild; **5:** David Rockefeller Jr.; **6:** Henry Kissinger; **7:** George Soros; **8:** Lloyd Blankfein.

There are groupings of globalists who exercise significant influence in our world today as well.

COMMITTEE OF 300

The Global Elite website identifies the Committee of 300, which it describes as the "Angelo-Jewish cousin-hood that dominates the financial and political systems of the world. This cousin-hood includes the Rothschild, Rockefeller, Oppenheimer, Goldmid, Mocatta, Montefiore, Sassoon, Warburg, Samuel, Kadoorie, Franklin, Worms, Stern and Cohen families." The website provides a "Current Membership List" that is impossible to verify, but it does include many well-known names.

"The Committee of 300 uses a network of roundtable groups, think tanks and secret societies which control the world's largest financial institutions and governments," according to the Global Elite website. "The most prominent of these groups include Chatham House, Bilderberg Group, Trilateral Commission, Council on Foreign Relations, Ditchley Foundation, Club of Rome, RAND Corporation, PNAC and of course Freemasonry." Others are highlighted in chapter 9 and in appendix B.

I save print space here by calling your attention to the website where the entire "Current Membership List" of the Committee of 300 is found: http://theglobalelite.org/globalists/.

AMERICA'S 60 FAMILIES

Another website, NNDB (http://www.nndb.com/lists/439/000 127058/), cites the work of Ferdinand Lundberg, a twentieth-century American journalist known for his criticism of American financial and political institutions, who in 1937 identified America's super-rich in a book, *America's 60 Families*. Lundberg wrote:

> The United States is owned and dominated today by a hierarchy of its sixty richest families, buttressed by no more than ninety families of lesser wealth.... These families are the living center of the modern industrial oligarchy which dominates the United States, functioning discreetly under a de jure democratic form of government behind which a de facto government, absolutist and plutocratic in its lineaments, has gradually taken form since the Civil War. This de facto government is actually the government of the United States—informal, invisible, and shadowy. It is the government of money in a dollar democracy.[561]

Those sixty families were identified using the 1924 tax records. Many of those families remain publicly known today as the wealthy elite and are closely linked to the globalist network. They are:

Rothschild (Bauer or Bower) family
Rockefeller family
Oppenheimer family
Goldsmid/Goldschmidt/Goldsmith family
Mocatta family
Montefiore family
Sassoon family
Warburg (del Banco) family
Samuel family
Kadoorie family
Worms family
Stern family
Cohen family
Schiff family
Morgan family

Lazard family
Schröder family
Harriman family
Royal Family of England
Windsor (Saxe-Coburg-Gotha) family
Hanover family
Cavendish (Kennedy) family
De Medici family
Lorraine family
Plantagenet family
Habsburg/Hapsburg family
Krupp family
Bruce (Bruis, Brix, or Broase) family
Carnegie family
Mellon family
Vanderbilt family
Du Pont family
Sinclair family
Astor family
Romanov family
Li family
Onassis family
Van Duyn (Dien, or Duyne) family
Thurn und Taxis family
Guinness family
Russell family
Bush family
Bundy family
Taft family
Disney d'Isigny ("from Isigny") family
Collins family
Freeman family

McDonald family
Goodyear family
Whitney family
Reynolds family
Getty family
Hearst family
Saudi (The House of Saud) family
Franklin family
Sloane family
Walton family
Koch family
Mars family
Cargill-MacMillan family
Johnson family
Cox family
Pritzker family
S.C. Johnson family
Perkins family
Kellogg family

Another group of people should be included as globalists elite, the neowealthy of the modern world. Most acquired their wealth thanks to entrepreneurial work.

Who are the "wealthiest people in the world"?

In 2017, *Business Insider* published an article, "The 30 Richest People on Earth," which identifies thirty people who control $1.23 trillion—more than the annual combined GDP of Spain, Mexico, or Turkey.[562]

My analysis of these people suggests many on this list are globalists elitists who endorse a progressive ideology. They also exercise significant control over global power centers. A few of the "wealthiest" from the *Business Insider's* list are profiled below to demonstrate their globalist membership.

BILL GATES—MICROSOFT
Net Worth: $85.2 Billion

Bill Gates is considered the richest man in the world with a net worth at $85.2 billion. His wealth comes from Microsoft, a company he cofounded and served as the CEO of until 2000. He and his wife founded the Bill & Melinda Gates Foundation, one of the most powerful charities in the world, which aims to lift millions out of poverty, and help eliminate HIV (the AIDS virus), malaria, and other infectious diseases.[563]

Gates' humanitarian efforts sound good on the surface, but further investigation suggests there are problems in paradise. He endorses much of the globalist agenda. Consider the following.

Gates, whose father was a Planned Parenthood leader,[564] is a big supporter of vaccines, and in a CNN interview with Dr. Sanjay Gupta, Mr. Gates celebrated the idea about how vaccines can help with "reducing the population growth," a globalist agenda item.[565]

Gatesfoundation.org gave the Global Alliance for Vaccines and Immunization campaign over $4 billion, but not without controversy. A report on vacnews.com said a Gates-funded effort in India gave an HPV (human papillomavirus) vaccine to children without parental consent, and death and sickness resulted.[566] Playing "Big Brother" without consent is a globalist-agenda item.

The Gates Foundation purchased five hundred thousand shares of Monsanto stock in 2010, which some allege is an attempt to "dominate and control the world's systems, including in the areas of technology, medicine, and now agriculture." Reportedly, the foundation spends considerable money in the name of humanitarianism to establish a global food monopoly dominated by genetically modified crops and seeds. This action suggests an effort to influence if not control a significant sector of the world's economy, a globalist agenda item.

A Mexican news source accused the foundation of hiding behind humanitarianism in order to profit. "Although Bill Gates might try to say that the Foundation is not linked to his business, all it proves is the opposite: most of their donations end up favoring the commercial investments of the tycoon, not really 'donating' anything, but instead of paying taxes to state coffers, he invests his profits in where it is favorable to him economically, including propaganda from their supposed good intentions," wrote Silvia Ribeiro in the Mexican news source *La Jornada* back in 2010.[567] Globalists elite tend to seek self-enrichment, which this account suggests.

Gates is also a proponent of global government and the United Nations, both parts of the globalist agenda. Gates said, as translated into German and back into English:

> Take the UN, it has been created especially for the security in the world. We are ready for war, because we have taken every precaution. We have NATO, we have divisions, jeeps, trained people. But what is with epidemics? How many doctors do we have as much planes, tents, what scientists? If there were such a thing as a world government, we would be better prepared.[568]

Gates' endorsement of one-world government is the key globalist goal.

The Gates Foundation is aligned with the progressive left's endorsement of CommonCore (education) state standards, which Gates "commended," and said they will "improve education for millions of students." The foundation gave $170 million to that cause in 2014.

Dr. Susan Berry rebuts Gates' characterization of Common Core in a *Breitbart* article:

> Gates assumes, first, that Americans believe students can only succeed if they attend college and, second, that they believe the only reason that some students do not attend college is poor academic standards. Working hard in school, having loving parents who are actively involved in their children's school and social lives, a stable family life that supports a solid work ethic and

achievement of goals, and developing one's own natural intelligence and skills—these are immaterial. Instead, it's 'the standards' that now make or break an American student.[569]

JEFF BEZOS—AMAZON
Net Worth: $73.1 Billion

Jeff Bezos earned his $73.1 billion through his e-commerce giant, amazon.com. He has other investments, including a privately owned spacecraft company, Blue Origin, and the *Washington Post*, which he purchased in 2013. In 2016, the *Post's* editorial board called for foreign workers to replace Americans. Specifically, the paper wrote "typically the [immigrants] do jobs—tending crops, washing dishes, mowing lawns—that native-born Americans do not want."

This editorial wasn't the first to mislead the public. An earlier editorial claimed Americans' wages were rising: "The rise of populists on the left and right [presumably Trump supporters] stems from wage stagnation and related trends…. But what if that gloomy picture is obsolete, to the extent it was ever true?" said the editorial.[570]

Bezos' mouthpiece, the *Post*, puts him by association into the progressive camp, which embraces immigration at the expense of American workers.

It wasn't surprising when Bezos announced his views about President Trump's executive order temporarily halting immigration. Bezos sent an e-mail to Amazon's employees stating: America is a nation of immigrants whose diverse backgrounds, ideas, and points of view have helped us build and invent as a nation for over 240 years. To our employees in the U.S. and around the world who may be directly affected by this order, I want you to know that the full extent of Amazon's resources are behind you.[571]

He continued:

> We reached out to congressional leaders on both sides of the
> aisle to explore legislative options. Our legal team has prepared a
> declaration of support for the Washington state attorney general
> who will be filing suit against the order. We are working other
> legal options as well.[572]

Ben Kew wrote for *Breitbart* in January 2017: "Jeff Bezos was
a prominent critic of Donald Trump during the presidential campaign, assembling a team of 20 people at his newspaper the *Washington Post* to investigate every aspect of Trump's past." Meanwhile, Trump
attacked Bezos, saying that Amazon had a "huge antitrust problem"
whilst "getting away with murder" on corporation taxes. The editorial
board of the *Washington Post* also called in 2016 for an influx of illegal
immigrants to fill low-paying jobs in America.[573]

MARK ZUCKERBERG—FACEBOOK
Net Worth: $58.5 Billion

Zuckerberg was only 19 and a sophomore at Harvard when he launched
thefacebook.com that in a few years became the ubiquitous social network known today as Facebook. Today, his personal wealth is reported
to be $58.5 billion, which at age 32, makes him the youngest of the fifty
richest people in the world.

Zuckerberg and his wife, Priscilla Chan, are reportedly generous
through an organization called the Chan Zuckerberg Initiative; for
example, they gave a $25 million gift in the fight against Ebola in 2015.

The Facebook creator is a very vocal, progressive globalist who
publicly praised as "inspiring" German Chancellor Angela Merkel's
open-door refugee policy. "I hope other countries follow Germany's
lead on this," Zuckerberg told a Berlin audience.[574]

Zuckerberg also publicly targeted those at Facebook who replaced "Black Lives Matter" in favor of "All Lives Matter." He told Facebook employees that their behavior was "malicious" and "disrespectful," and then he reminded his employees there are "specific issues affecting the black community in the United States."[575]

In May 2017, Zuckerberg spoke at a Harvard commencement: "For our society to keep moving forward we have a generational challenge, to not only create new jobs but to create a new sense of purpose." He continued, warning against the "pressure to turn inwards" in communities, and the shift towards isolationism, nationalism, and authoritarianism within nations. He called for measures to make progress on climate change, which "requires coming together not just as cities or nations, but also as a global community."[576]

LARRY ELLISON—ORACLE
Net Worth: $45.3 Billion

Ellison teamed with two others to start an electronics company that began with a contract for the CIA to build a relational database-management system named Oracle. That project morphed into today's Oracle Corporation. Like many other billionaires, Ellison is a generous philanthropist committing to give away at least half of his fortune.

Ellison is very much a globalist when it comes to immigration. Like Zuckerberg, Ellison supports comprehensive immigration reform. Oracle has pushed for an increase to the H-1B visa program, which displaces American high-tech workers with cheaper foreign workers.[577]

PERSPECTIVE ON THE WEALTHY GLOBALISTS:

I could provide additional profiles of the very wealthy to demonstrate how deep go their globalist tentacles. However, it should be sufficient to understand that wealth tends to have a corrupting influence, which is why there are numerous biblical injunctions about that danger. Wealth, more often than not, as demonstrated above, contributes to activities this volume identifies with the globalists-elite agenda. But do NOT misinterpret me here. I'm not saying that because you are wealthy you are a globalist elitist. There are many fine Christian people whom God has blessed with great wealth who have not bowed to the siren call of globalism.

This should be a warning to Christians, however. Jesus warned about wealth's influence in Mark 10:23–27:

> "How hard it will be for those who have wealth to enter the kingdom of God!" And the disciples were perplexed at these words. But Jesus said to them again, "Children, how hard it is to enter the kingdom of God! It is easier for a camel to go through the eye of a needle than for someone who is rich to enter the kingdom of God." They were greatly astounded and said to one another, "Then who can be saved?" Jesus looked at them and said, "For mortals it is impossible, but not for God; for God all things are possible."

The problem for man is whom we serve, God or wealth. God expects to have first place in our lives:

> No one can serve two masters. For you will hate one and love the other, or be devoted to one and despise the other. You cannot serve both God and money. (Luke 16:13, NLT)

How then should the Christian use the gift of wealth?

Christians blessed with wealth are expected to share it generously with the poor:

> If anyone has material possessions and sees his brother in need but has no pity on him, how can the love of God be in him? (1 John 3:17, NIV)

Command those who are rich in this present world not to be arrogant nor to put their hope in wealth, which is so uncertain, but to put their hope in God, who richly provides us with everything for our enjoyment. Command them to do good, to be rich in good deeds, and to be generous and willing to share. In this way they will lay up treasure for themselves as a firm foundation for the coming age, so that they may take hold of the life that is truly life. (1 Timothy 6:17–19, NIV)

Globalists' Secret Societies

There are many secret societies, and some are especially influential among the globalists elite. Chapter 9 profiled three secret societies—Bilderberg Conference, Council on Foreign Relations, and the Trilateral Commission—but there are many others. Three more secret societies are profiled below, especially those perceived as attractive to globalists elite. The difficulty is ascertaining whether these organizations indeed have any real influence on contemporary world affairs. Certainly in the past, they included very influential people, but modern society is changing, and their impact is unlikely to be what it was in the past.

It is too easy to paint all such "secret societies" with the same condemning brush. Most are exclusive, but not necessarily sinister—much less satanic; In fact, they may perform a useful service to their members and the world in general.

The following are in the globalist camp because of their membership, and they demonstrate spiritually dark histories.

FREEMASONRY

The Freemasons are one of the longest-lasting secret societies, and they included in their ranks some very influential people, including George Washington, Benjamin Franklin, and Winston Churchill. Freemasonry dates back to at least the early part of the eighteenth century in London, and today it has more thab six million members across multiple countries. Best known for its charitable work, this all-male fraternal organization is considered secret in part due to its special handshakes, chants, code words, and private rituals.

Freemasons had an impact on the formation of the United States, given that at least nine of the fifty-six signers of the Declaration of the American independence from Great Britain were Freemasons. Their influence included everyday symbols, such as the All-Seeing Eye and the phrase *Novus Ordo Seclorum* (translated "new world order") on the backside of the U.S. dollar bill.

The early English Masons adopted some pretty commendable aims: to improve themselves morally and spiritually through acts of brotherly love and assistance. Further, members were encouraged to believe in any one god, but were anticlerical and were expected to remain aloof from politics.

These factors earned the Masons enemies among the church and the political establishments. Combine that with their international appeal and "secret" practices, and one can understand the origin of all the conspiracy theories, such as the one that says Freemasons were behind the French and American Revolutions and that they seek a new world order.

UCLA history professor Margaret Jacob, an "expert" on Freemasonry, claims that those theories are wrong. As well, she denies that Freemasonry is a religion, a common allegation. Also, according to Jacob, the All Seeing Eye of providence is said to be Masonic. "In fact," explained Jacob, "it's commonplace in the eighteenth century, that particular set of symbols [eye and pyramid]."[578]

Evidently, Ms. Jacob isn't sufficiently informed about ancient history as her "expert" label suggests. Tom Horn writes in *Zenith 2016* that the All-Seeing Eye on the Great Seal of the United States is traceable to the Freemasons' influence. We know this in part, Horn wrote, because of the association between the accompanying uncapped Egyptian pyramid and the pagan deity Osiris-Apollo-related mottoes that reference the solar god represented by the "eye."[579]

Early Freemasons were also associated with the occult architecture of our nation's capitol, as well as the layout of the entire city, which is in the shape of a pentagram, a symbol used extensively in black magic. Horn, in the book referenced earlier, makes a strong argument for the continued evil influence of Freemasonry to the present.

American Freemasons ran into a rough patch in the nineteenth century with what became known as the "Morgan Affair," when a turncoat Mason member from New York threatened to expose the fraternity's secrets. As a result, he was hushed into Canada and never heard from again. That affair soured the organization's appeal for many years, but over time, Freemasonry rebuilt its reputation in the United States.[580] Today, there are an estimated two million Masons in North America and nearly five million worldwide.

The French, unlike the Americans, never turned their back on Freemasonry, however. "Freemasonry has always had a political role in France," said Pierre Mollier with the archives at the Grant Orient de France, that country's largest lodge. "We would never tell people who to vote for, but we're a moral authority."

Freemasons claim to keep an arm's distance from organized religion, while insisting "on a belief in what Masonic jargon calls the Grand Architect of the Universe."

There is not a lot of agreement among Masons across international borders, either. For example, French Masons aren't recognized by the United Grand Lodge in England or even with those here in America.

Jean-Claude Zambelli, a French Mason and French government employee who lived in the U.S. for decades, concluded:

It's just not the same Masonry. They [the Americans] do more charitable work, like the big Shriner hospital in San Francisco. We do a lot more work on ourselves. We're not a social club. We're here to progress spiritually. Otherwise, what good is all this? The Americans are proud to be Masons and show you their Mason rings. We find that shocking.[581]

French Masons tend to be more secretive than others, which convinces some they have something to hide and perhaps explains their membership growth. That expansion is perhaps encouraged by the secrecy, due in part to the loyalty among members that breeds networking for business and political purposes.

Sophie Coignard wrote the book, *A State within A State,* which explores French Masonry. She admits in the book that "most of the Masons I know are hyper-honest but it's also fair to say that in most of the big financial-political scandals of the past 20 years, you'll find Freemasons." Coignard identifies a number of Mason-related scandals as evidence, such as the 2001 Elf-Aquitaine African bribery scandal.[582]

There are differences of opinion about the role of the Freemasons in the contemporary United States as well. One view is shared by Henry Makow, who in his blog paints the Masons with a very dark brush. Makow said in a 2002 article, "Freemasonry Is Jewish Cabalism," that the group "is a satanic cult masquerading as a religion." Then he adds a caveats to his accusation by admitting, "only their inner circles are aware that the 'Craft' is in fact devoted to Satanism."[583]

A former Freemason disputes the conspiracy, satanic accusations. Sammy Lapoint states, "From everything I've witnessed as a Freemason, there is no grand conspiracy.... The whole notion that the so-called 'Illuminati' or Freemasons are behind everything is absurd and intellectually lazy."

Lapoint continues, "Freemasonry is just a fraternity and it's best suited for nerds, not evil doers. If you're looking for evil doers, investigate the misconduct of corporations and the military-industrial complex."[584]

That is an all-too-common popular view of Freemasonry. But other former Freemasons disagree, especially as it relates to Bible-believing Christians.

The Ex-Masons for Jesus website provides a very telling and contrary perspective about Freemasonry. It states that Freemasonry is not a Christian organization, but in fact welcomes members of all faiths. It goes on to state that Freemasonry is incompatible with Christianity and provides some alarming information for the Bible-believing Christian.[585]

"Freemasonry requires each Mason to believe that there is only one god and teaches that all men worship that one god, simply using a variety of different names," according to Ex-Masons for Jesus. That name for "god" includes "a Supreme Being by believing in the Horned god of Witchcraft," as well as faith in Vishnu for the Hindu.

Freemasonry really is a religion with its own form of seeking salvation. Specifically, there is a Freemason "Legend of the Third Degree," a ritual that states "the Master Mason represents a man saved from the grace of iniquity, and raised to the faith of salvation." This ritual and others "instruct Masons how to get into heaven."[586]

Since Freemasonry embraces any "god" and has its own ways of reaching heaven, it is clearly a religion. Obviously, Freemasons are blinded from the truth—which isn't surprising, given that society's very dark history.

In conclusion, Freemasonry is a large, somewhat disjointed, international, all-male fraternity that has historically attracted some of the most powerful men to its ranks. Today, perhaps with the exception of France, the organization, although shrouded in self-imposed secrecy, obviously occult practices, and an anti-Christian religious bias, is of dwindling true political consequence—in part because it lacks a cohesive international focus.

THE ORDER OF THE SKULL AND BONES

Yale University's best known "secret society" is informally known as "Bones," the Order of the Skull and Bones (S&B), which was founded in 1832 by students. The S&B is alleged to be part of a number of conspiracies, such as the aim to dominate the world.

The S&B was formed after a dispute between debating societies at Yale. It has a reputation for concealing the pasts of members and reportedly has some bizarre initiation practices, such as "new members are asked to lie naked in coffins before telling others about their deepest and darkest sexual secrets."[587]

Members, known as Bonesmen, include some of the nation's elite: John Kerry, George Bush, and William Taft. That shouldn't surprise the reader, given that Yale is a prestigious Ivy League institution that continues to draw some of the nation's best and brightest. The S&B carefully selects only a few students each year to join its ranks.

Like many other secret societies, the S&B is associated with some famous conspiracy theories, rangingfrom the nuclear bomb to the Kennedy assassination. Those theories remain alive because of the enforced silence among members.

Bonesmen refuse to answer questions about the society, which is backed by their infamous oath of *omerta* ("silence"), to never reveal secrets. In fact, they are instructed never to mention or discuss S&B with any "barbarian" (outsider).

The S&B has a long history of recruiting prime candidates and then grooming them for future service. Further, the organization uses its extensive network to advance its members into positions of power and influence vis-à-vis its alleged intimate ties to globalist organizations such as the Council on Foreign Relations, the Trilateral Commission, and the Bilderbergers (all profiled in chapter 9).

No doubt the Bonesmen are elitists. Alexandra Robbins wrote an expose about S&B, *Secrets of the Tomb*. Robbins wrote: "If the Wizard of Oz can represent Skull and Bones, then one must point out that, for a while, Oz needed its Wizard to provide balance and a constant current of reassurance." Evidently, according to Robbins, we the Munchkin mortals need the guidance of the elite S&B.[588]

The S&B do have other interesting links. Bonesman founder William H. Russell was from a wealthy opium-empire family who studied in Germany, and likely while there he associated with the infamous Order of the Illuminati. The German Illuminati, which was founded in 1776, was accused of subversion and revolution throughout Europe, and reportedly Illuminati agents even came to the U.S. to overthrow our new republic. A 1798 letter to President George Washington confirmed that Illuminati agents were in fact in the U.S. spreading their "diabolical tenets."

At that time, Yale President Timothy Dwight warned that the Illuminati threatened to "strike at the root of all human happiness and virtue…[seeking] the overthrow of religion, government, and human society civil and domestic." Dwight continued, saying that the Illuminati conspirators are committed to evil ends "that murder, butchery, and war, however extended and dreadful, are declared by them to be completely justifiable, if necessary for these great purposes."

The Bonesmen do have an interesting, bizarre history that feeds the conspiracies. Evidently, its elite members respect the tradition to keep the rituals secret and to collaborate at a special level with fellow members. What's not clear, and likely impossible to judge, is whether S&B members do secretly advance a sinister globalist agenda. However, any organization that operates in secret—fraternal, charity, or otherwise—will continue to raise suspicions in a constitutional republic accustomed to openness and transparency. Therefore, S&B membership should not be dismissed as inconsequential.

BOHEMIAN GROVE

In 2011, the *Washington Post* ran an article about the Bohemian Grove, "Bohemian Grove: Where the Rich and Powerful Go to Misbehave."

That article profiles the Grove as a bonding place for the richest and most powerful men in the world and asserts there is nothing sinister.[589]

There are suggestions the Bohemian Grove is more than just a place for rich men to blow off steam, and perhaps that's true. One theory about what actually happens at the Grove says, for example, that discussions there were responsible for the Manhattan Project, which produced the first nuclear bomb. What other very significant decisions might have been made there over the past 120 years?

The Grove has been called an Elks' Club for the rich and a scout camp for old guys equipped with rituals. The Bohemian Club, founded in San Francisco in 1872, started using the Grove as a retreat by the 1880s. It is a real, 2,700-acre campground seventy-five miles north of San Francisco near Monte Rio, California, where every summer for two weeks, well-known men meet to drink heavily, host secret talks, perform so-called druid worship (some say "revering the Redwoods"), and perform other bizarre rituals.

Those who gather at Bohemian Grove are America's ruling class, an eclectic group of prominent political personalities like former presidents, oligarchs, top military contractors, CEOs, art leaders, and more—all men, white, affluent, and Republican, according to the *Post*. They are told that "Weaving Spiders Come Not Here," translated: "Business deals are to be left outside the camp." So what exactly is done at this secret facility, if "weaving" is in fact "not" allowed?

Former President Herbert Hoover, a Grove member, reportedly called it "the greatest men's party on earth." Such statements pricked the attention of reporters over the years who have snuck inside the Grove for a close-up look.

At least two reports avail the outsider some insight into the Bohemian Grove experience based on their secretive invasions. Texas-based filmmaker Alex Jones infiltrated the camp in 2000, and with a hidden camera made pictures of a Bohemian Grove ceremony, "Cremation of the Care," in which members wear costumes and cremate "a coffin effigy called 'Care' before a 40-foot-owl, in deference to the surrounding Redwood trees." The ritual is intended to signify a "cathartic release of life's worries," according to an article in *Fortune*.[590]

This sort of behavior by the world's elite may be a "cathartic release," but it's seriously dangerous as well. These men are among only a few thousand in the world who dictate policies that impact all of us, and places like the Bohemian Grove are grooming venues. Dr. Stanley Monteith, author of *Brotherhood of Darkness*, warns that such men are part of an "occult hierarchy" that rules the world. "The movement is led by powerful men who reject Christianity, embrace the 'dark side,' and are dedicated to the formation of a world government and a world religion," Monteith wrote.[591]

A spokesman for the Grove labeled the "40-foot-owl" ceremony "a traditional musical drama celebrating nature and summertime." Jon Ronson, a documentary filmmaker, dismissed the drama as silliness in his book *Them: Adventures with Extremists*. "My lasting impression was of an all-pervading sense of immaturity: the Elvis impersonators, the pseudo-pagan spooky rituals, the heavy drinking. These people might have reached the apex of their professions but emotionally they seemed trapped in their college years."[592]

The Bohemian Grove Action Network, according to one of its members, exists "to expose that there is a ruling class in this country, and who they are."[593] The Network describes on its website the "Cremation of Care" ceremony is performed by "members wearing red-hooded robes, cremate a coffin effigy of 'Dull Care' at the base of a 40 foot owl altar." The Network adds that about 20 percent of those in attendance "engage in homosexual activity" and others "leave at night to enjoy the company of the many prostitutes who come from around the world for this event."[594]

Philip Weiss, another Grave infiltrator who at the time worked for *Spy* magazine, spent time at the camp in 1989. He wrote:

You know you are inside the Bohemian Grove when you come down a trail in the woods and hear piano music from amid a group of tents and then round a bend to see a man with a beer in one hand…urinating into the bushes. This is the most gloried-in ritual of the encampment, the freedom of powerful men to pee wherever they like, a right the club has invoked when trying to fight government anti-sex discrimination efforts and one curtailed only when it comes to a few popular redwoods just outside the Dining Circle.

Peter Phillips, a Sonoma State University sociologist who has written a great deal about the Bohemian Club, calls the club "the global dominance group."[595] Members see themselves as "the moral underpinnings of America's greatness," according to Alex Shoumatoff, writing for *Vanity Fair*. He continues, "The Bohemian Club is like the Opus Dei of the Protestant American establishment."[596]

It's not as serious as the discussions hosted annually at Davos, but, according to Shoumatoff, the lakeside talks at the Grove are enlightening. For example, Henry Kissinger spoke on the topic "Do We Need a Foreign Policy?" And evidently it is true that, in 1942, Edward Teller did in fact plan the Manhattan Project at the Grove.

Shoumatoff indicates there are 120 separate rustic camps scattered across a 109-acre main grove, mostly resting beneath ancient redwoods. Each member is assigned to a camp that has a rather odd name, like Derelicts, Five Easy Pieces, and Rattlers.

General Colin Powell, former chairman of the Joint Chiefs of Staff and secretary of state, attended a July session at the Grove in 2016. His e-mails were hacked and then released by WikiLeaks. A few of those e-mails addressed his time at the Grove.

Powell wrote that the Grove attendees accounted for "half the nation's GDP." Obviously, there were many wealthy members in attendance in 2016 and they performed silly comedy sketches like the one Powell did with Henry Kissinger, which made fun of actor Bill Cosby. In another e-mail, Powell wrote "Enjoy[ed] the cremation of care."[597]

Powell revealed there were numerous serious events as well. Major policy players held sessions to discuss pressing domestic and foreign policy issues. Powell himself hosted one session at the Owl's Nest, and General Joseph Ralston, former vice chairman of the Joint Chiefs of Staff, hosted another session to "discuss the situation in Russia and the Ukraine."[598]

A long article published in a 2001 edition of *The Progressive*, "Down with Rich Bohemians," concludes with an important question: "What's the Point?" Why should we care about the Bohemian Grove?[599]

That's simple. The Grove is important because it is evidence that the rich and powerful come together to build cohesiveness, which potentially benefits all of us—or, it could also mean something quite the opposite. The article points out that cohesion is built among the members at the Grove in two ways.

First, rich men gathering at the Bohemian Grove is evidence there is a socially cohesive upper class. Call them the globalists elite and recall what I wrote about them in chapters 8 and 9.

Second, such gatherings reinforce cohesion among the members, which can have a positive outcome, such as group solidarity, more interaction, and help in reaching future agreement. Obviously, if building cohesion is a key aim of the Grove experience, then the sponsors have something greater in mind than having fun in the giant redwoods.

It makes infinite good sense to have a place where the nation's leaders can get away and let their hair down to enjoy themselves and perhaps begin to build trust (cohesion) in a relaxed atmosphere in preparation for future encounters where established relationships are important for the nation's work.

Building cohesion is good, but policymakers in a constitutional republic have a moral obligation to be accountable to the public. Further, the occult influence and the suggestion of immoral behavior is shocking, illegal.

OTHER SECRET SOCIETIES

There are numerous other so-called secret societies that are forums for the globalists elite. A partial list of the others include:[600]

The Club of Rome
Philosophers of Fire
The Group of Eight (G-8)
Rhodes Scholar program
Black Lodge
Aspen Institute
Knights of Malta
World Federalists
The Circle of Initiates
Nine Unknown Men
Lucis Trust
Tavistock Institute
British Quator Coronati
Mumma Group
Nasi Princes
Milner Group-Round Table
World Economic Forum
Opus Dei
Hermetic Order of the Golden Dawn
Rosicrucians
Knights of the Garter
The Priory of Zion

Notes

1. Donald Trump, Donald Trump: "False Song of Globalism," You Tube, April 27, 2016, https://www.youtube.com/watch?v=L2QmClRt9AQ.
2. Ishaan Tharoor, "After Clinton, Trump's real enemy is 'globalism,'" *The Washington Post*, November 3, 2016.
3. Ishaan Tharor, "Trump's victory places U.S. at the front of a global right-wing surge," *The Washington Post*, November 9, 2016, https://www.washington-post.com/news/worldviews/wp/2016/11/09/trumps-victory-places-u-s-at-the-front-of-a-global-right-wing-surge/?utm_term=.e595698004bf.
4. https://www.goodreads.com/author/quotes/9951.David_Rockefeller.
5. William F. Jasper, "Joe Biden on Creating a 'New World Order,'" *The New American*, April 8, 2013, https://www.thenewamerican.com/usnews/politics/item/15036-joe-biden-on-creating-a-new-world-order.
6. Ibid.
7. Adolf Hitler quotes, accessed May 19, 2017. http://thinkexist.com/quotes/adolf_hitler/.
8. Liam Stack, "Globalism: A Far-Right Conspiracy Theory Buoyed by Trump," *The New York Times*, November 14, 2016, https://www.nytimes.com/2016/11/15/us/politics/globalism-right-trump.html.
9. Ibid.

10. Ibid.

11. Brandon Smith, "Phil's Stock World: The Dark Agenda Behind Globalism and Open Borders," Zerohedge, Chatham: Newstex. Oct 27, 2016.

12. "Globalism" as contested ideology: Making sense of Manfred Steger, slides accessed May 19, 2017, http://classes.maxwell.syr.edu/max/Microsoft%20PowerPoint%20-%20Globalism%20Steger.pdf.

13. Brandon Showalter, "Globalism Is Anti-Christ, Demonic, Theologians Argue," *The Christian Post*, September 28, 2016, http://www.christianpost.com/news/globalism-antichrist-demonic-theologians-wallace-henley-fay-voshell-jim-garlow-jeremy-rabkin-170131/.

14. Ibid.

15. Kidane Mengisteab, "Globalization: Africa," *New Dictionary of the History of Ideas*, Ed. Maryanne Cline Horowitz, Vol. 3. Detroit: Charles Scribner's Sons, 2005, p. 938–941. Gale Virtual Reference Library, go.galegroup.com

16. Calestous Juma, "Globalization as we know it has failed. Africa has an alternative," World Economic Forum, July 6, 2016, https://www.weforum.org/agenda/2016/07/globalization-as-we-know-it-has-failed-africa-has-an-alternative/.

17. Heather Long, "U.S. has lost 5 million manufacturing jobs since 2000," CNN, March 29, 2016, http://money.cnn.com/2016/03/29/news/economy/us-manufacturing-jobs/.

18. Ibid.

19. "Is Globalism a Job Killer?" *States News Service*, 30 June 2016.

20 Ibid.

21. Brooks Jackson, et al, "Trump's Address to Congress," Factcheck.org, March 1, 2017, http://www.factcheck.org/2017/03/trumps-address-to-congress/.

22. "Modern Immigration Wave Brings 59 Million to U.S., Driving Population Growth and Change Through 2065," Pew Research Center, September 28, 2015, http://www.pewhispanic.org/2015/09/28/modern-immigration-wave-brings-59-million-to-u-s-driving-population-growth-and-change-through-2065/.

23. Peter N. Peregrine, "Trade," *New Dictionary of the History of Ideas*, Ed. Maryanne Cline Horowitz, Vol. 6, Detroit: Charles Scribner's Sons, 2005, pp. 2353–2356.

24. Mark Pagel, "Does globalization mean we will become one culture?," BBC, November 18, 2014, http://www.bbc.com/future/story/20120522-one-world-order.

25. Vivien Stewart, A World-Class Education, ASCD, accessed May 19, 2017, http://www.ascd.org/publications/books/111016/chapters/Globalization-and-Education.aspx.

26. Sadegh Bakhtiari," Globalization and Education: Challenges And Opportunities," International Business & Economics Research Journal, Vol 5, No 2 (2006), https://www.cluteinstitute.com/ojs/index.php/IBER/article/view/3461/3508.

27. Michael W. Chapman, "Rev. Graham: Disney Is Pushing 'LGBT Agenda' into the Minds of Your Children—Watch Out!," CNS News, March 2, 2017, https://www.cnsnews.com/blog/michael-w-chapman/rev-graham-disney-pushing-lgbt-agenda-minds-your-children-watch-out.

28. Daniela Frendo, "Gender Stereotypes in TV series," Reel Rundown," October 17, 2013, https://reelrundown.com/tv/Gender-Stereotypes-in-TV-series.

29. Thomas D. Williams, "Obama's Push for Gay Rights in Africa Backfires," Breitbart, December 21, 2015, http://www.breitbart.com/national-security/2015/12/21/obamas-push-gay-rights-africa-backfires/.

30. Ibid.

31. John Ankerberg, "The Fatal Flaws of Moral Relativism," The John Ankerberg Show, accessed May 19, 2017, https://www.jashow.org/articles/worldview/moral-relativism/the-fatal-flaws-of-moral-relativism/.

32. Francis J. Beckwith, "Philosophical Problems with Moral Relativism," Christian Research Journal, Fall 1993, http://www.therazor.org/oldroot/Fall02/cri-1.htm.

33. Joseph Farah, "Moral Relativism in America," Worldnetdaily.com, February 27, 2013, http://www.wnd.com/2013/02/moral-relativism-in-america/#XlibJOLqrrx88iYW.99.

34. Ibid.

35. Daisy Luther, "Subliminal Messaging and Predictive Programming: How They Work And Why Some People Are Immune," Activist Post, October 10, 2016, http://www.activistpost.com/2016/10/subliminal-messaging-predictive-programming-work-people-immune.html.

36. Rob Schwartz, "Monarch Programming and Mind Control," Stranger Dimensions, April 24, 2013, http://www.strangerdimensions. com/2013/04/24/monarch-programming-and-mind-control/.

37. Rob Schwartz, "Predictive Programming: Who Controls the Future?," Stranger Dimensions, August 12, 2016, http://www.strangerdimensions. com/2016/08/12/predictive-programming-controls-future/ and "Origins and Techniques of Monarch Mind Control," https://hollywoodsublimi- nals.wordpress.com/project-monarch/ .

38. Creative Disruption in Marketing, https://en.wikipedia.org/wiki/ Creative_Disruption.

39. "China Battles Worst Air Pollution of the Year," December 21, 2016, http://learningenglish.voanews.com/a/china-battles-smog-as-worst-air- pollution-of-the-year-hits-beijing-and-other-cities/3645519.html.

40. "Global Trends in Oil & Gas Markets to 2025,"," LUKOIL, http://www. lukoil.be/pdf/Trends_Global_Oil_ENG.pdf.

41. Danielle Beurteaux, "How Does Globalization Affect Resources?," May 10, 2016, http://www.digitalistmag.com/digital-supply-networks/2016/05/10/ how-globalization-affects-resources-04200588.

42. Kimberly Amadeo, "U.S. Trade Deficit: Causes, Effects, Trade Partners," The Balance, April 12, 2017, https://www.thebalance. com/u-s-trade-deficit-causes-effects-trade-partners-3306276.

43. Rachel Kelley, "Globalization and health: great possibilities, great concerns," Orthopedics Today, September 2005, http://www.healio. com/orthopedics/business-of-orthopedics/news/print/orthopedics- today/%7B366999b4-c66e-4e27-8162-23d50d44a7f8%7D/ globalization-and-health-great-possibilities-great-concerns.

44. Jessie Hellman, "Trump reinstates ban on US funding for abortion over- seas," The Hill, January 23, 2017, http://thehill.com/policy/healthcare/ abortion/315652-trump-signs-executive-order-reinstating-global-gag- rule-on.

45. Pam Matthews, "What globalization in healthcare means to you," Health- careitnews, September 12, 2005, http://www.healthcareitnews.com/news/ what-globalization-healthcare-means-you.

46. Globalization and Religion, Encyclopedia of Religion, Encyclopedia.

com, Thomson Gale, 2005, accessed May 20, 2017, http://www.encyclo-pedia.com/environment/encyclopedias-almanacs-transcripts-and-maps/globalization-and-religion.

47. Ibid.

48. Sam Solomon and E Al Maqdisi, *Modern Day Trojan Horse: The Islamic Doctrine of Immigration* (Charlottesville, VA: ANM Publishers), 10.

49. As cited in Ann Corcoran, Refugee Resettlement and the Hijra to America, Civilization Jihad Reader Series, Center for Security Policy Press, March 30, 2015, p. 13. The cited material comes from Sam Solomon and E. Al Maqdisi, Modern Day Trojan Horse: The Islamic Doctrine of Immigration (Charlottesville, VA: ANM Publishers), 10.

50. Roland Oliphant, "Russia and the West have 'entered a new Cold War'," *Telegraph*, October 10, 2016, http://www.telegraph.co.uk/news/2016/10/22/unyielding-russia-and-us-heading-for-a-new-cold-war/'

51. Ibid.

52. The Decline of the Ottoman Empire: Part 3, Nationalism," Lost Islamic History, accessed May 20, , http://lostislamichistory.com/the-decline-of-the-ottoman-empire-part-3-nationalism/.

53. Buttonwood, "Globalisation backlash 2.0," *The Economist*, July 27, 2016, http://www.economist.com/blogs/buttonwood/2016/07/economics-and-politics-0.

54. Ibid.

55. Geoffrey Wheatcroft, "Who Needs NATO?," *New York Times*, June 15, 2011, http://www.nytimes.com/2011/06/16/opinion/16iht-edwheatcroft16.html.

56. John Bolton, "The Globalist Aren't Through," Review of Governing the World, the History of an Idea by Mark Mazower, *National Review*, November 12, 2012, accessed May 23, 2017, https://www.nationalreview.com/nrd/articles/331655/.

57. Buttonwood, "Globalisation backlash 2.0," *The Economist*, July 27, 2016, http://www.economist.com/blogs/buttonwood/2016/07/economics-and-politics-0.

58. Walter R. Mead, "The Tea Party and American foreign policy: what populism means for globalism." *Foreign Affairs*, Mar.–Apr. 2011, p. 28,

https://www.foreignaffairs.com/articles/united-states/2011-03-01/
tea-party-and-american-foreign-policy.

59. Ibid.

60. Ibid.

61. Buttonwood, "Globalisation backlash 2.0," *The Economist*, July 27,
    2016, http://www.economist.com/blogs/buttonwood/2016/07/
    economics-and-politics-0.

62. Ibid.

63. Ibid.

64. "Rush on Fox News Sunday with Chris Wallace," The Rush Lim-
    baugh Show, February 19, 2017, https://www.rushlimbaugh.com/
    daily/2017/02/19/rush-on-fox-news-sunday-with-chris-wallace/.

65. Ibid.

66. Ibid.

67 Ibid.

68. Ibid.

69. Ibid.

70. Ryan Landry, "The Elites Anticipated Nationalism vs. Globalism," Social
    Matter, December 13, 2015, http://www.socialmatter.net/2015/12/13/
    the-elites-anticipated-nationalism-vs-globalism/.

71. Ibid.

72. Ibid.

73. Ibid.

74. Kurt Nimmo, "WAPO: Rand Paul's Warning aout UN Gun Grabbers
    'Black Helicopter Stuff,'" State of the Nation, June 12, 2016, http://stateof-
    thenation2012.com/?p=40160.

75. "War of the Titansalists vs Nationalists," The Millennium
    Report, June 2016, http://themillenniumreport.com/2016/06/
    the-final-war-for-planet-earth-pits-the-globalists-against-the-nationalists/.

76. "Defense Intel Chief: Obama gave 'willful' aid to al-Qaeda," *The New
    American*. 31.17, September 7, 2015, p.8.

77. William F. Jasper, "The false gospel of globalism," *The New American*,
    31:15, August 3, 2015, p. 44.

78. Ibid.

79. Ibid.

80. Ibid.

81. Brandon Smith, "Global Elitism: The Character Traits of Truly Evil People," Alt-Market.com, February 20, 2013, http://alt-market.com/articles/1348-global-elitism-the-character-traits-of-truly-evil-people.

82. Ibid.

83. Alex Newman, "In African Union, globalist agenda becomes clear: the United States, the EU, and communist China are all funding the goal of a single African government, similar to the EU," *The New American*, 31:19, October 15, 2015, p. 21.

84. Ibid.

85. Ibid.

86. Mike Lofgren, "Introduction to the Deep State," accessed May 20, 2017, http://www.mikelofgren.net/introduction-to-the-deep-state/.

87. Ibid.

88. Bruce Stokes, "Most of the world supports globalization in theory, but many question it in practice," Pew Research, September 16, 2014, http://www.pewresearch.org/fact-tank/2014/09/16/most-of-the-world-supports-globalization-in-theory-but-many-question-it-in-practice/.

89. Ibid.

90. Ibid.

91. "What the world thinks about globalization," *The Economist*, November 18, 2016, http://www.economist.com/blogs/graphicdetail/2016/11/daily-chart-12.

92. Ibid.

93. Ibid.

94. Ibid.

95. Tyler Durden, "Phil's Stock World: Are Globalists Evil or Just Misunderstood," Weblog post, Phil's Stock World, Chatham: Newstex, May 19, 2016.

96. Ibid.

97. Jasper, William F. "Brexit: rejecting globalism." *The New American*, 8 Aug. 2016, p. 17.

98. Ibid.

99. Ibid.

100. Ibid.

101. "Franklin Delano Roosevelt Memorial," National Part Service, accessed May 20, 2017, https://www.nps.gov/frde/learn/photosmultimedia/quotations.htm.

102. Michael Marshall, "U.N. Created Through FDR's Determination, Schlesinger Says," University of Virginia School of Law, October 14, 2004, https://content.law.virginia.edu/news/2004_fall/un.htm.

103. John D. MacArthur, "Original Source of NOVUS ORDO SECLORUM," Great Seal, accessed May 20, 2017, http://greatseal.com/mottoes/seclorumvirgil.html.

The motto *Novus Ordo Seclorum* was coined by Charles Thomson in June 1782. He adapted it from a line in Virgil's *Eclogue IV*, a pastoral poem written by the famed Roman writer in the first century B.C. that expresses the longing for a new era of peace and happiness. How did it come about to be placed on the dollar bill? One day in 1934, while Secretary of Agriculture Henry A. Wallace was waiting to meet with Secretary of State Cordell Hull, he looked through a State Department publication titled, "The History of the Seal of the United States."

Wallace Recollects that Day (Excerpts from his letters written in 1951 and in 1955):

Turning to page 53, I noted the colored reproduction of the reverse side of the Seal. The Latin phrase *Novus Ordo Seclorum* impressed me as meaning the New Deal of the Ages.

I was struck by the fact that the reverse side of the Seal had never been used. Therefore I took the publication to President Roosevelt and suggested a coin be put out with the obverse and reverse sides of the Seal.

Roosevelt, as he looked at the colored reproduction of the Seal, was first struck with the representation of the "All Seeing Eye," a Masonic representation of The Great Architect of the Universe. Next he was impressed with the idea that the foundation for the new order of the ages had been laid in 1776, but that it would be completed only under the eye of the Great Architect. Roosevelt like myself was a 32nd degree Mason.

He suggested that the Seal be put on the dollar bill rather than a coin and took the matter up with the Secretary of the Treasury. He brought it up in a Cabinet meeting* and asked James Farley [Postmaster General and a Roman Catholic] if he thought the Catholics would have any objection to the "All Seeing Eye" which he as a Mason looked on as a Masonic symbol of Deity. Farley said "no, there would be no objection."

When the first draft came back from the Treasury, the obverse eagle side was on the left of the bill as is heraldic practice. Roosevelt insisted that the order be reversed so that the phrase "of the United States" would be under the obverse side of the Seal.

The new $1 silver certificates began to be printed in the summer of 1935.

104. Strobe Talbott, "America Abroad; They Come Bearing Hope," Time, October 7, 1991.

105. "The Final War for Planet Earth Pits the Globalists Against the Nationalists, WAR OF THE TITANS: Globalists vs Nationalists," *The Millennium Report*, June 13, 2016, http://themillenniumreport.com/2016/06/the-final-war-for-planet-earth-pits-the-globalists-against-the-nationalists/.

106. David Rockefeller as quoted by Christopher J. Larson in "David Rockefeller's Book: 'Memoirs' = Treason in Writing," accessed May 20, s017, http://saynototyranny.blogspot.com/2007/10/david-rockefellers-book-memoirs-treason.html.

107. Sheila Liaugminas, "Kissinger' hope for a new world order...led by Obama," Mercatornet, January 12, 2009, https://www.mercatornet.com/mobile/view/kissinger_hope_for_a_new_world_orderled_by_obama#sthash.WcpehTZe.dpuf.

108. "The Final War for Planet Earth Pits the Globalists Against the Nationalists, WAR OF THE TITANS: Globalists vs Nationalists," The Millennium Report, June 13, 2016, http://themillenniumreport.com/2016/06/the-final-war-for-planet-earth-pits-the-globalists-against-the-nationalists/.

109. "The Globalist Agenda: How the Elite Control Your Mind and Life," accessed May 20, 2017, https://www.globalistagenda.org/elitebeliefs.htm.

110. The Final War for Planet Earth Pits the Globalists Against the Nationalists, WAR OF THE TITANS: Globalists vs Nationalists," The Millennium Report, June 13, 2016, http://themillenniumreport.com/2016/06/the-final-war-for-planet-earth-pits-the-globalists-against-the-nationalists/.

111. Andrew M. Łobaczewski, *Political ponerology: a science on the nature of evil adjusted for political purposes*, Red Pill Press, Ltd, 1998 and Helinä

Häkkänen-Nyholm, Psychopathy and Law: A Practitioner's Guide, John
Wiley & Sons, Mar 23, 2012, p. 178.

112. "10 Most Famous Psychopaths in History," Posi-
tiveMed, September 30, 2014, http://positivemed.
com/2014/09/30/10-famous-psychopaths-history/.

113. "The Globalist Agenda: How the Elite Control Your Mind and Life,"
accessed May 20, 2017, https://www.globalistagenda.org/elitebeliefs.htm.

114. Ibid.

115. Jon Rappoport, "UC Berkeley Riots Night: Globalist Dupes on Parade,"
Wordpress.com, February 3, 2017, https://anoutsidersojourn2.wordpress.
com/2017/02/03/uc-berkeley-riots-night-globalist-dupes-on-parade/.

116. Michael Bodley, "UC Berkeley cancels right-wing provocateur's talk amid
violent protest," San Francisco Chronicle, February 2, 2017, http://www.
sfgate.com/bayarea/article/Protesters-storm-Milo-Yiannopoulos-event-at-
UC-10901829.php.

117. "Milo Yiannopoulos event at UC Berkeley canceled after violent protests," CBS News, February 2, 2017, http://www.cbsnews.com/news/
milo-yiannopoulos-uc-berkeley-event-canceled-after-violent-protests/.

118. Jon Rappoport, "UC Berkeley Riots Night: Globalist Dupes on Parade,"
Wordpress.com, February 3, 2017, https://anoutsidersojourn2.wordpress.
com/2017/02/03/uc-berkeley-riots-night-globalist-dupes-on-parade/.

119. Ibid.

120. "Ads Offer Protesters $2500 to Disrupt Trump Inauguration," Sput-
nik International, January 17, 2017, https://sputniknews.com/
us/201701171049697952-ads-offering-thousands-protest-trump/ .

121. Servando Gonzalez, "How the CFR Globalist Conspirators Miscalculated," newswithviews.com, June 10, 2016, http://www.newswithviews.
com/Gonzalez/servando162.htm.

122. Ibid.

123. "The Fabien Society," accessed May 20, 2017, https://en.wikipedia.org/
wiki/Fabian_Society.

124. Sadiq Khan, ed., "Our London: The Capital Beyond 2015," Fabian Ideas
634, Fabian Society, accessed May 20, 2017, http://www.fabians.org.uk/
wp-content/uploads/2013/12/Our_London_WEB.pdf.

125. Richard Butrick, "The Obama Sell Game," The American Thinker,

November 1, 2013, http://www.americanthinker.com/blog/2013/11/the_obama_sell_game.html#ixzz4bg4FDGDP.

126. Jerry Bowyer, "Barack Obama, Fabian Socialist," *Forbes*, November 3, 2008, https://www.forbes.com/2008/11/03/obama-fabian-socialist-oped-cx_jb_1103bowyer.html.

127. Servando Gonzalez, "How the CFR Globalist Conspirators Miscalculated," newswithviews.com, June 10, 2016, http://www.newswithviews.com/Gonzalez/servando162.htm.

128. Ibid.

129. Ben Wolfgang, "Clinton: 'I do not want to repeal the 2nd Amendment,'" *The Washington Times*, August 3, 2016, http://www.washingtontimes.com/news/2016/aug/3/hillary-clinton-i-do-not-want-repeal-2nd-amendment/

130. John R. Lott, "Four ways Hillary Clinton will work to end gun ownership as president," Fox News, June 6, 2016, http://www.foxnews.com/opinion/2016/06/06/four-ways-president-hillary-clinton-will-work-to-end-gun-ownership.html.

131. Servando Gonzalez, "How the CFR Globalist Conspirators Miscalculated," newswithviews.com, June 10, 2016, http://www.newswithviews.com/Gonzalez/servando162.htm.

132. Richard J. Barnet, *The Alliance*, Simon & Schuster, NY, 1983, p. 360.

133. "Globalist Movements: The Trilateral Commission," EndTimesTruth, accessed May 20, 2017, http://endtimestruth.com/globalist-movements/.

134. "Does the Bible prophesy a one-world government and a one-world currency in the end times?," Gotquestions.org, accessed May 20, 2017, https://www.gotquestions.org/one-world-government.html.

135. Interview with Manfred B. Steger, Department of Sociology, University of Hawaii, Honolulu, Hawaii, March 13, 2017.

136. "What is the one world order?," Gotquestions.org, accessed May 20, 2017, https://www.gotquestions.org/new-world-order.html.

137. Marc Clausen, "Globalism versus Globalization," Bereans in the gate.com, July 22, 2016, http://bereansatthegate.com/globalism-versus-globalization/.

138. Ibid.

139. D.C. McAlliser, "The Sordid History of Liberals Calling Republicans

Racists," PJ Media, September 13, 2016, https://pjmedia.com/blog/the-sordid-history-of-liberals-calling-republicans-racists/.

140. Glenn Beck, *Liars: How Progressives Exploit Our Fears for Power and Control*, Simon & Schuster, Inc., New York, NY, 2016, p.3.

141. Ibid.

142. Christopher Burkett, "Remaking the World: Progressivism and American Foreign Policy," The Heritage Foundation, September 24, 2013, http://www.heritage.org/political-process/report/remaking-the-world-progressivism-and-american-foreign-policy.

143. Ibid.

144. Glenn Beck, *Liars: How Progressives Exploit Our Fears for Power and Control*, Simon & Schuster, Inc., New York, NY, 2016, p.10.

145. Christopher Burkett, "Remaking the World: Progressivism and American Foreign Policy," The Heritage Foundation, September 24, 2013, http://www.heritage.org/political-process/report/remaking-the-world-progressivism-and-american-foreign-policy.

146. John Fonte & John Yoo, "Progressivism Goes Global," The Hudson Institute, September 28, 2016, https://hudson.org/research/12872-progressivism-goes-global.

147. Steven Pifer, "What's the deal with Senate Republicans and the test ban treaty?," The Brookings Institute, September 26, 2016, https://www.brookings.edu/blog/order-from-chaos/2016/09/26/whats-the-deal-with-senate-republicans-and-the-test-ban-treaty/

148. John Fonte & John Yoo, "Progressivism Goes Global," The Hudson Institute, September 28, 2016, https://hudson.org/research/12872-progressivism-goes-global.

149. Timothy Cama, "GOP: Obama circumventing Senate in Paris climate deal talks," The Hill, October 20, 2015, http://thehill.com/policy/energy-environment/257511-gop-senators-obama-circumventing-congress-in-climate-deal-talks.

150. John R. Bolton, Should We Take Global Governance Seriously?, *Chicago Journal of International Law: Vol. 1*: No. 2, Article 2, http://chicagounbound.uchicago.edu/cjil/vol1/iss2/2/.

151. Ibid.

152. "Council on Foreign Relations," Democratic Internationalism, Docu-

ments.mx, January 2, 2016, http://documents.mx/documents/demo-cratic-internationalism.html.

153. John Fonte & John Yoo, "Progressivism Goes Global," The Hudson Institute, September 28, 2016, https://hudson.org/research/12872-progressivism-goes-global.

154. Ewen MacAskill, "Clinton: It is a 'great regret' the US is not in International Criminal Court," The Guardian, August 6, 2009, https://www.theguardian.com/world/2009/aug/06/us-international-criminal-court.

155. John Fonte & John Yoo, "Progressivism Goes Global," The Hudson Institute, September 28, 2016, https://hudson.org/research/12872-progressivism-goes-global.

156. Ibid.

157. Ibid.

158. Manfred Steger, "Globalization: A Very Short Introduction," Oxford University Press, April 2013, http://www.veryshortintroduc-tions.com/view/10.1093/actrade/9780199662661.001.0001/actrade-9780199662661-chapter-2.

159. "Globalization Since the Fourteenth Century," A Quick Guide to the World History of Globalization, accessed May 20, 2017, https://www.sas.upenn.edu/~dludden/global1.htm.

160. Manfred Steger, "Globalization: A Very Short Introduction," Oxford University Press, April 2013, http://www.veryshortintroduc-tions.com/view/10.1093/actrade/9780199662661.001.0001/actrade-9780199662661-chapter-2.

161. Ibid.

162. Ibid.

163. "Current World Population," Worldometers.info, accessed May 20, 2017, http://www.worldometers.info/world-population/.

164. James Watkins, "Genghis Khan: The Father of Globalization," Ozy.com, November 29, 2016, http://www.ozy.com/flashback/genghis-khan-the-father-of-globalization/71997.

165. John W. Whitehead, "What did Charles Darwin really believe?," Huffing-tonpost.com, updated November 17, 2011, http://www.huffingtonpost.com/john-w-whitehead/what-did-charles-darwin-r_b_166521.html.

166. Michael Bargo, Jr., "What Darwin Said About God," *The American*

Thinker, September 4, 2011, http://www.americanthinker. com/2011/09/what_darwin_said_about_god.html#ixzz4hdOI2HXa.

167. John W. Whitehead, "What did Charles Darwin really believe?," Huffing-tonpost.com, updated November 17, 2011, http://www.huffingtonpost. com/john-w-whitehead/what-did-charles-darwin-r_b_166521.html.

168. Peter Corning, Nature Magic: Synergy in Evolution and the Fate of Humankind, Cambridge University Press, May 5, 2003, accessed May 24, 2017, https://books.google.com/books?id=Elwzu8vUmhQC&pg =PA108&lpg=PA108&dq=%E2%80%9CThe+growth+of+large+bu siness+is+merely+a+survival+of+the+fittest.%E2%80%9D&source= bl&ots=5ISfIWSEe_&sig=qDa-8Vk_Sgno7dm7MQ7DI5g8sZc&hl =en&sa=X&ved=0ahUKEwjy6dDBt4jUAhVBNSYKHcXJB4gQ6A EIKjAC#v=onepage&q=%E2%80%9CThe%20growth%20of%20 large%20business%20is%20merely%20a%20survival%20of%20the%20 fittest.%E2%80%9D&f=false.

169. John W. Whitehead, "What did Charles Darwin really believe?," Huffing-tonpost.com, updated November 17, 2011, http://www.huffingtonpost. com/john-w-whitehead/what-did-charles-darwin-r_b_166521.html.

170. Bradley C.S. Watson, "Darwin's Constitution," National Review, May 17, 2010, p. 29.

171. John W. Whitehead, "What did Charles Darwin really believe?," Huffing-tonpost.com, updated November 17, 2011, http://www.huffingtonpost. com/john-w-whitehead/what-did-charles-darwin-r_b_166521.html.

172. "Hegel and his dialectic: A philosophy of history," The AgeoftheSage.org, accessed May 20, 2017, http://www.age-of-the-sage.org/philosophy/his-tory/hegel_philosophy_history.html.

173. Dr. Thomas West and Dr. John Grant, Hillsdale College, Hillsdale Dialogues, February 20, 2015, http://blog.hillsdale.edu/online-courses/ hegel-and-early-progressivism.

174. Ibid.

175. Ibid.

176. John William Burgess, Reconstruction and the Constitution, 1866-1876, Charles Scribner's Sons, New York, NY, 1905, p. 133. https:// archive.org/details/reconstructionco00burg.

177. Glenn Beck, *Liars: How Progressives Exploit Our Fears for Power and Control,* Simon & Schuster, Inc., New York, NY, 2016, p.20.

178. Ronald J. Pestritto, Woodrow Wilson and the Roots of Modern Liberalism, Rowman & Littlefield Publishing Inc., New York, 2005, p. 25, accessed May 24, 2017, https://books.google.com/books?id=RLu8UbOPyTAC &printsec=frontcover&dq=Woodrow+Wilson+and+the+Roots+of+M odern+Liberalism&hl=en&sa=X&ved=0ahUKEwiUtMi3vojUAhUEO yYKHf5gAV8Q6AEIJjAA#v=onepage&q=Woodrow%20Wilson%20 and%20the%20Roots%20of%20Modern%20Liberalism&f=false.

179. Paula Span, "How did the man hailed as the savior of humanity suddenly become America's most hated president?," American History;Aug2011, Vol. 46 Issue 3, p, 36, http://connection.ebscohost.com/c/arti-cles/61354313/how-did-man-hailed-as-savior-humanity-suddenly-become-americas-most-hated-president.

180. Woodrow Wilson and Ronald J. Pestritto, Woodrow Wilson: The Essential Political Writings, Lexington Books, 2005, p.. 121, accessed May 24, 2017, https://books.google.com/books?id=sHttQqlEb50C&pg=PA 121&dq=All+that+progressives+ask+or+desire+is+permission+%5B in+an%5D+era+when+%E2%80%98development,%E2%80%99 +%E2%80%98evolution,%E2%80%99+is+the+scientific+word,+ %5Bto%5D+interpret+the+Constitution+according+to+the+Darw inian+principle;+all+they+ask+is+recognition+of+the+fact+that+a+ nation+is+a+living+thing+and+not+a+machine.%E2%80%9D&hl =en&sa=X&ved=0ahUKEwjbsfmwwIjUAhXDNiYKHZBNCIYQ 6AEIIjAA#v=onepage&q=All%20that%20progressives%20ask%20 or%20desire%20is%20permission%20%5Bin%20an%5D%20 era%20when%20%E2%80%98development%2C%E2%80%99%20 %E2%80%98evolution%2C%E2%80%99%20is%20the%20 scientific%20word%2C%20%5Bto%5D%20interpret%20the%20 Constitution%20according%20to%20the%20Darwinian%20 principle%3B%20all%20they%20ask%20is%20recognition%20 of%20the%20fact%20that%20a%20nation%20is%20a%20living%20 thing%20and%20not%20a%20machine.%E2%80%9D&f=false.

181. Glenn Beck, *Liars: How Progressives Exploit Our Fears for Power and Control*, Simon & Schuster, Inc., New York, NY, 2016, p. 60.

182. Ibid, p.64.

183. James S. McMaster, McMaster's Commercial Cases for Banker, Treasurer

and Credit Man, McMaster Company, 1917, p.97, accessed May 24, 2017, https://books.google.com/books?id=o0MZAAAAYAAJ&pg=PA 97&dq=%E2%80%9CWe+stand+firm+in+armed+neutrality.%E2% 80%9D&hl=en&sa=X&ved=0ahUKEwjm9efowYjUAhVLLyYKHe U6Cq8Q6AEIJjAA#v=onepage&q=%E2%80%9CWe%20stand%20 firm%20in%20armed%20neutrality.%E2%80%9D&f=false.

184. Glenn Beck, *Liars: How Progressives Exploit Our Fears for Power and Control*, Simon & Schuster, Inc., New York, NY, 2016, p.71.

185. "Hillary Clinton Honored with The Woodrow Wilson Award for Public Service," Wilson Center, April 26, 2012, https://www.wilsoncenter.org/event/hillary-clinton-honored-the-woodrow-wilson-award-for-public-service#sthash.SnR5XPmH.dpuf.

186. Paula Span, "How did the man hailed as the savior of humanity suddenly become America's most hated president?," American History; Aug 2011, Vol. 46 Issue 3, p, 36, http://connection.ebscohost.com/c/articles/61354313/how-did-man-hailed-as-savior-humanity-suddenly-become-americas-most-hated-president.

187. "Quotes," Globalist Agenda, accessed May 22, 2017, http://www.globalistagenda.org/quotes.htm.

188. William L. Anderson, "The Legacy of Progressivism," Ludwig von Mises Institute, Auburn, Alabama, 1991, as published in The Political Junkie Handbook, ed. Michael Crane, S.P.I. Books, New York, 2004, p.46, accessed May 24, 2017, https://books.google.com/books?id=2ChqGIvW-rsC&pg=PA46&dq=Sinclair+and+%E2%80%9CAmerican+heart%E 2%80%9D+and+The+Pure+Food+and+Drug+Act+of+1906.&hl=en &sa=X&ved=0ahUKEwjXgLGvxYjUAhWFNSYKHazrD9cQ6AEIJj AA#v=onepage&q=Sinclair%20and%20%E2%80%9CAmerican%20 heart%E2%80%9D%20and%20The%20Pure%20Food%20and%20 Drug%20Act%20of%201906.&f=false.

189. "Stretching Executive Power in Wartime," Editorial, New York Times, May 27, 2007, https://campaigningforhistory.blogs.nytimes.com/2007/05/27/stretching-executive-power-in-wartime/?_r=0.

190. Ibid.

191. Glenn Beck, *Liars: How Progressives Exploit Our Fears for Power and Control*, Simon & Schuster, Inc., New York, NY, 2016, p. 106.

192. William Beach, "We're Spending More Than Ever and It Doesn't Work." The Daily Signal, January 14, 2009, http://dailysignal.com/2009/01/14/were-spending-more-than-ever-and-it-doesnt-work/.

193. Ibid.

194. Bradely C.S. Watson, "Darwin's Constitution," *National Review*, May 17, 2010, pp. 28–34.

195. Ibid.

196. Ibid.

197. Townsend Hoopes and Douglas Brinkley, FDR and the Creation of the U.N., Yale University Press, New York Times on the Web, accessed May 20, 2015, http://www.nytimes.com/books/first/h/hoopes-fdr.html.

198. "The United States and the Founding of the United Nations, August 1941–October 1945," Bureau of Public Affairs, U.S. Department of State, accessed May 20, 2017, https://2001-2009.state.gov/r/pa/ho/pubs/fs/55407.htm.

199. Michael Marshall, "U.N. Created Through FDR's Determination, Schlesinger Says," University of Virginia School of Law, October 14, 2004, https://content.law.virginia.edu/news/2004_fall/un.htm.

200. Ross Douthat, "The Myth of Cosmopolitanism," *New York Times*, July 2, 2016, https://www.nytimes.com/2016/07/03/opinion/sunday/the-myth-of-cosmopolitanism.html.

201. "The Globalists," The Global Elite, accessed May 22, 2017, http://theglobalelite.org/globalists/.

202. Ferdinand Lundberg, *America's 60 Families*, The Vanguard Press, New York, 1937, https://archive.org/stream/LundbergFerdinandAmericas60Families1937PDFscan/Lundberg,%20Ferdinand%20-%20America%27s%2060%20Families%20(1937)_djvu.txt.

203. Jonathan Kandell, "David Rockefeller, Philanthropist and Head of Chase Manhattan, Dies at 101," *New York Times*, March 20, 2017, https://www.nytimes.com/2017/03/20/business/david-rockefeller-dead-chase-manhattan-banker.html.

204. Ibid.

205. "Family Planning," The Rockefeller Foundation, accessed May 20, 2017, http://rockefeller100.org/exhibits/show/health/family-planning.

206. "Woman Reveals Intense Suffering Caused by Norplant Abortifacient,"

Population Research Institute, November 6, 2014, https://www.pop.org/content/woman-reveals-intense-suffering-caused-norplant-abortifacient.

207. William F. Jasper, "David Rockefeller, 'Mr. Globalist,' Dead at 101," *The New American*, March 20, 2017. https://www.thenewamerican.com/culture/biography/item/25654-david-rockefeller-mr-globalist-dead-at-101.

208. "Kinsey Reports," The Rockefeller Foundation, accessed May 20, 2017, http://rockefeller100.org/exhibits/show/health/kinsey-reports.

209. Robert H. Knight, "How Alfred C. Kinsey's Sex Studies Have Harmed Women and Children," Concerned Women for America, accessed May 20, 2017, http://concernedwomen.org/images/content/kinsey-women_11_03.pdf.

210. Brett Curtiss, "Inclusive Economies, Sexual Orientation, and Gender Identity and Expression," The Rockefeller Foundation, accessed May 20, 3017, https://www.rockefellerfoundation.org/blog/inclusive-economies-sexual-orientation/.

211. Jonathan Kandell, "David Rockefeller, Philanthropist and Head of Chase Manhattan, Dies at 101," *New York Times,* March 20, 2017, https://www.nytimes.com/2017/03/20/business/david-rockefeller-dead-chase-manhattan-banker.html.

212. Inderjeet Parmar, "To relate knowledge and action: The impact of the Rockefeller Foundation on Foreign Policy thinking during America's rise to globalism 1939-1945," Minerva Vol. 40, No. 3, 2002, pp. 235–263.

213. Yates, Steven. "Openly attacking American sovereignty: globalists are now openly revealing their true goal of submerging the United States in a world government." *The New American*, 17 Apr. 2006, p. 29+. *Academic.*

214. Ibid.

215. Ibid.

216. David Rockefeller as quoted by Christopher J. Larson in "David Rockefeller's Book: 'Memoirs' = Treason in Writing," p. 405, accessed May 20, s017, http://saynototyranny.blogspot.com/2007/10/david-rockefellers-book-memoirs-treason.html.

217. Alex Newman, "New Report: Exposes Rockefeller Dynasty's Role in 'Climate' Scam," *The New American*, February 6, 2017, pp. 22–24.

218. Ibid.

219. Ibid.

220. Alana Goodman, "Memo Shows Secret Coordination Effort Against ExxonMobil by Climate Activists, Rockefeller Fund," *Washington Free Beacon*, April 14, 2016, http://freebeacon.com/issues/memo-shows-secret-coordination-effort-exxonmobil-climate-activists-rockefeller-fund/.

221. Alex Newman, "New Report: Exposes Rockefeller Dynasty's Role in 'Climate' Scam," The New American, February 6, 2017, pp. 22–24.

222. Ibid.

223. Gregg William Norman, "Kissinger: Cover-up king; hailed by President Bush as a respected public servant, Henry Kissinger has actually been the faithful servant of a corrupt international elite bent on total power. (Cover Story: Conspiracy)." *The New American*, 30 Dec. 2002, p. 10+.

224. Ibid.

225. Henry A. Kissinger, AZ Quotes, accessed May 20, 2017, http://www.azquotes.com/quote/653697.

226. Greg Gandin, "Henry Kissinger, Hillary Clinton's Tutor in War and Peace," *The Nation*, February 5, 2016, https://www.thenation.com/article/henry-kissinger-hillary-clintons-tutor-in-war-and-peace/.

227. Grigg, William Norman. "Kissinger: cover-up king; hailed by President Bush as a respected public servant, Henry Kissinger has actually been the faithful servant of a corrupt international elite bent on total power. (Cover Story: Conspiracy)." *The New American*, 30 Dec. 2002, p. 10+.

228. Ibid.

229. Ibid.

230. Amy Chozick, "Hillary Clinton's Ties to Henry Kissinger Come Back to Haunt Her," *New York Times*, February 12, 2016, accessed May 24, 2017, https://www.nytimes.com/politics/first-draft/2016/02/12/hillary-clintons-ties-to-henry-kissinger-come-back-to-haunt-her/?_r=0.

231. Alex Newman, "Globalist Henry Kissinger Outlines 'New World Order,'" *The New American,* September 1, 2014, p.26, https://www.thenewamerican.com/world-news/item/19030-globalist-henry-kissinger-outlines-new-world-order.

232. Jeffrey Goldberg, "The Lessons of Henry Kissinger," *The Atlantic*, December 2016, p.53, https://www.theatlantic.com/magazine/archive/2016/12/the-lessons-of-henry-kissinger/505868/.

233. Martha Sherrill, "In 1993 we interviewed Hillary Clinton about religion and politics. Here's what she said." *Washingtonpost.com*, 17 Oct. 2016.

234. Ibid.

235. Ibid.

236. Ibid.

237. Ibid.

238. Ibid.

239. "Clinton, Hillary Rodham 1988–1989, 1991," DOCPLAYER, accessed May 20, 2015, http://docplayer.net/1137975-Clinton-hillary-rod-ham-1988-1989-1991.html.

240. Milo Beckman, "Don't vote for Hillary Clinton because you have to—vote for her because she's a true progressive." *Quartz*, 26 Oct. 2016.

241. Harper Neidig, "Ex-FBI official: Clintons are a 'crime family,'" *The Hill*, October 30, 2016, http://thehill.com/blogs/ballot-box/presidential-races/303458-former-fbi-official-clintons-are-a-crime-family.

242. "Bill and Hillary Inc. The Clintons' financial affairs." *The Economist*, 1 Oct. 2016, p. 26.

243. Ibid.

244. Cited in William F. Jasper, "The Clinton Crime Cesspool," *The New American,* December 5, 2016, pp. 17–24.

245. Ibid.

246. Julia Hahn, "Leaked Hillary Clinton Speech to Foreign Bank: 'My Dream Is a Hemispheric Common Market with Open Trade and Open Borders,'" Breitbart, October 7, 2016, http://www.breitbart.com/2016-presidential-race/2016/10/07/leaked-hillary-clinton-speech-to-foreign-bank-my-dream-is-a-hemispheric-common-market-with-open-trade-and-open-borders/.

247. Cited in William F. Jasper, "The Clinton Crime Cesspool," *The New American,* December 5, 2016, pp. 17–24.

248. "REPORT: Hillary And Staff Had Access to Top-Secret Info for Years after Leaving State Dept.," Hannity.com, accessed May 20, 2017, http://www.hannity.com/articles/hanpr-election-493995-493995/report-hillary-and-staff-had-access-15699519/.

249. "Bill and Hillary Inc. The Clintons' financial affairs." *The Economist*, 1 Oct. 2016, p. 26.

250. Tyler Durden, "Doug Band to John Podesta: 'If This Story Gets Out, We Are Screwed,'" ZeroHedge, October 30,

2016, http://www.zerohedge.com/news/2016-10-30/doug-band-john-podesta-if-story-gets-out-we-are-screwed.

251. Cited in William F. Jasper, "The Clinton Crime Cesspool," *The New American*, December 5, 2016, pp. 17–24.

252. "Here's How to Explain Soros' $1 Billion Losing Bet against Trump," *The Street*, January 17, 2017, https://www.thestreet.com/story/13954459/1/here-s-how-to-explain-soros-1-billion-losing-bet-against-trump.html.

253. George Gimein, "George Soros Is Mad as Hell He made billions antici-pating blowups. Now he thinks George Bush is creating one," *Fortune*, October 27, 2003, http://archive.fortune.com/magazines/fortune/fortune_archive/2003/10/27/351671/index.htm.

254. Cliff Kincaid, "The Hidden Soros Agenda: Drugs, Money, the Media, and Political Power," Accuracy in Media, Octo-ber 27, 2004, http://www.aim.org/special-report/the-hidden-soros-agenda-drugs-money-the-media-and-political-power/.

255. Ibid.

256. Tayyab Baloch, "Soros Media Plots Color Revoluation in Amer-ica" Katehon, February 8, 2017, http://katehon.com/article/soros-media-plots-color-revolution-america.

257. Ibid.

258. Jay Syrmopoulos, "Globalist Soros Exposed Funding Over 50 Organizations in Women's March on DC," The Free Thought Project, January 22, 2017, http://thefreethoughtproject.com/soros-exposed-funding-womens-march-dc/#A9vzFvDSZTXSrHb1.99.

259. J. D. Heyes, "George Soros letter reveals globalist plan to destroy the First World by eliminating national borders with global migrant blitzkreig invasions," Natural News, November 6, 2015, http://www.naturalnews.com/051869_George_Soros_national_borders_migrant_invasion.html.

260. Cliff Kincaid, "The Hidden Soros Agenda: Drugs, Money, the Media, and Political Power," Accuracy in Media, Octo-ber 27, 2004, http://www.aim.org/special-report/the-hidden-soros-agenda-drugs-money-the-media-and-political-power/.

261. Ibid.

262. "Leaked Documents Reveal Expansive Soros Funding to Manipulate Fed-eral Elections," *States News Service*, 7 Nov. 2016.

263. Ibid.

264. Joe Schoffstall, "Soros-Tied Networks, Foundations Joined Forces to Create Trump 'Resistance' Fund," *Washington Free Beacon*, April 1, 2017, http://freebeacon.com/issues/SOROS-tied-networks-foundations-joined-forces-create-trump-resistance-fund/.

265. Charlotte Allen, "Soros and Simony," First Things, December 2016, https://www.firstthings.com/article/2016/12/soros-and-simony.

266. William F. Jasper, "George Soros: The 'God' Who Should Be Jailed," *New American,* February 6, 2017, pp. 10–14, https://www.thenewamerican.com/culture/biography/item/25189-george-soros-the-god-who-should-be-jailed.

267. Tayyab Baloch , "Soros Media Plots Color Revolutation in America," Katehon, February 8, 2017, http://katehon.com/article/soros-media-plots-color-revolution-america.

268. Ibid.

269. Ibid.

270. Ibid.

271. Amy Brittain and Sari Horwitz, "Justice Scalia spent his last hours with members of this secretive society of elite hunters," *The Washington Post*, February 24, 2016, https://www.washingtonpost.com/world/national-security/justice-scalia-spent-his-last-hours-with-members-of-this-secretive-society-of-elite-hunters/2016/02/24/1d77af38-db20-11e5-891a-4ed04f4213e8_story.html?utm_term=.a0ddda32e9f6.

272. G. William Domhoff, "Social Cohesion & the Bohemian Grove," Who Rules America, accessed May 20, 2017, http://www2.ucsc.edu/whorulesamerica/power/bohemian_grove.html.

273. "10 Crazy College Secret Societies," ZEN College Life, accessed May 20, 2017, http://www.zencollegelife.com/10-crazy-college-secret-societies/.

274. Ibid.

275. Bonnie H. Erickson, "Secret Societies and Social Structure," Social Forces, Vol. 60:1, September 1981, pp. 188-210, https://academic.oup.com/sf/article-abstract/60/1/188/1938308/Secret-Societies-and-Social-Structure?redirectedFrom=fulltext.

276. David Bay, "A Transcript of Secret Societies," The Cutting Edge Radio Program, accessed May 20, 2017, http://www.cuttingedge.org/ce1037.html.

277. "Brotherhood of the Snake," accessed May 22, 2017, https://www.bibliote-capleyades.net/vida_alien/godseden/godseden03.htm#Brotherhood of the Snake.

278. The Israelites rebelled against God who sent venomous snakes among them to get their attention. The snakes compelled the Israelites to approach Moses to declare, "We sinned when we spoke against the Lord and against you. Pray that the Lord will take the snakes away from us (Numbers 21:7, NIV)." Moses did pray and God said to Moses, "Make a snake and put it up on a pole, anyone who is bitten can look at it and live (Numbers 21:8, NIV)." The modern medical symbol of a bronze snake on a pole originated with this account.

279. Beth Rowland, "Home Grown Terrorists," America's Civil War, Historynet, July 2015, pp. 49-53. http://www.historynet.com/home-grown-terrorists.htm.

280. Ibid.

281. Ibid.

282. Jim Marrs, Rule by Secrecy, as cited in BookCase Kroupnov Website, accessed May 20, 2017, http://www.bibliotecapleyades.net/sociopolitica/sociopol_rulebysecrecy.htm.

283. Ibid.

284. Ibid.

285. Ibid.

286. "Bilderbergers give John Edwards the nod?" *The New American*, 9 Aug. 2004, p. 5.

287. Ibid.

288. Jason Simpkins, "The World's Most Powerful Secret Societies: The Bilder-bergs," Outsider Club, January 21, 2014, https://www.outsiderclub.com/secret-societies-the-bilderbergs-david-rockefeller-trilateral-commission-council-on-foreign-relations/751.

289. "Kingmakers Don't Even Change Loation Let Alone Plans for the Nation," *States News Service*, 8 Mar. 2016.

290. Ibid.

291. Alex Newman, "Where Big Business and Big Government Meet," *The New American*, July 7, 2014, pp. 21–26.

292. "Bilderbergers give John Edwards the nod?" *The New American*, August 9, 2004, p. 5.

293. Ibid.

294. Alex Newman, "Where Big Business and Big Government Meet," *The New American*, July 7, 2014, pp. 21–26.

295. Ibid.

296. Ibid.

297. The Logan Act (18 U.S.C.A. § 953 [1948]) is a single federal statute making it a crime for a citizen to confer with foreign governments against the interests of the United States. Specifically, it prohibits citizens from negotiating with other nations on behalf of the United States without authorization. http://legal-dictionary.thefreedictionary.com/Logan+Act.

298. "Who We Are," FAQs, Council on Foreign Relations, accessed May 20,, 2017, http://www.cfr.org/about/faqs.html.

299. "Our History," Council on Foreign Relations, accessed May 20, 2017, http://www.cfr.org/about/history/cfr/inquiry.html.

300. Ibid.

301. "Covenant of the League of Nations," accessed May 20, 2017, https://en.wikipedia.org/wiki/Covenant_of_the_League_of_Nations.

302. Ibid.

303. Alex Newman, "Some of Trump's Picks Have Troubling Links to Globalism, CFR," The New American, February 25, 2017, https://www.thenewamerican.com/usnews/politics/item/25475-some-of-trump-s-picks-have-troubling-links-to-globalism-cfr.

304. James Perloff, "Council on Foreign Relations," *The New American*, August 3, 2009, pp. 10-16, https://www.thenewamerican.com/usnews/foreign-policy/item/1213-council-on-foreign-relations.

305. Edith Kermit Roosevelt, "Elite Clique Holds Power in U.S.," *Indianapolis News*, December 23, 1961, p. 6, cited in http://www.ourrepubliconline.com/Author/104.

306. William F. Jasper, "David Rockefeller, 'Mr. Globalist,' Dead at 101," *The New American*, March 20, 2017, https://www.thenewamerican.com/culture/biography/item/25654-david-rockefeller-mr-globalist-dead-at-101.

307. James Perloff, "Council on Foreign Relations," *The New American*, August 3, 2009, pp. 10-16, https://www.thenewamerican.com/usnews/foreign-policy/item/1213-council-on-foreign-relations.

308. "Advisory Committee on Postwar Foreign Policy,"
   accessed May 20, 2017, https://en.wikipedia.org/wiki/
   Advisory_Committee_on_Postwar_Foreign_Policy.

309. "United Nations," accessed May 20, 2017, https://en.wikiquote.org/
   wiki/United_Nations.

310. James Perloff, "Council on Foreign Relations," *The New American*,
   August 3, 2009, pp. 10-16, https://www.thenewamerican.com/usnews/
   foreign-policy/item/1213-council-on-foreign-relations.

311. Ibid.

312. Ibid.

313. "Novus Ordo Seclorum: The New World Order," Overlords of Chaos,
   accessed May 20, 2015, http://www.overlordsofchaos.com/html/1965-
   69.html.

314. Alex Newman, "Some of Trump's Picks Have Troubling Links to Globalism, CFR," The New American, February 25, 2017, https://www.
   thenewamerican.com/usnews/politics/item/25475-some-of-trump-s-
   picks-have-troubling-links-to-globalism-cfr.

315. Diane Kepus, "What Have 'We' Done to Our Country?,"
   News with Views, May 19, 2017, https://newswithviews.com/
   what-have-we-done-to-our-country/.

316. Damien Sharkov, "Will New National Security Adviser
   McMaster Clash with Donald Trum on Russia?" *Newsweek*, February 22, 2017, http://www.newsweek.com/
   what-will-trumps-new-pick-mcmasters-clash-russia-559278.

317. Bob Adelmann, "Trump names ExxonMobil Chief Rex Tillerson secretary
   of state," New American, December 13, 2016, https://www.thenewamer-
   ican.com/usnews/politics/item/24827-trump-names-exxonmobil-chief-
   rex-tillerson-secretary-of-state.

318. W. E. B., "The Council on Foreign Relations (CFR) and
   The New World Order," Conspiracy Archive, December 21,
   2013, http://www.conspiracyarchive.com/2013/12/21/
   the-council-on-foreign-relations-cfr-and-the-new-world-order/.

319. Richard Brookhiser, "The Grey/Lurid World of the Trilateral Commision,
   National Review, November 13, 1981, pp. 1328-1333, https://www.unz.
   org/Pub/NationalRev-1981nov13-01328.

320. "Globalist and Grey Cardinal Zbigniew Brezezinski Dies at 89," The Globalist Elite, TGE News, May 28, 2017, accessed May 29, 2017 http://theglobalelite.org/globalist-grey-cardinal-zbigniew-brzezinski-dies-89/?utm_source=feedburner&utm_medium=e-mail&utm_campaign=Feed%3A+TheGlobalElite+%28The+Global+Elite%29.

321. Richard Brookhiser, "The Grey/Lurid World of the Trilateral Commision, National Review, November 13, 1981, pp. 1328-1333, https://www.unz.org/Pub/NationalRev-1981nov13-01328.

322. Ibid.

323. Ibid.

324. Ibid.

325. Ibid.

326. Ibid.

327. Ibid.

328. Ibid.

329. Ibid.

330. Laurence H. Shoup, *The Presidency: The Carter Presidency and Beyond Power and Politics in the 1980s*, book review, *Christian Science Monitor*, July 14, 1980, accessed May 20, 2017, http://www.csmonitor.com/1980/0714/071450.html.

331. Patrick Wood, "Trilateral Commission Exposed," Agenda 21 News, December 4, 2012, http://agenda21news.com/2012/12/trilateral-commission-exposed/.

332. Ari Kaufman, "America's Three Worst Presidents," *American Thinker*, February 18, 2008, http://www.americanthinker.com/articles/2008/02/americas_three_worst_president.html.

333. "Jimmy Carter on Budget & Economy," On the Issues, accessed May 20, 2017, http://www.ontheissues.org/celeb/Jimmy_Carter_Budget_&_Economy.htm.

334. Richard Brookhiser, "The Grey/Lurid World of the Trilateral Commision, National Review, November 13, 1981, pp. 1328-1333, https://www.unz.org/Pub/NationalRev-1981nov13-01328.

335. Ibid.

336. Ibid.

337. Robert Alan Goldberg, Enemies Within: The Culture of Conspiracy in

Modern America, Yale University Press, 2008, p. 52, accessed May 25, 2017, https://books.google.com/books?id=Z8e5YELGGFAC&pg=PA5 2&lpg=PA52&dq=goldwater+and+%22a+skillful,+coordinated+effort+ to+seize+control+and+consolidate+the+four+centers+of+power%22&s ource=bl&ots=cUYGdHQ16t&sig=thRgoFdz91nYR-NLTzUeW2ByR 4A&hl=en&sa=X&ved=0ahUKEwjn8fnag4vUAhXB8CYKHTnxD foQ6AEIKDAB#v=onepage&q=goldwater%20and%20%22a%20 skillful%2C%20coordinated%20effort%20to%20seize%20con-trol%20and%20consolidate%20the%20four%20centers%20of%20 power%22&f=false.

338. David Weigel, "Ron Paul on the Trilateral Commission," Slate, December 23, 2011, http://www.slate.com/blogs/weigel/2011/12/23/ron_paul_on_ the_trilateral_commission.html.

339. "David Rockefeller's book *Memoirs* admits secretly conspiring for a NOW," OpenGov—Open Government Brainstorm, accessed May 25, 2017, http://opengov.ideascale.com/a/dtd/David-Rockefeller-s-book-Mem-oirs-admits-secretly-conspiring-for-a-NWO/4007-4049.

340. Heinz Duther, The Trilateral Commission and the New World Order, IAC Society, 2010, p. 42, https://books.google.com/books?id=Jvbl5o9_ rm8C&pg=PA2&dq=%E2%80%9CIt+transcends+and+influences+ national+systems.++It+requires+new+and+more+intensive+forms+o f+international+cooperation+to+realize+its+benefits+and+to+counte ract+economic+and+political+nationalism.%E2%80%9D&source= gbs_selected_pages&cad=2#v=onepage&q=%E2%80%9CIt%20tran-scends%20and%20influences%20national%20systems.%20%20It%20 requires%20new%20and%20more%20intensive%20forms%20of%20 international%20cooperation%20to%20realize%20its%20benefits%20 and%20to%20counteract%20economic%20and%20political%20 nationalism.%E2%80%9D&f=false.

341. Jon Rappoport, "The TPP, Monsanto, Rockefeller, Tri-lateral Commission, Brzezinski," accessed May 20, 2017, https://jonrappoport.wordpress.com/2015/05/27/ the-tpp-monsanto-rockefeller-trilateral-commission-brzezinski/.

342. Eric Bradner, "Trump's TPP withdrawal: 5 things to know," CNN, January 23, 2017, http://www.cnn.com/2017/01/23/politics/ trump-tpp-things-to-know/.

343. Jon Rappoport, "Trump: what dangers does he face from Globalists?" Trilateral Commission, CFR, WEF/Davos, Bilderberg?," Robert Scott Bell Show, December 6, 2016, http://www.robertscottbell.com/government/trump-what-dangers-does-he-face-from-globalists-TRILATERAL-commission-cfr-wefdavos-bilderberg-by-jon-rappoport/.

344. Rachel Alexander, "Agenda 21: Conspiracy Theory or Real Threat," Townhall.com, July 2, 2011, http://townhall.com/columnists/rachelalexander/2011/07/02/agenda_21_conspiracy_theory_or_real_threat/page/full.

345. Caitlin Dickson, "Agenda 21: The UN Conspiracy that Just Won't Die," *The Daily Beast*, April 13, 2014, http://www.thedailybeast.com/articles/2014/04/13/agenda-21-the-un-conspiracy-that-just-won-t-die.html.

346. Andrew Cohen, "Is the UN Using Bake Paths to Achieve World Domination?," The Atlantic, February 7, 2012, http://www.theatlantic.com/national/archive/2012/02/is-the-un-using-bike-paths-to-achieve-world-domination/252572/ .

347. Rachel Alexander, "Agenda 21: Conspiracy Theory or Real Threat," Townhall.com, July 2, 2011, http://townhall.com/columnists/rachelalexander/2011/07/02/agenda_21_conspiracy_theory_or_real_threat/page/full.

348. Jon Rappoport, "Things You Really Should Know About the Global Domination Agenda: The TPP, Monsanto, Rockefeller, Trilateral Commission, Brzezinski," Activistpost.com, September 21, 2015, http://consciouslifenews.com/really-about-global-domination-agenda-tpp-monsanto-rockefeller-trilateral-commission-brzezinski/1197862/#.

349. "The Progressive, Statist, Globalist Agenda," Words of Wisdom, accessed May 21, 2017, https://themadpiper.wordpress.com/tag/history/.

350. "Famous Quotations on Banking," The Money Masters, accessed May 21, 2017, http://www.themoneymasters.com/the-money-masters/famous-quotations-on-banking/.

351. Ibid.

352. Sol Palha, "Federal Reserve Cartel's Main objectives; Manipulate Markets and The Masses," Safe Haven, March 31, 2016,http://www.safehaven.com/article/40958/federal-reserve-cartels-main-objectives-manipulate-markets-and-the-masses.

353. Josiah Stamp, director of the bank of England, accessed May 21, 2015, http://www.harmlesswise.com/conspiracy/quotes/14.

354. "Famous Quotations on Banking," The Money Masters, accessed May 21, 2017, http://www.themoneymasters.com/the-money-masters/famous-quotations-on-banking/.

355. "Quotes from International Bankers and Fathers of America," *Thoughts about Gold, Silver, and other stuff,* accessed May 21, 2017, http://www.rapidtrends.com/quotes-from-international-bankers-and-fathers-of-america/.

356. "Federal Reserve System," Wikiquote, accessed May 21, 2017, https://en.wikiquote.org/wiki/Federal_Reserve_System.

357. "Economy," Wikipedia, accessed May 21, 2017, https://en.wikipedia.org/wiki/Economy.

358. "Free Market," ARI, accessed May 21, 2017, http://aynrandlexicon.com/lexicon/free_market.html.

359. "Context: a financial element in the larger centers has owned the Government - FDR," Metabunk.org, accessed May 21, 2017, https://www.metabunk.org/context-a-financial-element-in-the-larger-centers-has-owned-the-government-fdr.t338/.

360. Jeff Cox, "5 biggest banks now own almost half the industry," CBNC, April 15, 2015, http://www.cnbc.com/2015/04/15/5-biggest-banks-now-own-almost-half-the-industry.html.

361. John Maxfield, "Who Owns JPMorgan Chase?," The Motley Fool, February 19, 2013, https://www.fool.com/investing/general/2013/02/19/who-owns-jpmorgan-chase.aspx.

362. Ananya Bhattacharya, "China now runs 4 of the world's 5 biggest banks," CNN Money, August 4, 2015, http://money.cnn.com/2015/08/04/investing/worlds-biggest-banks-china/.

363. "The Largest Banks in The World," Worldatlas, accessed May 21, 2017, http://www.worldatlas.com/articles/the-largest-banks-in-the-world.html.

364. "Why is it important to separate Federal Reserve monetary policy decisions from political influence?," FAQs, Board of Governors of the Federal Reserve System, accessed May 21, 2017, https://www.federalreserve.gov/faqs/why-is-it-important-to-separate-federal-reserve-monetary-policy-decisions-from-political-influence.htm.

365. Ibid.

366. Paul Davidson, "Trump defends U-turn on China's currency manipulation," USA Today, April 16, 2017, https://www.usatoday.com/story/money/2017/04/16/trump-defends-u-turn-china-currencys-practices/100548546/.

367. Jeff Faux, "Free Trade and Moral Hypocrisy," *The Globalist,* July 21, 2016, https://www.theglobalist.com/free-trade-and-moral-hypocrisy/.

368. Ibid.

369. Michael Bastasch, "UN Climate Chief: We Should 'Make Every Effort' To Reduce Population Increases," The Daily Caller, April 6, 2015, http://dailycaller.com/2015/04/06/un-climate-chief-we-should-make-every-effort-to-reduce-population-increases/.

370. Ibid.

371. Ibid.

372. Michael Bastasch, "Al Gore once again suggests 'fertility management' to fight global warming," The Daily Caller, January 27, 2014, http://dailycaller.com/2014/01/27/al-gore-once-again-suggests-fertility-management-to-fight-global-warming/.

373. Ibid.

374. Sarah Knapton, "Humans 'will become God-like cyborgs within 200 years,'" The Telegraph, May 25, 2015, http://www.telegraph.co.uk/culture/hay-festival/11627386/Humans-will-become-God-like-cyborgs-within-200-years.html.

375. Ibid.

376. Peter Ubel, "Is the profit motive ruining American healthcare?," *Forbes*, February 12, 2014, https://www.forbes.com/sites/peterubel/2014/02/12/is-the-profit-motive-ruining-american-healthcare/#59a3c93837b9.

377. Ibid.

378. "Aldous Huxley Control Humans," YouTube, accessed May 21, 2017, https://www.youtube.com/watch?v=x9cbOLKkxzs.

379. "In Searching For A New Enemy To Unite Us, We Came Up With The Threat Of Global Warming," Climatism, January 24, 2014, https://climatism.wordpress.com/2014/01/24/in-searching-for-a-new-enemy-to-unite-us-we-came-up-with-the-threat-of-global-warming/.

380. Brian Viner, "Why the world isn't running out of oil," *The Telegraph*, February 19, 2013, http://www.telegraph.co.uk/news/earth/energy/oil/9867659/Why-the-world-isnt-running-out-of-oil.html.

381. Ibid.

382. "How Much Coal Is Left, U.S. Energy Administration Information, accessed May 21, 2017, https://www.eia.gov/energyexplained/index.cfm?page=coal_reserves.

383. "Providing Insight into Climate Change," Friends of Science, accessed May 21, 2017, https://friendsofscience.org/index.php?id=3.

384. Ibid.

385. "Former Presidents and Other High-Profile Leaders Warn About the 'Invisible Government' Running the United Statesk" Global Elite News, September 14, 2013, http://theglobalelite.org/former-presidents-warn-invisible-government-running-united-states/.

386. Almon Leroy Way, Jr., "The American System of Government: Politics & Government in the U.S.A., accessed May 21, 2017, http://www.proconservative.net/CUNAPolSci201PartOneC.shtml.

387. Ibid.

388. "Majority in U.S. Prefer State Over Federal Government Power, Gallup, July 11, 2016, http://www.gallup.com/poll/193595/majority-prefer-state-federal-government-power.aspx.

389. Joseph Postell, "From Administrative State to Constitutional Government," The Heritage Foundation, December 14, 2012, http://www.heritage.org/political-process/report/administrative-state-constitutional-government.

390. Ibid.

391. "What is the purpose of the Federal Reserve System?," FAQs, Board of Governors of the Federal Reserve System, accessed May 21, 2017, https://www.federalreserve.gov/faqs/about_12594.htm .

392. Zoe Thomas, "Why do many Americans mistrust the Federal Reserve?," BBC, December 15, 2015, http://www.bbc.com/news/business-35079495.

393. "Community Reinvestment Act," FAQs, Board of Governors of the Federal Reserve System, accessed May 21, 2017, https://www.federalreserve.gov/consumerscommunities/cra_about.htm.

394. Matt Palumbo, "Overselling TARP: The Myth of the $15 Billion Profit,"

National Review, January 6, 2015, http://www.nationalreview.com/article/395822/overselling-tarp-myth-15-billion-profit-matt-palumbo.

395. Louis Jacobson, "Rand Paul says Barack Obama 'spent nearly a trillion dollars on make-work government jobs,'" Politifact, January 30, 2014,http://www.politifact.com/truth-o-meter/statements/2014/jan/30/rand-paul/rand-paul-says-barack-obama-spent-nearly-trillion-/.

396. Richard Conniff, "The Political History of Cap and Trade," *Smithsonian Magazine*, August 2009, http://www.smithsonianmag.com/air/the-political-history-of-cap-and-trade-34711212/#Eyef3djVTZLEQXHx.99.

397. "Cap and trade primer: eight reasons why cap and trade harms the economy and reduces jobs," Institute of Energy Research, accessed May 21, 2017, http://instituteforenergyresearch.org/studies/cap-and-trade-primer-eight-reasons-why-cap-and-trade-harms-the-economy-and-reduces-jobs/.

398. Becket Adams, "Obama Fact Check: Is Only Bush Responsible for Bailouts and Is GM Really 'Number One'?," *The Blaze*, January 26, 2012, http://www.theblaze.com/news/2012/01/26/obama-fact-check-bush-responsible-for-bailouts-and-gm-is-number-one/.

399. Jeff Sommer, "*Gripes About Obamacare Aside, Health Insurers Are in a Profit Spiral,*" *New York Times, March 18, 2017,* https://www.nytimes.com/2017/03/18/business/health-insurers-profit.html.

400. Penny Starr, "Hillary Clinton: United Nations Is 'Single Most Important Global Institution,'" CNS News, September 8,2010, http://www.cnsnews.com/news/article/hillary-clinton-united-nations-single-most-important-global-institution.

401. Joseph Klein, "The Clinton Agenda of Global Government and 'Progressive Internationalism'," *Frontpage Magazine*, September 20, 2016, http://www.frontpagemag.com/fpm/264226/clinton-agenda-global-government-and-progressive-joseph-klein.

402. Ibid.

403. Ibid.

404. Logan Anderson, "What Hillary Clinton's first job out of law school can tell us about who she is today," hillaryclinton.com, July 26, 2016, https://www.hillaryclinton.com/feed/what-hillary-clintons-first-job-out-of-law-school-can-tell-us-about-who-she-is-today/.

405. Ibid.

406. AWR Hawkins, "Six Wikileaks E-mails on Hillary Clinton and Gun Control," Breitbart, October 18, 2016, http://www.breitbart.com/big-government/2016/10/18/six-wikileaks-hillary-clinton-gun-controls/.

407. AWR Hawkins, "Hillary Clinton: Australia Gun Ban 'Worth Looking At' In U.S.," Breitbart, October 16, 2015, http://www.breitbart.com/big-government/2015/10/16/hillary-clinton-australia-gun-ban-worth-looking-u-s/.

408. Susan Smith, "Guns & Politics: In Her Own Words, Hillary On Gun Control," The Daily Caller, October 1, 2016, http://dailycaller.com/2016/10/01/guns-politics-in-her-own-words-hillary-on-gun-control/.

409. Marc A. Thiessen, "Hillary Clinton is a threat to religious liberty," *The Washington Post*, October 13, 2016,https://www.washingtonpost.com/opinions/hillary-clinton-is-a-threat-to-religious-liberty/2016/10/13/878cdc36-9150-11e6-a6a3-d50061aa9fae_story.html?utm_term=.f1dc0f812052.

410. Ben Johnson, "Hillary Clinton: 'I've been fighting to defend religious freedom for years,'" Life Site News, August 22, 2016, https://www.lifesitenews.com/news/hillary-clinton-ive-been-fighting-to-defend-religious-freedom-for-years.

411. Amy Chozick, "Hillary Clinton Says U.S. Should Lead Effort to Help Syrian Migrants," *New York Times*, September 9, 2015, https://www.nytimes.com/politics/first-draft/2015/09/09/hillary-clinton-says-u-s-should-lead-effort-to-help-syrian-migrants/.

412. "Hillary Clinton: U.S. should take 65,000 Syrian refugees," Face the Nation, CBS News, September 20, 2015, http://www.cbsnews.com/news/hillary-clinton-u-s-should-take-65000-syrian-refugees/.

413. "The Yearbook of International Organizations," Union of International Associates, accessed May 22, 2017, https://www.uia.org/yearbook.

414. "Intergovernmental Organizations (IGOs)," Harvard Law School, accessed May 21, 2017, http://hls.harvard.edu/dept/opia/what-is-public-interest-law/public-international-law/intergovernmental-organizations-igos/.

415. Ibid.

416. Stephanie Morrow, "What Kind of Power Does The UN Wield Internationally?," accessed May 21, 2017, https://www.legalzoom.com/articles/what-kind-of-power-does-the-un-wield-internationally.

417. "Criticism of the United Nations," Wikipedia, accessed May 21, 2017, https://en.wikipedia.org/wiki/Criticism_of_the_United_Nations.

418. "What is NATO?," North Atlantic Treaty Organization, accessed May 21, 2017, http://www.nato.int/nato-welcome/index.html.

419. "The EU in brief," European Union, accessed May 21, 2017, https://europa.eu/european-union/about-eu/eu-in-brief_en.

420. Katie Mansfield, "EU POWER GRAB: Brussels to launch its own prosecutor's office despite sovereignty concerns," Express, April 4, 2017, http://www.express.co.uk/news/world/787656/european-union-prosecutors-office-tax-fraud-germany-france.

421. "Our Mission," Organization of the Oil Exporting Countries, accessed May 21, 2017, http://www.opec.org/opec_web/en/about_us/23.htm.

422. Tim Worstall, "Now OPEC Faces The Problem of All Economic Cartels: Enforcement," Forbes, December 1, 2016, https://www.forbes.com/sites/timworstall/2016/12/01/now-opec-faces-the-problem-of-all-economic-cartels-enforcement/#7333979148be.

423. "What is the WTO?," World Trade Organization, accessed May 21, 2017, https://www.wto.org/english/thewto_e/whatis_e/whatis_e.htm.

424. "Top Reasons to Oppose the WTO," Global Exchange, accessed May 21, 2017, http://www.globalexchange.org/resources/wto/oppose.

425. "Who We Are," Organization of American States, accessed May 21, 2017, http://www.oas.org/en/about/who_we_are.asp.

426. "OAS Meets amid Strong Criticism from Latin America's Left," Telesur Television, June 13, 2016, http://www.telesurtv.net/english/news/OAS-Meets-amid-Strong-Criticism-from-Latin-Americas-Left-20160613-0015.html.

427. Brianna Lee and Danielle Renwick, "The Organization of American States," Council on Foreign Relations, May 17, 2017, http://www.cfr.org/americas/organization-american-states/p27945.

428. "African Charter on Democracy, Elections and Governance," African Commission on Human and People's Rights, accessed May 21, 2017, http://www.achpr.org/instruments/charter-democracy/.

429. Simon Allison, "The African Union often comes under fire, but even critics admit that Africa is in much better shape with the continental body than without it," Institute for Security Studies, September 9, 2014, https://issafrica.org/iss-today/think-again-in-defence-of-the-african-union.

430. "Profile: African Union," BBC, February 5, 2015, http://www.bbc.com/news/world-africa-16910745.

431. "FY 2017 Budget Request Highlights," USAID, accessed May 21, 2017, https://www.usaid.gov/results-and-data/budget-spending.

432. Peter Willets, "The Role of NGOs in Global Governance," World Politics Review, September 27, 2011, http://www.worldpoliticsreview.com/articles/10147/the-role-of-ngos-in-global-governance.

433. "The path through the fields," *The Economist*, November 3, 2012, http://www.economist.com/news/briefing/21565617-bangladesh-has-dysfunctional-politics-and-stunted-private-sector-yet-it-has-been-surprisingly.

434. Didde Lykke and Michala Bendixen, "New bill wants Danish refugee council out of the refugee appeals board," Refugees.DK, August 24, 2016, http://refugees.dk/en/news/2016/august/new-bill-wants-danish-refugee-council-out-of-the-refugee-appeals-board/.

435. "CARE's History," CARE International, accessed May 21, 2017, http://www.care-international.org/who-we-are/cares-history.

436. Ibid.

437. Amber William, "BREAKING: America Is Under Attack By These 187 Groups Funded By George Soros," My Daily Informer, April 24, 2017, http://www.mydailyinformer.com/breaking-america-is-under-attack-by-these-187-groups-funded-by-george-soros/.

438. "Edward B. Taylor," Truman State University, accessed May 21, 2017, http://rgraber.sites.truman.edu/edward-b-taylor/.

439. Angelo M. Codevilla, *The Rise of Political Correctness*, Claremont Review of Books, Fall 2016, pp. 37–43.

440. Ibid.

441. Ibid.

442. Ibid.

443. Ibid.

444. Ibid.

445. "Aleksandr I. Solzhenitsyn," Archives, *New York Times*, September 15, 1973, http://www.nytimes.com/1973/09/15/archives/peace-and-violence-aleksandr-i-solzhenitsyn.html.

446. "Education," Solutions, Heritage Foundation, accessed May 21, 2017, http://solutions.heritage.org/culture-society/education/.

447. Daren Jonescu, "Public Education: Progressivism's Unbeatable Advantage," *American Thinker*, October 15, 2016, http://www.americanthinker.com/articles/2016/10/public_education_progressivisms_unbeatable_advantage.html.

448. Ibid.

449. Glenn H. Reynolds, "Glenn Reynolds: How PC culture is killing higher education," USA Today, March 28, 2016, https://www.usatoday.com/story/opinion/2016/03/28/emory-university-student-activists-trump-2016-chalk-free-speech-column/82322316/.

450. Ibid.

451. Eric Metaxas, "Political Correctness is killing Colleges: Emotions or Education?," ChristianHeadlines.com, January 23, 2017, http://www.christianheadlines.com/columnists/breakpoint/political-correctness-is-killing-colleges-emotions-or-education.html.

452. Ibid.

453. Ibid.

454. Ibid.

455. Edward Bernays, "Propaganda," ThirdWorldTraveler.com, 2005, accessed May 21, 2017, http://www.thirdworldtraveler.com/Propaganda/Propaganda_Bernays.html.

456. Dan Merica and Sophie Tatum, "Clinton expresses regret for saying 'half' of Trump supporters are 'deplorables,'" CNN, September 12, 2016, http://www.cnn.com/2016/09/09/politics/hillary-clinton-donald-trump-basket-of-deplorables/.

457. Bianca-Marina Mitu, "Culture and Television, the Televisual Globalization," Economics, Management, and Financial Markets, Vol. 6(2), 2011, pp. 896-900.

458. Jason Dowd, "Celebrities Pushing Politics – Have They Gone Too Far," AME Magazine, January 5, 2017, http://theamemagazine.com/magazine/2017/01/05/celebrities-pushing-politics-have-they-gone-too-far/.

459. "Imagine (John Lennon song)," Wikipedia, accessed May 21, 2017, https://en.wikipedia.org/wiki/Imagine_(John_Lennon_song).

460. Brandon Showalter, "Globalism Is Anti-Christ, Demonic, Theologians Argue," Christian Post, September 28, 2016, http://www.christianpost.com/news/globalism-antichrist-demonic-theologians-wallace-henley-fay-voshell-jim-garlow-jeremy-rabkin-170131/.

461. Ibid.

462. William Boykin interview 26 April 2017.

463. Ibid.

464. Mark Juergensmeyer, The New Cold War? Religious Nationalism Confronts the Secular State, University of California Press, p.5, https://books.google.com/books?id=qBJmeM6DiBAC&pg=PA5&lpg=PA5&dq=bruce+lawrence+and+%E2%80%9Cagainst+the+secular+ideology+that+often+accompanies+modern+society.%E2%80%9D&source=bl&ots=lJSf1yopMh&sig=YfhbbNOU2hRaM9GZ6tlBMLvLyb4&hl=en&sa=X&ved=0ahUKEwjrwu3nz9TTAhXD6iYKHZVtAnMQ6AEIIjAA#v=onepage&q=bruce%20lawrence%20and%20%E2%80%9Cagainst%20the%20secular%20ideology%20that%20often%20accompanies%20modern%20society.%E2%80%9D&f=false.

465. Mark Juergensmeyer, Global Rebellion, Religious Challenges to the Secular State, from Christian Militias to al Qaeda, University of California Press, 2009, https://www.amazon.com/Global-Rebellion-Religious-Challenges-Comparative/dp/0520261577.

466. Ibid, p.30.

467. Ibid.

468. Ibid., p. 253.

469. Ibid.

470. Timothy Samuel Shah et al, Rethinking Religion and World Affairs, Oxford University Press, 2012, p. 3.

471. Ibid., p.17.

472. Samuel Huntington, "The Clash of Civilizations?" Foreign Affairs, vol. 71, no. 3 (Summer 1993): 26.

473. Braden P. Anderson, "Religion and Its Discontents: A Review of The Myth of Religious Violence," Book Review, The Intersection of Theology and

Culture, February 15, 2011, https://theotherjournal.com/2011/02/15/religion-and-its-discontents-a-review-of-the-myth-of-religious-violence/.

474. Assaf Moghadam, "A Global Resurgence of Religion?" (Unpublished paper, Weatherhead Initiative Project on "Religion and Global Politics," August 2003), Table: "Global Trends in Religious Adherence, 1900–2025, by Religion." Laurie Goodstein ("Study Finds One in 6 Follows No Religion," *The New York Times*, December 18, 2012) reports the results of a recent Pew Survey of Americans which despite the growth of this category still finds that over 83% identify with some religion. See http://www.nytimes.com/2012/12/18/world/pew-study-finds-one-in-6-follows-no-religion.html?_r=0.

475. Monica Duffy Toft, "Religion, Rationality, and Violence" in Snyder, ed., *Religion and International Relations Theory*, 118.

476. Brandon Showalter, "Globalism Is Anti-Christ, Demonic, Theologians Argue," Christian Post, September 28, 2016, http://www.christianpost.com/news/globalism-antichrist-demonic-theologians-wallace-henley-fay-voshell-jim-garlow-jeremy-rabkin-170131/.

477. Jan Larue interview April 28, 2017.

478. Michael S. Heiser, *The Unseen Realm*, Lexham Press, 2015, p. 376.

479. Ibid.

480. Brandon Showalter, "Globalism Is Anti-Christ, Demonic, Theologians Argue," Christian Post, September 28, 2016, http://www.christianpost.com/news/globalism-antichrist-demonic-theologians-wallace-henley-fay-voshell-jim-garlow-jeremy-rabkin-170131/.

481. Ibid.

482. Jan Larue interview April 28, 2017.

483. William Boykin interview April 26, 2017.

484. Leo Hohmann, "Is Globalism Actually Demonic?," Worldnetdaily.com, October 16, 2016, http://www.wnd.com/2016/10/is-globalism-actually-demonic/.

485. Ibid.

486. Tyler Durden, "Are Globalists Evil Or Just Misunderstood?," ZeroHedge, May 18, 2016, http://www.zerohedge.com/news/2016-05-18/are-globalists-evil-or-just-misunderstood.

487. Terry James interview May 26, 2017.

488. Jan Larue interview April 28, 2017.

489. William Boykin interview April 26, 2017.

490. Carl Teichrib interview May 1, 2017.

491. Carl Teichrib, "Things Change Fast," Forcing Change, Vol. 9, Issue 10, October 2015, accessed May 27, 2017 http://www.understandthetimes. org/rome2016/seg2/romeseg2.shtml.

492. Ibid.

493. Ibid.

494. Ibid.

495. Terry James interview May 26, 2017.

496. Wilfred Hahn, "The Bible on the Next World Leader," Rapture Ready, February 10, 2017, http://www.raptureready.com/2015/01/06/ the-bible-on-the-next-world-leader-by-wilfred-hahn/.

497. Ibid.

498. George F. Will, "The Disciplining of Austria," *The Washington Post*, February 10, 2000, p. A23.

499. "Profile: Controversy and Joerg Haider," BBC News, February 29, 2000.

500. Jonathan Rauch, "The New Europe: Ready for Everything, Except Democracy," *The National Journal*, February 19, 2000.

501. Anne Applebaum, "Austria Ostracized: The European union Showboats about Haider," *The Weekly Standard*, February 28, 2000, pp. 17–19.

502. Barry Schweid, "U.S. Limits Austria Govt. Contacts," Associated Press, February 4, 2000.

503. "Leading European right-wing populists attend Koblenz meeting," DW, January 21, 2017, http://www.dw.com/en/leading-european-right-wing- populists-attend-koblenz-meeting/a-37220481.

504. Peter Hitchens, "Escape From the EU," *The American Conservative,* September/October 2016, p.20–23.

505. Oscar Lopez, "Can a sputtering economy and fears of ISIS lift France's marine Le Pen into the Elysee Palace?," *Newsweek*, May 5, 2017, pp. 26–29.

506. Peter Foster, "Dutch election result: Mark Rutte sees off Geert Wilders challenge as Netherlands rejects far-Right," *The Telegraph*, March 15, 2017, http://www.telegraph.co.uk/news/2017/03/15/ dutch-election-results-geert-wilders-andmark-rutte-vie-power/.

507. Dalibor Rohac, Edit Zgut and Lorant Gyori, "Populism in Europe and its Russian love affair," AEI Paper & Studies, January 2017, p.5, https://www.aei.org/wp-content/uploads/2017/01/Populism-in-Europe-and-Its-Russian-Love-Affair.pdf.

508. Soeren Kern, "Germany confiscating homes to use for migrants," Gatestone Institute, May 14, 2017, https://www.gatestoneinstitute.org/10352/germany-migrants-property-rights.

509. "Europe's far-right leaders speak on Trump at conference," *CNN Wire*, 21 Jan. 2017.

510. Ibid.

511. Ibid.

512. May Bulman, "Who Is Beppe Grillo and what is Five Star Movement?," *The Independent,* December 5, 2016, http://www.independent.co.uk/news/world/europe/who-is-beppe-grillo-five-star-movement-italy-referendum-party-matteo-renzi-resigns-a7456106.html.

513. Ed Pilkington, "Obama angers midwest voters with guns and religion remark," *The Guardian,* April 14, 2008, https://www.theguardian.com/world/2008/apr/14/barackobama.uselections2008.

514. Steve Schmutzer, "The Man for Such a Time as This," Rapture Ready, April 27, 2017, http://www.raptureready.com/2017/04/27/the-man-for-such-a-time-as-this-by-steve-schmutzer/.

515. Ibid.

516. Heather Long, "U.S. has lost 5 million manufacturing jobs since 2000," CNN, March 29, 2016, http://money.cnn.com/2016/03/29/news/economy/us-manufacturing-jobs/.

517. Matthew McCaffrey, "Can Capitalism Survive," Mises Institute, November 4, 2009, https://mises.org/library/can-capitalism-survive.

518. Fareed Zakaria, "Everyone seems to agree globalization is a sin. They're wrong," *The Washington Post,* January 19, 2017, https://www.washingtonpost.com/opinions/everyone-seems-to-agree-globalization-is-a-sin-theyre-wrong/2017/01/19/49bded68-de8b-11e6-918c-99ede3c8cafa_story.html?utm_term=.183f8c23865c.

519. Steve Schmutzer, "The Man for Such a Time as This," Rapture Ready, April 27, 2017, http://www.raptureready.com/2017/04/27/the-man-for-such-a-time-as-this-by-steve-schmutzer/.

520. Dalibor Rohac, Edit Zgut and Lorant Gyori, "Populism in Europe and its Russian love affair," *AEI Paper & Studies*, January 2017, p. 3, https://www.aei.org/wp-content/uploads/2017/01/Populism-in-Europe-and-Its-Russian-Love-Affair.pdf.

521. Jonathan Haidt, "When and why nationalism beats globalism," *Policy*, Vol. 32 No. 3, Spring 2016, pp. 46–53.

522. Mike Allen, "Obama promises to 'remake the world,'" *Politico*, July 24, 2008, http://www.politico.com/story/2008/07/obama-promises-to-remake-the-world-012028.

523. David Brooks, "We Take Care of Our Own," *New York Times*, July 15, 2016, https://www.nytimes.com/2016/07/15/opinion/we-take-care-of-our-own.html.

524. Jonathan Haidt, "When and why nationalism beats globalism," *Policy*, Vol. 32 No. 3, Spring 2016, pp. 46–53.

525. Ibid.

526. Ibid.

527. Ibid.

528. Ibid.

529. Ibid.

530. Ibid.

531. Robert L. Maginnis, *Never Submit: Will the Extermination of Christians Get Better Before It Gets Worse?* Defender Publishing Group, 2015, https://www.amazon.com/Never-Submit-Extermination-Christians-Before/dp/0990497496.

532. Jonathan Haidt, "When and why nationalism beats globalism," *Policy*, Vol. 32 No. 3, Spring 2016, pp. 46-53.

533. Ibid.

534. William Boykin interview April 26, 2017.

535. Michael Heiser interview May 1, 2017.

536. William Boykin interview April 26, 2017.

537. John Ehrman, "A half-century of controversy: The Alger Hiss case," Central Intelligence Agency, accessed May 22, 2017, https://www.cia.gov/library/center-for-the-study-of-intelligence/kent-csi/vol44no5/html/v44i5a01p.htm.

538. Ibid.

539. Ibid.

540. "China's chase of the 'golden visa' abroad, by the numbers," *New York Times*, May 16, 2017, accessed May 27, 2017, http://www.startribune.com/china-s-chase-of-the-golden-visa-abroad-by-the-numbers/422473434/.

541. Ibid.

542. Michael Heiser interview May 1, 2017.

543. William Boykin interview April 26, 2017.

544. Peter Hitchens, "The Cold War Is Over," First Things, October 2016, pp. 33–38.

545. "Attack by Stratagem," *Sun Tzu's Art of War*, accessed May 22, 2017, https://suntzusaid.com/book/3.

546. Michael Heiser interview May 1, 2017.

547. Philip Doecke interview May 11, 2017.

548. Carl Teichrib interview May 1, 2017.

549. Fay Voshell, "Globalism: The Religion of Empire," *American Thinker*, September 4, 2016, http://www.americanthinker.com/articles/2016/09/globalism_the_religion_of_empire_.html.

550. Ibid.

551. Peter J. Leithart, "Kingdom First," First Things, August 2016, https://www.firstthings.com/blogs/leithart/2016/08/kingdom-first.

552. Steven J. Cole, "Lesson 1: The Man Who Cried About a Wall (Nehemiah 1:1–11)," Bible.org, accessed May 22, 2017, https://bible.org/seriespage/lesson-1-man-who-cried-about-wall-nehemiah-11-11.

553. Ray C. Stedman, "Nehemiah: Rebuilding the Walls," Ray Stedman.org, accessed May 22, 2017, https://www.raystedman.org/bible-overview/adventuring/nehemiah-rebuilding-the-walls.

554. Ibid.

555. Ibid.

556. Ibid.

557. Peter Jones, "Truth Exchange: An Interview with Peter Jones," Ligonier Ministries, accessed May 22, 2017, http://www.ligonier.org/learn/articles/truth-exchange/.

558. Carl Teichrib, "Things Change Fast," Forcing Change, Vol. 9, Issue 10, October 2015, accessed May 27, 2017 http://www.understandthetimes.org/rome2016/seg2/romeseg2.shtml.

559. Peter J. Leithart, "Kingdom First," First Things, August 2016, https://www.firstthings.com/blogs/leithart/2016/08/kingdom-first.

560. "World Trade in 2015-2016," World Trade Organization, accessed May 22, 2017, https://www.wto.org/english/res_e/statis_e/wts2016_e/WTO_Chapter_03_e.pdf.

561. Ferdinand Lundberg, *America's 60 Families*, The Vanguard Press, New York, 1937, https://archive.org/stream/LundbergFerdinandAmericas60Families1937PDFscan/Lundberg,%20Ferdinand%20-%20America%27s%2060%20Families%20(1937)_djvu.txt.

562. Emmie Martin and Tanza Loudenback, "The 30 richest people on earth," *Business Insider,* March 2, 2017, http://www.businessinsider.com/30-richest-people-on-earth-2017-3/#30-ma-huateng-1.

563. Ibid.

564. "Transcript: Bill Moyers Interviews Bill Gates," NPR, May 9, 2003, http://www.pbs.org/now/transcript/transcript_gates.html.

565. D. Samuelson, "The two most EVIL globalists of our time: George Soros and Bill Gates," NewsTarget, January 4, 2017, http://www.newstarget.com/2017-01-04-the-three-most-evil-globalists-alive-today-george-soros-jeff-bezos-and-bill-gates.html.

566. "India Holds Bill Gates Accountable For His Vaccine Crimes," Vactruth, October 5, 2014, https://vactruth.com/2014/10/05/bill-gates-vaccine-crimes/.

567. Ethan A. Huff, "Bill Gates, Monsanto, and Eugenics: A Corporate takeover of global agriculture," *Natural News*, March 1, 2012, http://www.frontierlandpost.com/bill-gates-globalist-front-man.html.

568. Michael Bauchmuller and Stefan Braun, "Bill Gates interview: Den taglichen tod nehmen wir nicht wahr," Sueddeutsche Zeitung, January 28, 2015, http://www.sueddeutsche.de/wirtschaft/bill-gates-im-interview-den-taeglichen-tod-nehmen-wir-nicht-wahr-1.2324164.

569. Susan Berry, "Bill Gates: Common Core Opponents 'Shrouded in Myths,'" Breitbart, February 13, 2013, http://www.breitbart.com/big-government/2014/02/13/bill-gates-common-core-opponents-shrouded-in-myths/.

570. Neil Munro, "Jeff Bezos' Washington Post: Import Foreign Workers to Replace Spoiled Americans," Breitbart, August 26,

2016, http://www.breitbart.com/immigration/2016/08/26/
washington-post-jeff-bezos-scab-workers-replace-americans/.

571. Ben Kew, "Amazon's Jeff Bezos Exploring Legal
Challenge to Trump Travel Ban," Breitbart, January
31, 2017, http://www.breitbart.com/tech/2017/01/31/
amazons-jeff-bezos-exploring-legal-challenge-to-trump-travel-ban/.

572. Ibid.

573. Ibid.

574. Allum Bokhari, "Mark Zuckerberg: German Refugee Policies
'Inspiring,' U.S. Should 'Follow Their Lead,'" Breitbart,
February 26, 2016, http://www.breitbart.com/tech/2016/02/26/
germanys-open-door-policies-inspiring-says-facebook-ceo-zuckerberg/.

575. Allum Bokhari, "Mark Zuckerberg Blasts Facebook Staff for
Replacing 'Black Lives Matter' with 'All Lives Matter,'" Breitbart,
February 26, 2016, http://www.breitbart.com/tech/2016/02/26/
zuckerberg-reprimands-facebook-staff-for-rejecting-black-lives-matter/.

576. Hannah Boland, "Resist 'turn inwards' and isolationism,
says Mark Zuckerberg," *The Telegraph*, May 25, 2017,
http://www.telegraph.co.uk/technology/2017/05/25/
resist-turn-inwards-isolationism-says-mark-zuckerberg/.

577. Adelle Nazarian, "Rubio Fundraises with Oracle's Larry
Ellison in Silicon Valley," Breitbart, June 9, 2015, http://
www.breitbart.com/big-government/2015/06/09/
rubio-fundraises-with-oracles-larry-ellison-in-silicon-valley/.

578. "Inside the secret world of the Freemasons," CBS News,
December 8, 2013, http://www.cbsnews.com/news/
inside-the-secret-world-of-the-freemasons/.

579. Thomas Horn, *Zenith 2016*, Defender, 2013, pp. 292–293.

580. Joshua Levine, "France: Where Freemasons Are Still Feared," Bloomberg,
April 19, 2012, https://www.bloomberg.com/news/articles/2012-04-19/
france-where-freemasons-are-still-feared.

581. Ibid.

582. Ibid.

583. Henry Makow, "Freemasonry—The Elephant in the Room,"
henrymakow.com, accessed May 22, 2017, https://www.henrymakow.
com/300902.html#sthash.2WJ2859M.dpuf.

584. Sammy R. LaPoint, "What I've learned as a Freemason and why I left the order," Midnight in the Desert, October 21, 2015, http://midnightinthedesert.com/ what-ive-learned-as-a-freemason-and-why-i-left-the-order/.

585. "Honest Answers to Important Questions," Ex-Masons for Jesus, accessed May 27, 2017, http://www.emfj.org/answers.htm.

586. Ibid.

587. Richabh Banerji, "9 Of The Most Dangerous Secret Societies In The World," *India Times*, November 27, 2015, http://www.indiatimes.com/ culture/who-we-are/9-of-the-most-dangerous-secret-societies-in-the-world-247678.html.

588. William F. Jasper, "Bipartisan Bonesmen," *The New American*, March 8, 2004, pp. 10-15, https://www.thenewamerican.com/usnews/politics/ item/15248-bipartisan-bonesmen.

589. Elizabeth Flock, "Bohemian Grove: Where the rich and powerful go to misbehave." *Washingtonpost.com*, June 15, 2011, https://www. washingtonpost.com/blogs/blogpost/post/bohemian-grove-where-the-rich-and-powerful-go-to-misbehave/2011/06/15/AGPV1sVH_blog.html?utm_ term=.b81cf72a0b76.

590. Adam Laskinsky, "Burning Man vs Bohemian Grove," Fortune, August 26, 2014, http://fortune.com/2014/08/26/ burning-man-vs-bohemian-grove/.

591. Stanley Monteith, "The Occult Hierarchy: Part I," Radio Liberty (May 2005), accessed May 25, 2017 https://tobefree.wordpress.com/2011/03/07/ dr-stanley-monteiths-newsletters-from-radio-liberty-with-footnotes/.

592. Jon Ronson, Them: Adventures with Extremists. Simon and Schuster, 2002, p. 321.

593. Daniel H. Johnson, "Bohemian Grove Action Network," The Hall-Hoag Collection, Brown University, March 18, 2014, accessed May 25, 2017, https://blogs.brown.edu/hallhoag/2014/03/18/ bohemian-grove-action-network/.

594. "Bohemian Grove Fact Sheet," Bohemian Grove Network, accessed May 25, 2017, http://www.thirdworldtraveler.com/Global_Secrets_Lies/ BohemianGrove_Facts.html.

595. Peter Phillips, "Inside the Global Dominance Group," CounterPunch, February 9, 2006, http://www.counterpunch.org/2006/02/09/inside-the-global-dominance-group/.

596. Alex Shoumatoff, "Bohemian Tragedy," *Vanity Fair*, April 1, 2009, http://www.vanityfair.com/culture/2009/05/bohemian-grove200905.

597. Aaron Kline, "Colin Powell's Hacked E-mails Reveal Insider Details of Secretive Bohemian Grove Summit for World's Elite," Breitbart, September 16, 2016, http://www.breitbart.com/jerusalem/2016/09/16/colin-powells-hacked-e-mails-reveal-insider-details-secretive-bohemian-grove-summit-worlds-elite/.

598. Ibid.

599. G. William Domhoff, "The Power Elite at Summer Camp," Who Rules America, accessed May 22, 2017, http://whorulesamerica.net/power/bohemian_grove.html.

600. "Role of Secret Societies In Bringing Forth The Coveted New World Order," Global Elite News, February 22, 2013, accessed May 26, 2017, http://theglobalelite.org/role-of-secret-societies-in-bringing-forth-the-coveted-new-world-order/.